Sew Kawaii!

Sew Kawaii!

22 Simple Sewing Projects for Cool Kids of All Ages

Choly Knight

Fox Chapel
Publishing

Step-by-step photography by Matthew McClure.

ISBN 978-1-56523-568-7

Library of Congress Cataloging-in-Publication Data

Knight, Choly.

Sew kawaii! : 22 simple sewing projects for cool kids of all ages / Choly Knight.

p. cm.

Includes index.

ISBN 978-1-56523-568-7 (pbk.)

1. Sewing. 2. Popular culture--Japan. I. Title.

TT715.K59 2011

646.2--dc23

2011019595

To learn more about the other great books from Fox Chapel Publishing, or to find a retailer near you, call toll-free 800-457-9112 or visit us at *www.FoxChapelPublishing.com.*

Note to Authors: We are always looking for talented authors to write new books in our area of woodworking, design, and related crafts. Please send a brief letter describing your idea to Acquisition Editor, 1970 Broad Street, East Petersburg, PA 17520.

Printed in China
First printing

About the Author

Choly Knight is from Orlando, Florida. She has been crafting for as long as she can remember, and has drawn, painted, sculpted, and stitched everything in sight. She took up sewing clothing in 1997 and has yet to put her sewing machine away. After studying studio art and earning a BA in English, she now enjoys trying to find numerous different ways to combine her passions for writing, fine art, and craft art. In addition to having created all of the designs, projects, and patterns appearing in this book, she also appears as the model for each clothing item. She focuses on handcrafted clothing, accessories, and other creations inspired by Japanese art, anime, and style, and specializes in cosplay (costume play) hats and hoodies. She sells her wares at anime conventions and in her Etsy shop: *www.Etsy.com/shop/ShoriAmeshiko*.

Dedication:

To Matt and Ali, who have always supported my kawaii endeavors.

Contents

What is "kawaii?"

Kawaii is the Japanese word for cute, adorable, or lovable. And just as in English, it is used to describe many things, such as a darling child, a sweet animal, or a favorite outfit. In Japan, cuteness is a large part of everyday life, with iconic characters like Hello Kitty found everywhere, even representing banks and airline companies.

Since the creation of Sanrio and Hello Kitty in the 1970s, cuteness has been a constantly growing trend in Japan among children and adults alike. With the hectic and demanding lifestyle many people have in Japan and around the world, kawaii items are a welcome escape into a mindset that is more innocent and naïve.

Kawaii has grown all over the world to inspire lovable, iconic characters that are eye-catching in their simplicity. Today, you'll continue to find kawaii characters from Sanrio, and also new companies like San-X, Q-Lia, and Toki Doki. These companies focus on creating adorable characters that are featured on stationery, accessories, clothing, and plush toys. In this book, I will give you the skills and guidance to create your own kawaii goods!

Cute, Adorable, Loveable: かわいい
Kawaii (ka-WAI-EE)

Learn to Speak Japanese

In addition to featuring adorable characters, the projects here are also inspired by the crazy Harajuku style seen on the streets of Tokyo. So, these projects are not only great for those with an eye for design and cute characters, but also those who like to take chances with their fashion statements.

These projects range from the very simple to more complex, but all of them are quite attainable with some knowledge about sewing techniques and a patient hand. You can start by making something small and simple, like a key chain, and with enough practice you'll find yourself making a full poncho—a real garment. I promise both will be just as satisfying to create.

Whether you make these projects for yourself or for others, you'll find that using soft and comforting fabrics to create sweet and adorable characters is much more motivating than a typical drab beginner's project. As soon as you start to see the character's face come together, nothing will stop you from finishing. So, choose a project and get sewing!

About Metric

Throughout the book, you'll notice that every measurement is accompanied by a metric equivalent. Inches are rounded off to the nearest 0 or 5mm unless precision is necessary. Yards are converted to meters. Please be aware that while this book will show 1 yard = 1 meter, the actual conversion is 1 yard = .9 meters, a difference of about 3⅓" (33mm). Using these conversions, you will always have a little bit extra fabric if purchasing by the metric quantity.

How to Use This Book

This book is chock-full of cute and approachable projects you'll actually want to make. Whether you've never sewed before or are well-practiced with your sewing machine, there is something in these pages you'll want to make for yourself. If you're new to sewing, check out the getting started chapter (page 10) and keep your eye on the helpful sidebars throughout the text. Each photo-illustrated sewing project is clearly labeled with a difficulty level (see below, left). Have a look at the directory below to find a project for your skill level. Every pattern and illustration you'll need are located in the back of the book, starting on page 143. Lastly, you'll notice fun "Learn Japanese!" tips at the beginning of each project—you can even learn another language while you sew! Pick a kawaii project, and let's get sewing!

Difficulty Levels

☺ **Very Easy:** Great first projects! So straightforward you can breeze right through them.

♡ **Easy**: Good for a third or fourth project, when you're ready to learn a few new skills.

✿ **Experienced Beginner:** Great for when you're ready to move beyond simple beginner projects and into something with a little more detail.

☆ **Intermediate:** Good for when you already know most sewing techniques and how to work your way around a pattern.

Very Easy

Easy

Experienced Beginner

Intermediate

Getting Started

Making the projects in this book requires some basic sewing tools and techniques, along with a few new ones. Whether you have any experience sewing or not, you'll still be able to make the projects in this book with the information given here. Jump in and discover different types of fabrics; tools you'll need to get started; closures and notions; applique; hand sewing; and all the techniques and terms you'll need to know.

Dritz
MADE IN CHINA

Fabrics

Knit fabrics are created by knitting threads together. This is just like a sweater, only on a much smaller scale. The fabric will stretch a little or considerably depending on the construction. Knits include jersey, interlock, fleece, and spandex.

Fabrics can be classified into two types: wovens and knits. Both types are used to demonstrate projects in this book. After you experiment with woven and knit fabric, you'll be able to choose your favorite type—though I do recommend that beginners start with woven fabrics. All of these fabrics and supplies can be found at your local fabric store or online. In many cases, the projects will call for so little fabric that the remnant bin will have just what you need. Greater varieties of minky and plush fabrics can be found online, where you can buy swatches for a small fee and try all the textures there are to offer.

Fabrics are manufactured in a variety of widths, with those sold in retail stores being commonly 45" (1145mm), 60" (1525mm), and sometimes 36" (915mm). This information can be found in the product description of the fabric in the store and online. All projects made here with fleece and minky assume you will be working with 60" (1525mm)-wide fabric, as nearly all of these types of fabric come in this width. The fabric requirements for all other projects in this book assume that at least 45" (1145mm)-wide fabric is being used. Be sure to accommodate for this if your fabric is narrower, especially if it was purchased internationally or from a specialty supplier.

Woven fabrics

Woven fabrics are constructed by weaving fibers together, much like a basket. This gives the fabric a solid construction that will not stretch more than a minimal amount. Light- to medium-weight fabrics of this type are great for beginners because they do not shift or stretch while they are being worked on, and yet are still easy to sew through. Some projects may also call for lining fabric, which is used to cover the inside of a project. Fabrics made specifically for lining are typically light and thin polyester materials, though quilting cotton can be used as well.

Woven fabrics are created by weaving threads together. The resulting fabric will be sturdy and won't stretch much. Wovens include quilting cotton, corduroy, flannel, terrycloth, and twill.

> Plush and faux fur fabrics are available in an impressive variety. Minky fabric is a variation of fleece that comes in many great varieties and textures, from short, smooth piles to long, fluffy piles, and even novelty piles, such as rosebud.

Knit fabrics

Knit fabrics, on the other hand, are constructed by knitting threads together. This is done much like a sweater, yet on a smaller scale. The resulting fabric will have a little or considerable amount of stretch depending on the knitting technique and material used. Fleece is one of the major knit fabrics used in this book, as it is versatile and great for beginners. Fleece is a plush, medium-weight polyester material that has a slight stretch. It is easy to work with, and its stretchiness can accommodate simple mistakes made with seams and fit. Other knits, such as interlock and jersey, are thinner and stretch farther. These fabrics can be more difficult to work with because of their slinky texture and tendency to stretch out of shape while sewing, but the tips in the Jellyfish Dress project (page 121) can help you with these problems.

Plush fabrics

The last group of fabrics appearing in this book is those for plush animals. These fabrics can include faux fur, minky, and even fleece. Most, but not all, plush fabrics are knits. Knits are highly recommended for plushies because their stretchy quality makes for rounder and softer curves in the stuffed animals. A knit with a furry surface is even better, as the fur covers any noticeable seams or minor mistakes.

Tip: Napped Fabrics

Most plush fabrics and some woven fabrics have what is called nap or pile. This is the raised surface of the fabric that creates its fuzzy texture. Fabrics with noticeable nap include minky, faux fur, suede, and corduroy.

This nap will usually have a right and wrong direction, much like an animal's fur. Brush the fabric against the nap, and the fabric is left with fibers sticking up at awkward angles. Brush the fabric with the nap, and result is smooth and shiny. Fabrics with a shorter pile may not be as obvious, but you can often feel the difference.

When cutting these fabrics, be sure the nap aligns with the direction of the grain line in the pattern. Typically, the nap should be facing down, allowing you to brush your project from top to bottom. This is particularly important with plushies.

Brushing the nap in the wrong direction results in the fabric catching shadows in the pile and looking darker. This is true for any fabric, but easy to see on long-pile varieties.

Brushing in the right direction smoothes the nap so it reflects light. The fabric will appear lighter.

Basic Sewing Tools

Basic sewing tools, such as needles, scissors, and thread, are all that's necessary for nearly every project in this book. Items like these are often found in beginner sewing kits.

Basic sewing tools you'll need include (from L to R): Seam ripper, machine needles, safety pins, pinking shears, fabric markers and pencils, embroidery thread, and all-purpose thread.

Sewing machine

The kind of machine used for these projects will need to do a straight stitch and zigzag stitch. Stitch length adjustment is also very important. Other helpful features are a zipper foot for attaching zippers and a stretch stitch.

Thread

All-purpose thread works well for all the projects listed, though there are other kinds of specialty thread that can be used optionally. All-cotton quilting thread can be used for quilting projects, and rayon and embroidery threads add a beautiful sheen for machine embroidery.

Sewing machine needles

Universal needles can be used for all the projects in this book. However, if you find you are encountering skipped stitches or broken thread, a more specific needle can be the solution. Needles are made to match the weight of the fabric and whether it is woven or knit. Also be sure to change your needle after every project, as they can get dull and break easily after repeated use.

Hand-sewing needles

Many of the projects in this book will call for a bit of hand-sewing for small details and closing up seams. Standard hand-sewing needles are called "sharps," and range from sizes 7 to 11. Anything larger goes into hand embroidery and tapestry range. Experiment with whatever size in the standard range feels most comfortable to you. Be aware that you get what you pay for—cheap needles will often bend and break easily. Hand-sewing stitches and techniques are listed later in this chapter.

Fabric marker/pencil

Fabric markers are indispensable in making temporary marks on fabric to note darts, appliqué details, and locations for arms, ears, etc. The pigment is typically air or water soluble so the marks can be erased after the project is finished. Be sure to get a light pencil for dark materials and a dark marker for light materials.

Iron and ironing board

Ironing is most crucial when making crisp seams for garments or applying appliqué pieces. It is not necessary to iron the seams in some plushie and accessory projects, so the instructions will indicate whether pressing is needed. An iron with a temperature gauge and steam control is important, as some fabrics have low tolerance for heat. Always be sure to test-iron fabric scraps first. If ironing damages the fabric, manually pressing the seam with your fingers can work just as well. Use a press cloth if necessary on fluffier fabrics.

Additional sewing tools

Sewing scissors or shears
Seam ripper
Tape measure
Straight pins
Safety pins

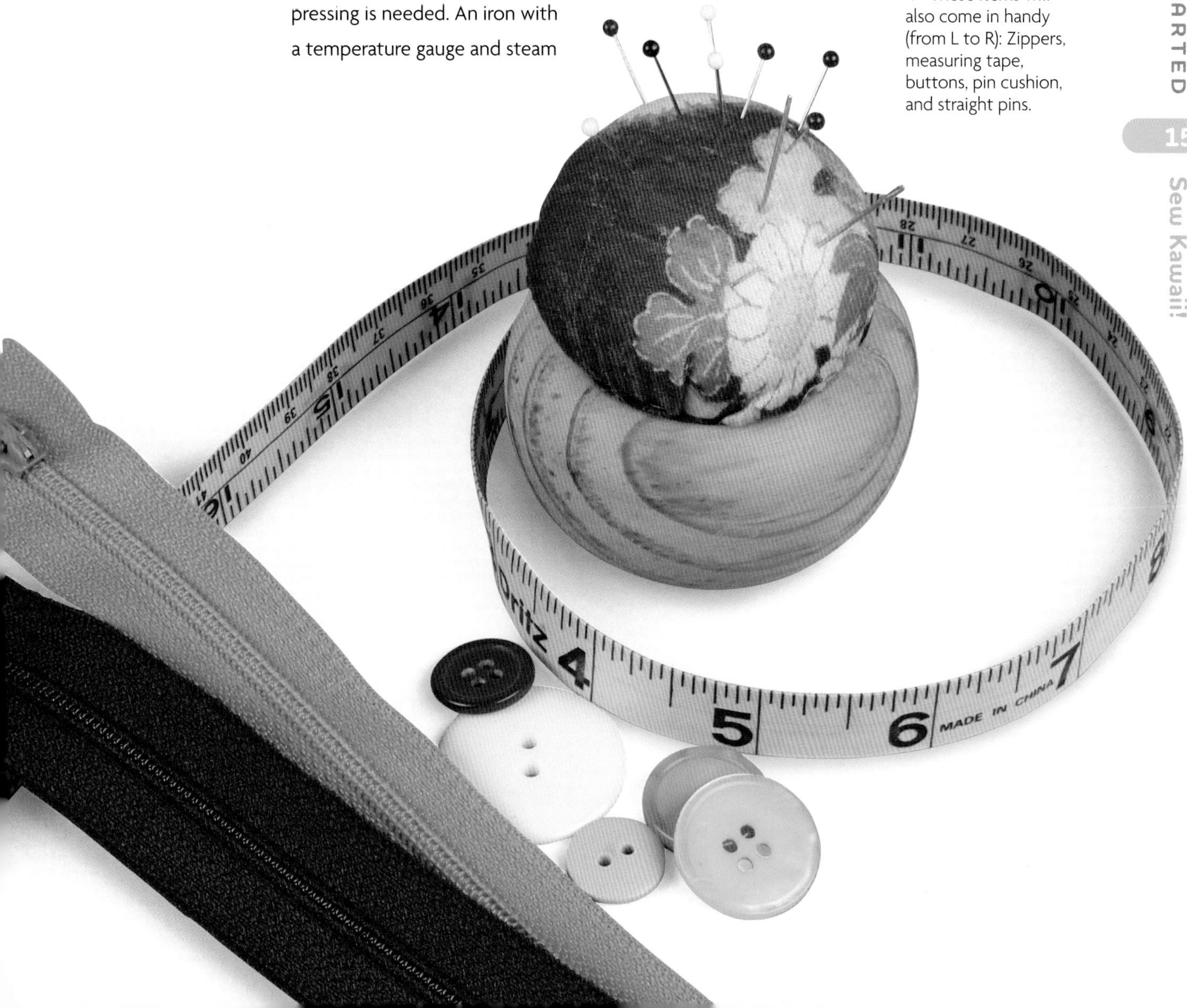

▼ These items will also come in handy (from L to R): Zippers, measuring tape, buttons, pin cushion, and straight pins.

Closures and Other Notions

You'll encounter a variety of closures, such as zippers and hook-and-loop tape, during your perusal of this book. These items are vital in the construction of hoodies, pouches, and a few other projects. This section also includes fun decorative trimmings, as well as stuffings.

Zippers

Zippers come in a variety of colors and lengths, and can be selected to match the color of your project. Read the package carefully to make sure you are selecting the correct size, because a 7" (180mm) zipper package can look the same as a 20" (510mm) zipper package.

Hook-and-loop tape

This tape comes in black and white, and in both adhesive and sew-on varieties. The sew-on variety is much better for these projects, as it will stand up to extended use.

Elastic

Elastic is available in many textures and widths. The instructions for each project will indicate which width to use. The braided and knit varieties offer the best stretch and flexibility. Decorative elastic will not be necessary for the projects here, because the elastic will be hidden in casing.

Ribbon

The ribbon used in these projects is for an added decorative touch—one you can easily customize for yourself utilizing the variety of colors and patterns available. Common types are grosgrain ribbon and satin ribbon. Grosgrain has a stiffer and sturdier construction, making it easy to work with. Satin ribbon is softer and more flexible, but can also be a little trickier to sew in place.

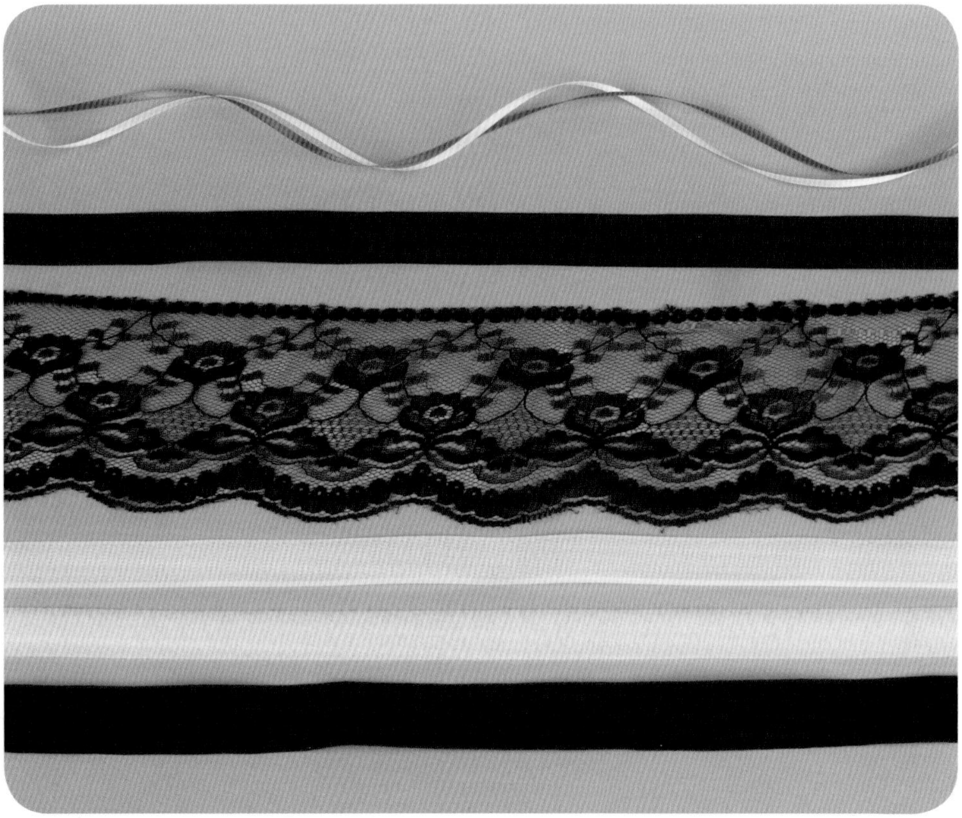

Trims, such as ribbon and lace, are used for decoration in this book, while hook-and-loop tape and elastic are more vital as closures.

^ Plushies can be stuffed with batting, micro pellets, or micro beads, all providing different textures to the finished product.

Lace

Lace comes in many different colors, in both polyester and crocheted cotton. It is used for decorative details in this book, so choose a color that suits your main fabric well. Stretch lace is another variety that is mostly used for lingerie and isn't recommended for the projects here.

Batting and filling

Batting is the material used to fill up plushies. This soft, fluffy stuff comes in polyester, cotton, wool, and hypoallergenic varieties. Batting also comes in a flat form specifically for quilts. Quilt batting is made in the same variety of fibers as regular batting, but in a flat, pressed form that is sewn between the layers of a quilt. It can be purchased by the yard or in packages big enough for an entire blanket.

Also useful as filler are micro beads and pellets. Micro pellets are small plastic beads that weigh plushies down and give them a squishier feel. Micro beads are even smaller and lighter, and give a similar feel to plushies without the added weight. In some projects, both batting and micro pellets are used to give one specific part of the animal weight.

Basic Machine Stitches

A reliable sewing machine with a straight stitch and zigzag stitch can do just about anything, and definitely all the projects in this book! Varying the stitches' width and length makes them adaptable to a variety of applications. If your machine has specialty stitches, experiment with them first, because they can result in faster or more professional-looking results. However, it's still important to get to know these basic stitches well, as they are some of the strongest weapons in your arsenal!

Tip

Unless otherwise noted, seams are sewn with the right sides together.

Straight stitches

Shorter stitches (left in photo) are used when finishing a dart, and for sewing light and delicate fabrics, such as silk and satin.

Medium length stitches (center in photo) are a basic all-around stitch for a majority of fabrics. Note the reverse stitches made by the machine's backstitch lever or button. This function makes the machine run backward in order to lock down your beginning and ending stitches.

Long stitches (right in photo) are great for basting or gathering, when doing so by hand would be too time-consuming.

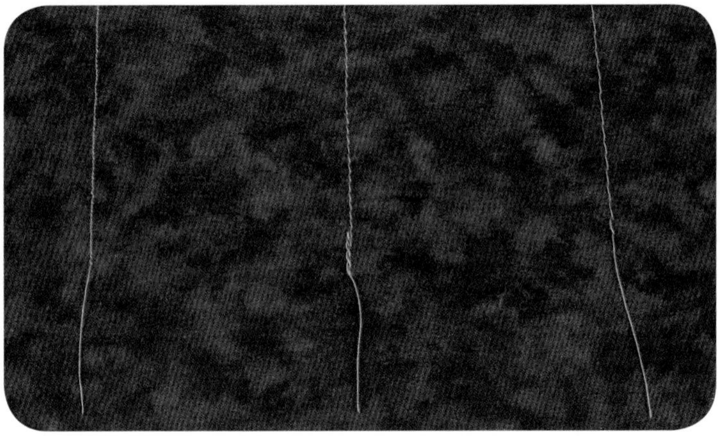

^ The straight stitch: short, medium, and long (L to R).

Zigzag stitches

A zigzag with medium width and length (left in photo) is a great basic zigzag, especially useful for finishing raw edges of seam allowances.

A zigzag with wide width and short length (center in photo), also called a satin stitch, is a decorative stitch that makes a clean, thick line with the thread. It is great for borders on appliqué.

A zigzag with a narrow width and long length (right in photo) serves as a stretch stitch. When done on knit fabrics, it gives a little bit when stretched.

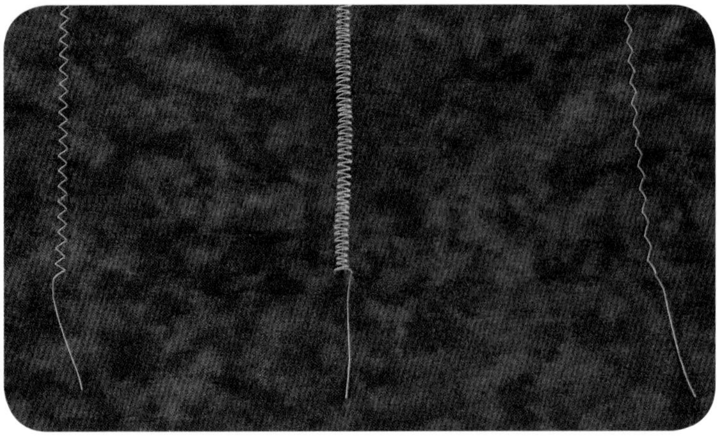

^ The zigzag stitch: medium, wide and short, narrow and long (L to R).

Tip: Basting Seams

Using a basting stitch to temporarily hold fabric together is a very helpful technique to use when pins are too awkward or imprecise. This extra step works well when sewing a piece with a curved shape to one with a straight shape, and other similar scenarios. Taking the extra step here can avoid headache at the machine when fabric pieces just don't want to line up properly. The photos here illustrate Step 8 from the Llama Plush project (page 96), but these tips can be applied to any project where you need more control in getting pieces matched up evenly.

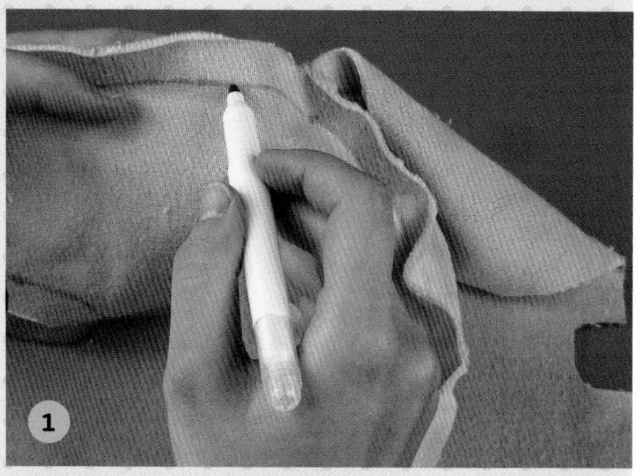

Mark the fabric. Use a washable fabric marker to mark where the seams will go, especially at pivot points.

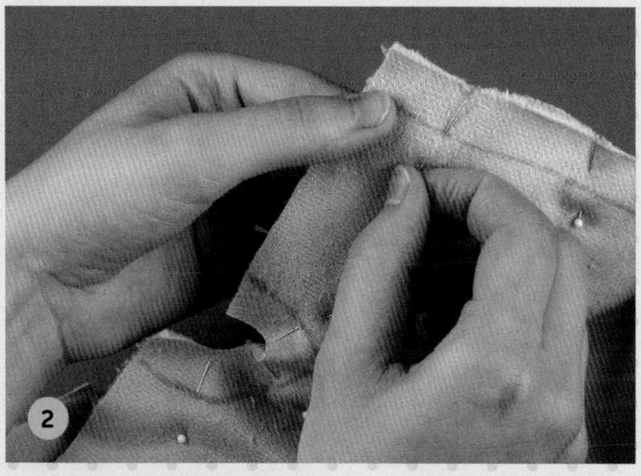

Pin the pieces in place. Match up the seam lines and pin the fabric pieces in place.

Sew a basting hand stitch near the seam lines. Use a basting hand stitch (see page 24) about ⅛" (3mm) inside the seam line while unpinning. Use the control you have with doing it by hand to make sure the curves are precise and even.

Machine stitch on the seam lines. Go back and resew the seams along the actual seam lines. The pieces will be held in place much better than with pins, and there is no fear of pricking yourself!

Remove the basting stitches. If you wish, pull out the thread from the hand-sewn basting stitches. You can leave them in, because they'll be on the inside of the seam.

On Appliqué

Appliqué comes from the French word for apply, and in sewing means applying one kind of fabric or material onto another. It is a very useful skill to know, and is used in this book to put adorable animals and faces onto the projects we'll be making. There are many different techniques for doing appliqué. I have listed here three reliable methods that can be suited to your particular skill level. Read on for more information on fabrics, techniques, and other things to keep in mind while working with appliqué.

▲ Sturdy and light- to medium-weight fabrics are best for headache-free appliqué. These include quilting cotton, flannel, felt, and fleece.

Appliqué fabrics

The appliquéd fabric you'll be applying to your main fabric should not have much stretch, and should be relatively thin to medium weight. I've found that flannel, quilting cotton, felt, and fleece are very reliable standbys. They also come in a multitude of colors, making assembly of an appliqué picture very easy.

Flannel is perhaps the most versatile because it is available in beautiful colors, has a soft touch, and has a nice weight that is easy to sew through. Its one drawback is that it unravels, and any raw edges will need to be covered or sealed.

Quilting cotton is also a good choice. The variety of colors and patterns you can find add an eye-catching look to many projects. Like flannel, cotton also unravels, and because it lacks the plush thickness of flannel, it often shows a bit of strain from the dense stitching needed to cover the raw edges.

Felt has a great advantage in that it doesn't unravel. Quality felt will cut with crisp edges, allowing the features of your project to really stand out. Because the material doesn't unravel, it is not necessary to stitch around the edges to prevent fraying. My major qualm with felt, however, is that it is a very rough material that pills easily in the wash.

Fleece is a softer alternative. A knit fabric, fleece also does not fray. A problem with fleece sometimes is that it is a bit thicker than the other fabrics, and can be hard on some sewing machines not accustomed to the work. For this reason, it is always good to test your appliqué techniques on scrap fabric before starting a project.

Appliqué supplies

Beyond your sewing machine, thread, scissors, iron, and other tools you'll already have on hand, you'll need two additional supplies to do appliqué: fusible web and stabilizer.

Fusible web is a kind of adhesive that comes in an iron-on paper-backed sheet. Ironing the paper to the back of your appliqué fabric transfers adhesive to the fabric. After peeling the paper away, your fabric then holds the adhesive, much like an iron-on patch. When you iron your appliqué to a base fabric, the adhesive keeps everything from shifting and puckering while you sew. Fusible web is available in different strengths of adhesive: light adhesive for appliqués you intend to sew down, and stronger ones for appliqués you do not intend to sew, but still will use regularly. This product can be found in small folded sheets, larger rolls, or by the yard.

Stabilizer is a stiff fiber used to back pieces of embroidery to keep the fabric taut and strong while sewing. Without stabilizer, your fabric can stretch out and warp from all the stitches you'll be doing in the fabric. The stabilizer is also a better material for your sewing machine's feed dogs to grab onto, making maneuvering the fabric much easier. Stabilizer comes in water-soluble, light tear-away, and firm cut-away varieties. Use light to medium-weight tear-away stabilizer for the projects in this book.

Fusible web and stabilizer are the only special supplies you need to do any appliqué in this book. These items can be found in many varieties and sizes.

Appliqué techniques

There are three general methods for applying appliqué. Practice all three and decide which you prefer. Your skill level and the eventual use of the project you're making will both contribute to your decision as well. All of the projects in this book will be shown appliquéd with the satin stitch, but remember, you can swap out satin stitch for any other technique explained here.

The iron-on appliqué method is not as strong as sewing, but works well for a quick and easy appliqué.

The iron-on technique is best for accessories that won't be getting heavy use or washing, as the appliquéd pieces will be held on only by fusible web adhesive. For the same reason, you'll want to use a non-fraying fabric for your appliqué, such as felt or fleece. Following the product instructions, apply heavy-duty no-sew fusible web to the back of your appliquéd pieces, and use the project's pattern as a guide to iron the appliqués to your main fabric. No sewing is needed, and if you follow the product instructions correctly, your pieces should stay on nicely.

The straight-stitch technique requires a little bit of sewing, but is still very easy. The finished result will have raw edges exposed, so use a non-fraying fabric such as fleece or felt. Following the product instructions, apply light fusible web to your appliquéd pieces; using the pattern as a guide, iron the appliqués onto the main fabric. Use a piece of light tear-away stabilizer beneath your project while sewing a short straight stitch around the edges of the piece. This will hold down your appliqué much better than

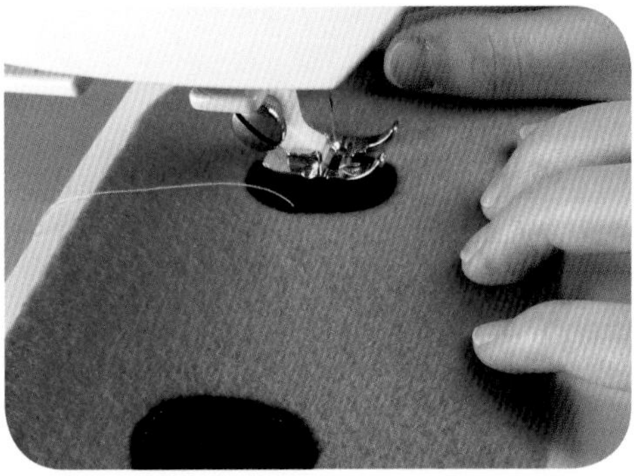

The straight-stitch appliqué method is very simple and secure, but will require using a non-fraying appliqué fabric.

adhesive alone, while still keeping the process simple. After sewing, tear away the stabilizer carefully around your stitches.

The satin-stitch technique renders the most professional look, although it takes the most time. A satin stitch is essentially a very wide and short zigzag stitch. The short length of the stitches, when done effectively, will cover the fabric underneath, leaving a thick line covering the edge of your appliqué. It's a good idea to test this stitch on a piece of scrap fabric first to hone your coordination. This technique will cover any raw edges of the fabric, so you are free to use fabrics that may fray, such as flannel or cotton. For an even more professional look, use embroidery thread instead of all-purpose. Your satin stitch will have a lovely shine that stands out nicely.

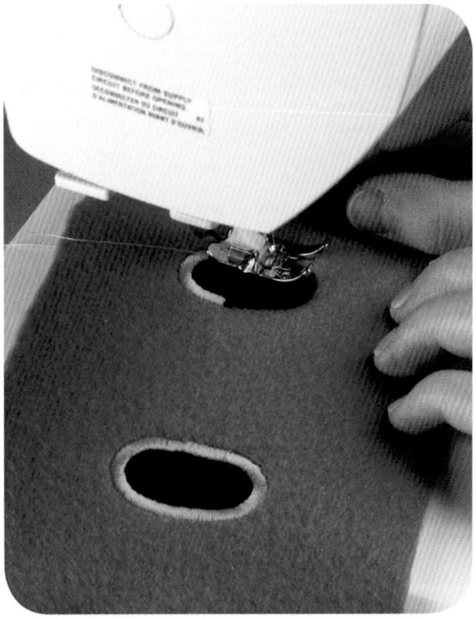

The most time-consuming of all appliqué techniques, the satin stitch also looks the most professional after some time practicing.

Follow the product's instructions to iron a light fusible web to the back of your appliqué, and then iron the appliqué to the front of your main fabric. Use a piece of medium-weight stabilizer beneath your main fabric while sewing. Set the sewing machine to a very short width (usually the shortest), and relatively wide stitch (between average and the widest width). Position your needle to sew over the edge of your appliqué and begin sewing very carefully, as the machine will move slowly. You'll have to make turns very consistently and with patience, and also check your stitches to make sure they cover your fabric edge.

If you don't have the patience for the satin stitch, or feel that your machine can't handle the dense stitches, a zigzag is a nice alternative. Increase the length of your stitches and the process will be much faster. The result will look similar while still encasing the raw edges. Some of the appliqué fabric will show through underneath, so if you don't want your stitches to stand out, pick a thread that is the same color as your appliqué fabric. After sewing, remember to carefully tear away the stabilizer from your stitches. If you discover your fabric has stretched or warped a bit, a quick ironing will smooth out any problems.

Hand Sewing

The projects in this book call for very little hand sewing, making them quick, easy, and great for beginners. Most of the hand sewing is needed to close up openings in projects that have been turned right-side out, so it's good to know just a few basic hand stitches to get started.

Backstitch

This is a strong and versatile stitch used for seams. Begin by sewing down through the fabric; come up where you want the far side of the next stitch to be, and sew down where you want the near side to be. Repeat, always sewing the far side of the stitch first, and then the near side. Think of it as a "two steps forward, one step back" pattern.

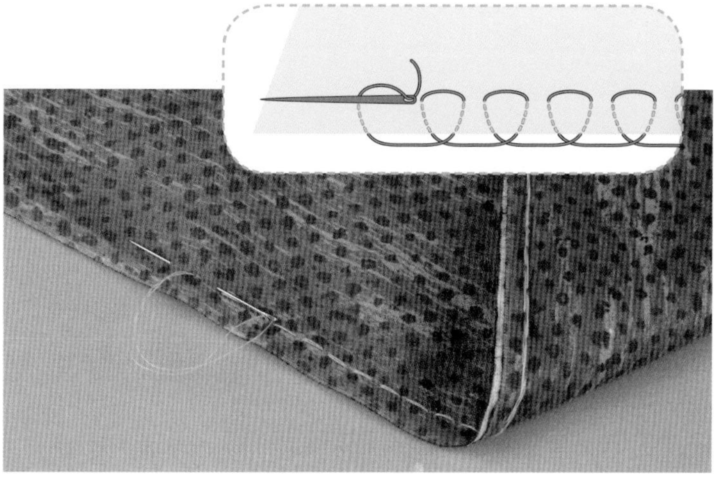

Backstitch. A strong and versatile stitch used for seams.

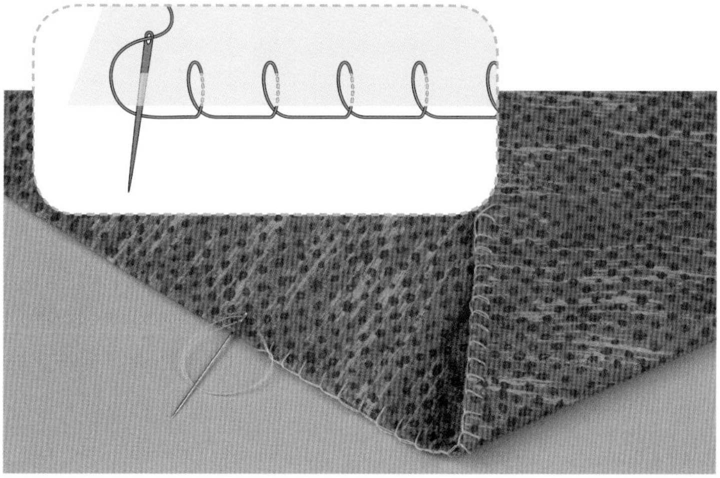

Blanket Stitch. A stitch that makes a decorative edging, but also encases the edges slightly, preventing fraying.

Blanket stitch

This stitch makes a decorative edging, but also encases the edges slightly, preventing fraying. Begin by sewing down through the fabric; bring the needle around the edge of the fabric and sew from the top down again. Before tightening the thread, guide the needle through the loop that the thread creates and move on to the next stitch. This will make a sort of chain, with the thread traveling along the edge of the fabric. If you do not bring the thread through the loop, you'll end up with a whipstitch.

Basting stitch

This stitch is composed of long, even stitches, and is used to temporarily hold fabric together or gather fabric. Begin by sewing down through the fabric. Proceed by sewing up and down through the fabric so the stitches are roughly the same length—about 1" (25mm) works well—on the top and bottom of the fabric.

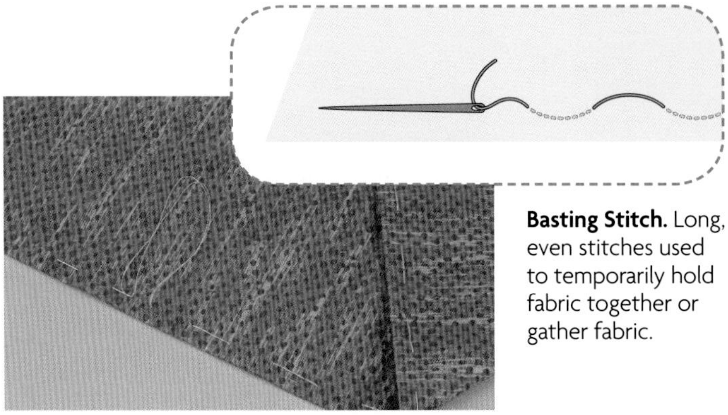

Basting Stitch. Long, even stitches used to temporarily hold fabric together or gather fabric.

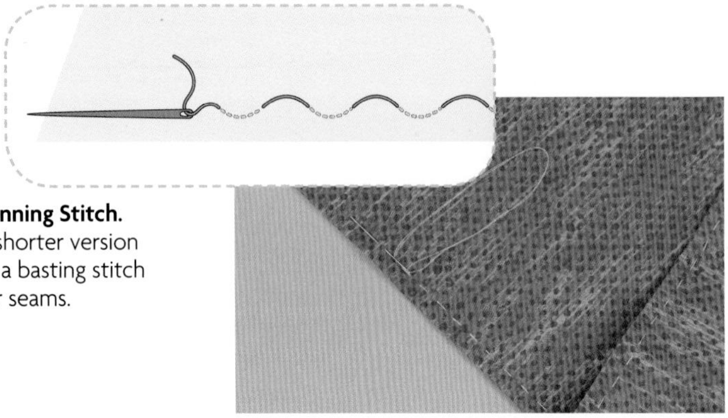

Running Stitch. A shorter version of a basting stitch for seams.

Running stitch

This is a shorter version of a basting stitch for seams. Begin by sewing down through the fabric. Proceed by sewing up and down through the fabric so the stitches are roughly the same length—about ¼" (5mm) works well—on the top and bottom of the fabric.

Ladder stitch

See this technique in action in the "Sewing an Opening Closed" sidebar (page 25). Hold the folded edges together firmly and begin by sewing into the edge of one side, between the two folded layers. Come up through the fabric about ¼" to ⅛" (3 to 5mm) along the folded edge. Repeat this on the other side, moving gradually toward the other end of the opening. When the thread is tightened, the thread will sit inside the folds and pull the edges together.

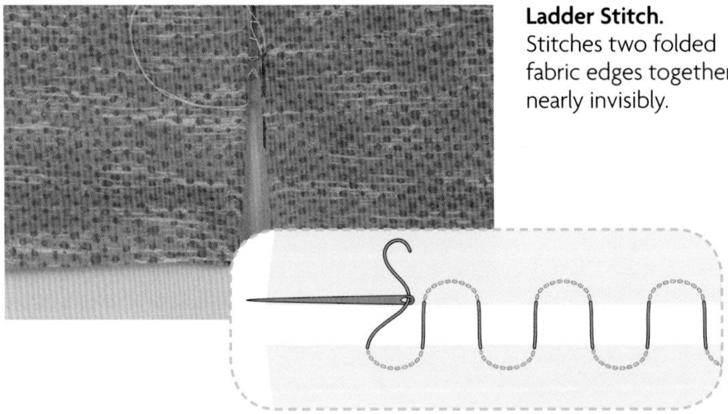

Ladder Stitch. Stitches two folded fabric edges together nearly invisibly.

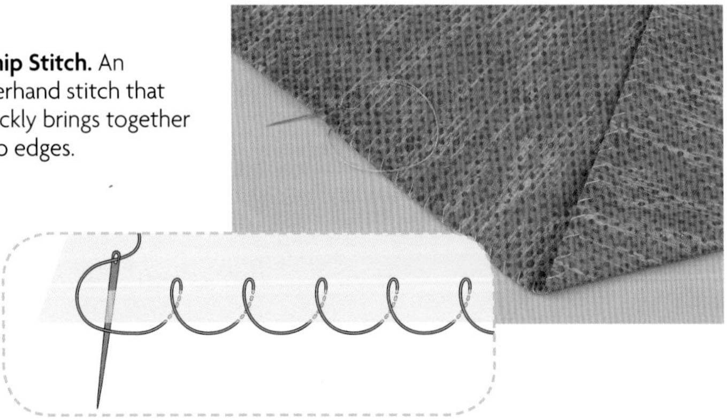

Whip Stitch. An overhand stitch that quickly brings together two edges.

Whip stitch

This is an overhand stitch that quickly binds together two edges. Begin by sewing down through the fabric; bring the needle around the edge of the fabric and sew down again. This will create diagonal stitches down the edge of the fabric.

Tip: Sewing an Opening Closed

When you need to sew closed the opening of a plushie or other accessory, there are a few techniques you can use to ensure your seam is completely invisible.

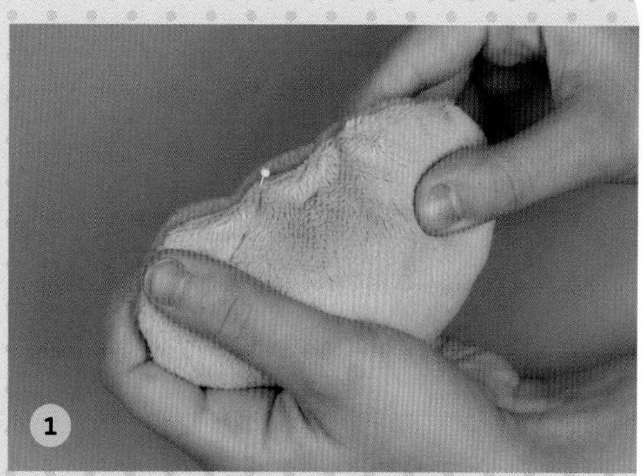

Fold and pin. Fold the edges of your plush's opening inside, and pin the opening closed.

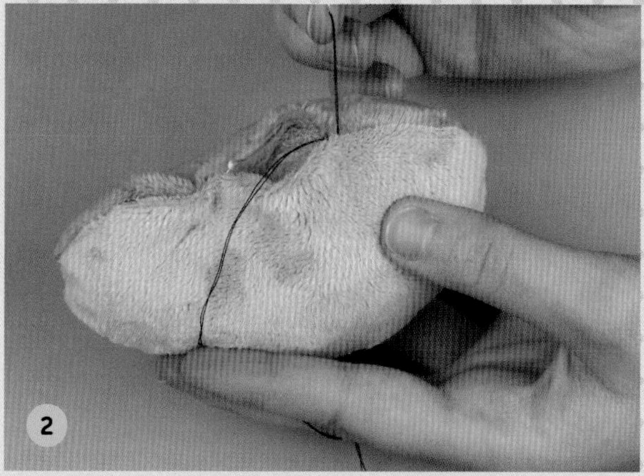

Make the starting knot. Make a knot at the end of your thread, and bring the needle into the fabric through the inside of the opening. This encases the knot and thread tail inside the plush. Make a few knots around your machine stitches by bringing your needle up underneath the machine stitches. Bring the needle through the loop made in the thread and tighten, similar to a square knot.

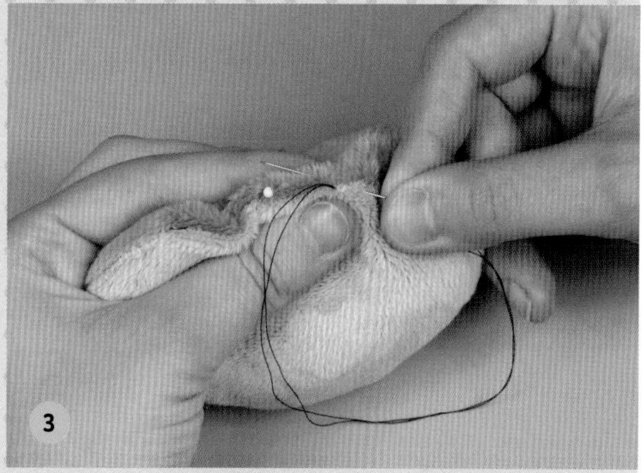

Sew with the ladder stitch. Use the ladder stitch to take small ⅛" (3mm) stitches from one side of your fabric to the other. Lightly tug on your thread to keep it taut and completely hide the stitches.

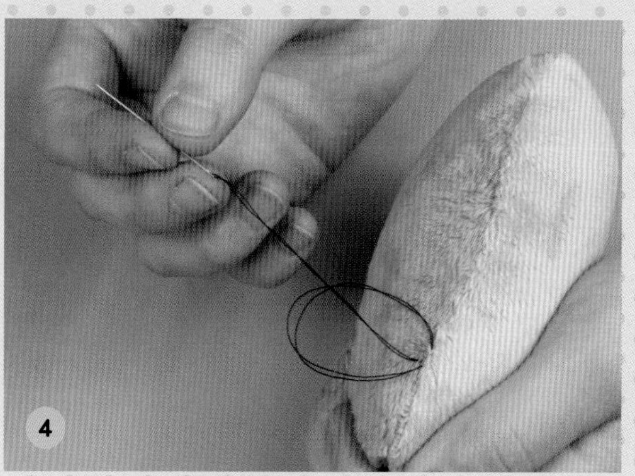

Make the ending knot. At the end of your seam, bring your needle through the loop made in the thread to create more knots around the machine stitches.

Cut the thread tail. Insert your needle close beside your finishing knots, and bring the needle back out a few inches away, through the plushie. Tug lightly, and your knot may pop into the fabric. Clip the thread while still tugging and your thread tail will be deep inside your plush, completely hidden!

Sewing Techniques and Terms

Clipping corners and curves

Whenever turning something right side out, any corners or curves made in your fabric should be trimmed, clipped, and/or notched. Trimming involves cutting down the overall size of the excess fabric. Clipping is creating a straight cut in on the excess fabric, and notching is removing a V of the excess. These actions eliminate extra bulk and also give curves more room to stretch, resulting in a smoother look. Trim the excess fabric on convex corners and curves to ⅛"–¼" (3–6mm) or clip them. Concave curves should be clipped every 1" (25mm), close to the seam. Concave corners should be clipped into the corner, within ⅛"–¼" (3–6mm) of the seam.

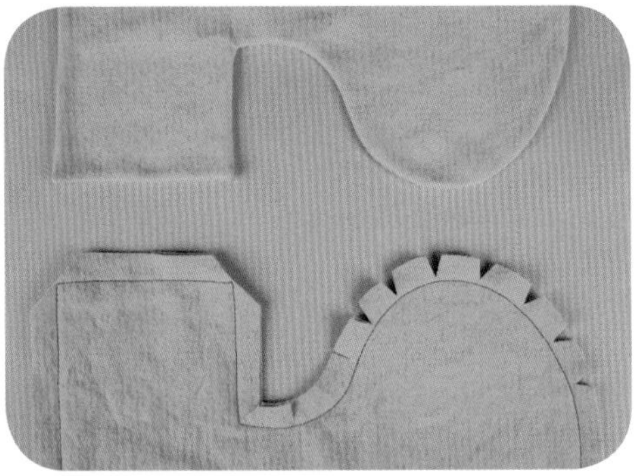

Trimming the seam allowances and clipping the corners and curves of your shapes makes them very smooth when turning them right side out.

Darts

Darts are tucks made to take in extra fabric and create a more pronounced shape in a finished piece. The sewing pattern will show a triangular shape that should be traced onto the fabric. Fold the fabric, right sides together, along the middle of the triangle to make each side of the dart match up. These lines are stitching lines. To make the dart, start at the outer edge of the triangle shape and sew inward. At the end, reduce your stitch length to nearly the shortest length and run off the edge. Avoid doing a backstitch at the end, as this can cause extra bulk at the apex of your point. If the dart is big enough, cut it open and press it open. If not, press it to one side.

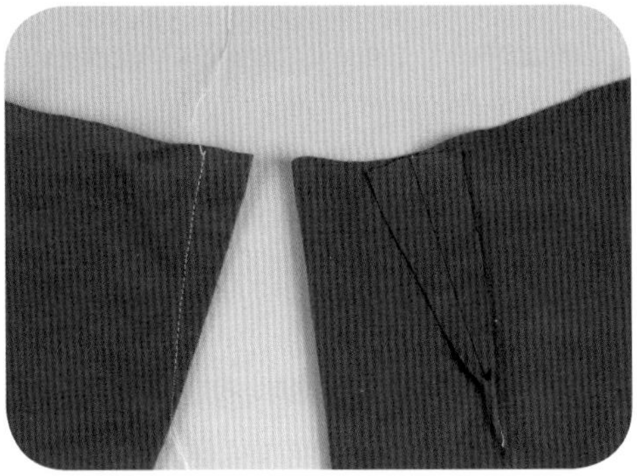

Darts are triangular-shaped tucks made in a fabric to create shape.

Finishing edges

As mentioned before, woven fabrics will unravel when the edges are left uncased. In some of the projects in this book, raw edges are not encased, so I suggest finishing them. This can be done with pinking shears, a kind of scissor with a zigzag that prevents fraying. There are also many liquid sealants on the market that put light glue on your fabric edges, and lastly, you can also sew a zigzag stitch along the edge of your fabric—the extra stitches keep the fabric from fraying and unraveling.

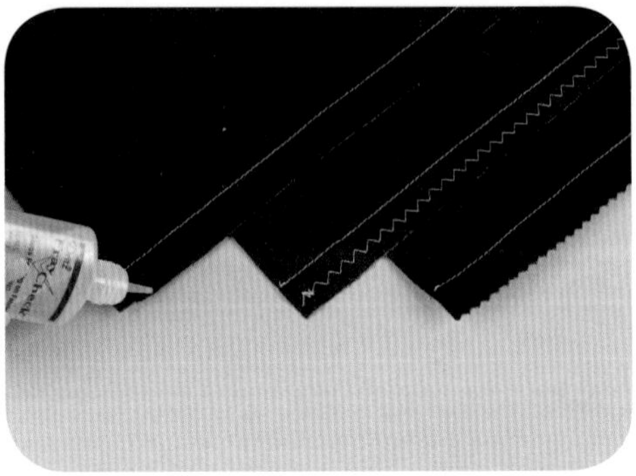

Using fray-blocking glue, a zigzag stitch, or cutting with pinking shears can help stop fraying in fabrics where the edges are left raw.

Gathering

In sewing, gathering means creating ruffles in fabric. This technique is typically done by machine or hand sewing a long basting stitch close to the edge of your fabric. Make sure it is done within the seam allowance to prevent threads showing on your finished project. Hold one side taut (or knot it), and begin pulling on the bobbin threads from the other side to ruffle the fabric. Multiple rows of stitching should be done for particularly long pieces of fabric. When the fabric is ruffled to the desired length or density, you can sew a quick knot on each end to temporarily hold the ruffles. Proceed to sew your gathered fabric into your project as usual.

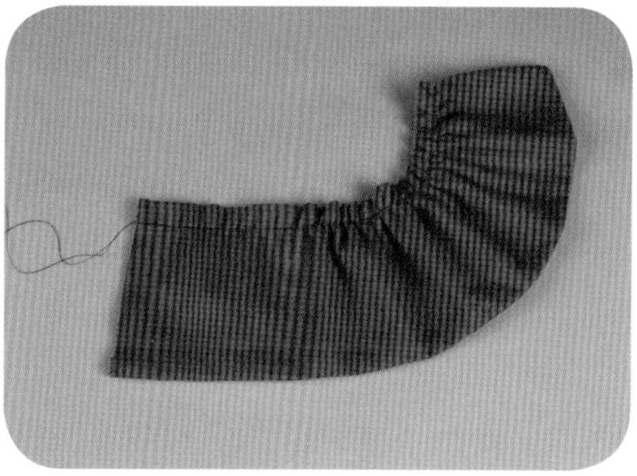

Pulling on the threads of a loosely sewn bit of fabric is called gathering, and is how ruffles are made in fabric.

Grain line

The grain line of a fabric follows how it was knitted or woven; it goes parallel to the selvage (the machine-finished edges of the fabric). Each pattern piece will have a grain line arrow to show how it needs to be placed and cut on the fabric to ensure proper stretching and direction. If you find that your pattern pieces don't fit on your fabric, you can turn them 90° to make them fit if necessary.

Hemming

Hemming is folding up the raw edge of fabric to finish it. The pattern will tell you how much to fold the fabric when hemming. Though there are many ways to hem fabric, the standard technique is to fold the fabric over once and press, then fold the fabric over again and press. Sew along the edge, keeping a steady distance from the edge, to finish the look.

Hemming is simply folding up the raw edges of a fabric and sewing it down to make a clean finish.

Seam allowance

The seam allowance in your project is the space between the edge of your fabric and where the seam is made. The western standard for most patterns is typically ⅝" (16mm) for garments and other projects. This is wide enough to give room for error in case any mistakes are made and seams need to be redone. With some smaller project pieces, the seam allowance may be shortened to ⅜" (10mm) to avoid extra bulk from the seam allowance. Always be sure to check what the seam allowance is for your project to ensure accuracy. When sewing, make sure your needle is a consistent distance from the edge of your fabric and your projects will turn out wonderfully. Use the measurement lines on the throat plate of your machine as a reliable guideline.

1

Key Chains

These adorable key chains are a great way to dive into the projects in this book. They use very little fabric, so nothing goes to waste, and their simple food shapes mean they only take minutes to construct. If you lack a sewing machine, the key chains can be done completely by hand—simply refer to the hand-sewing techniques on page 23. Whether you make these to adorn your cell phone, keys, purse, or just keep you company on your desk, you might find yourself making an entire army of food friends!

Dumpling Key Chain Plush

Difficulty: Very Easy

Patterns on page 144.

This little key chain has barely any sewing at all, so it is great for beginners. With a few simple stitches, it looks just like a delicious crimped dumpling. Fleece or felt are ideal for this project because there will be raw edges and neither fabric unravels. Use a golden brown color to make it look like it has been fried, while a cream fabric looks like a steamed dumpling. Try other colors to imagine different flavors!

Materials

- 6" x 7" (150 x 180mm) square of fleece or felt
- Fabric for appliqué
- Thread to match fleece/felt
- Thread to match appliqué fabric
- Batting
- Fusible web
- Stabilizer

Tools

- Fabric marker
- Fabric scissors
- Fabric pins
- Hand-sewing needle
- ⅜" (10mm) eyelet and eyelet setting tools
- Key chain or lanyard
- Key ring (optional)

Dumpling: 餃子
Gyoza (GYOH-zah)
Learn to Speak Japanese

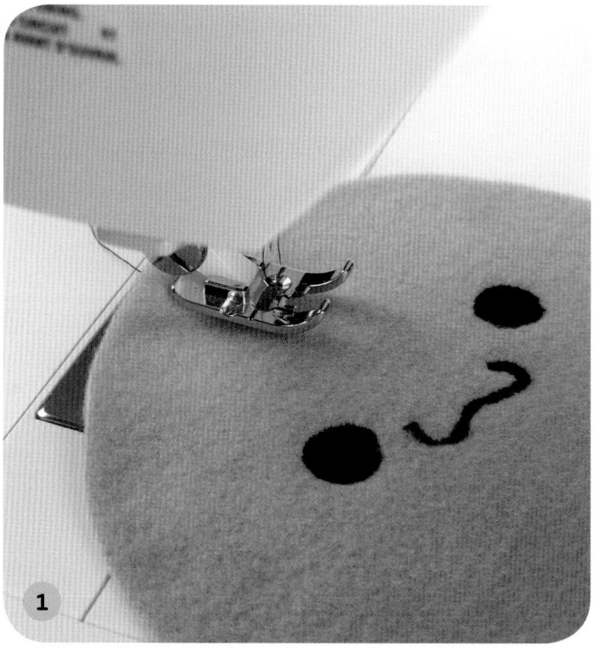

Appliqué the Dumpling face. Cut the pattern pieces from your fabric and make all applicable markings. Apply fusible web to the appliqué pieces. Iron the appliqué pieces to the main fabric according to the pattern guidelines. Sew the appliqué fabric down along its edges and sew along the pattern guideline to form the mouth.

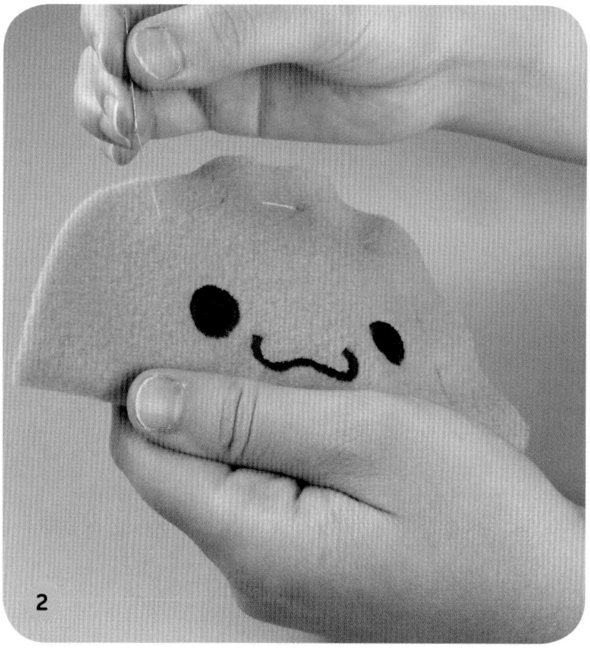

Sew the Dumpling closed. Fold the Dumpling in half, following the pattern fold line. Run a gathering stitch along the stitching line, stopping 2" (50mm) short to leave room for stuffing. Don't cut your thread yet, because you'll continue stitching after stuffing.

Stuff the Dumpling. Stuff the Dumpling lightly with batting. Continue stitching along the rest of the dumpling as before. Before you end your stitching and tie a knot, tug lightly at the thread to cinch the Dumpling's body until it looks crimped. Knot your seam while tugging the thread.

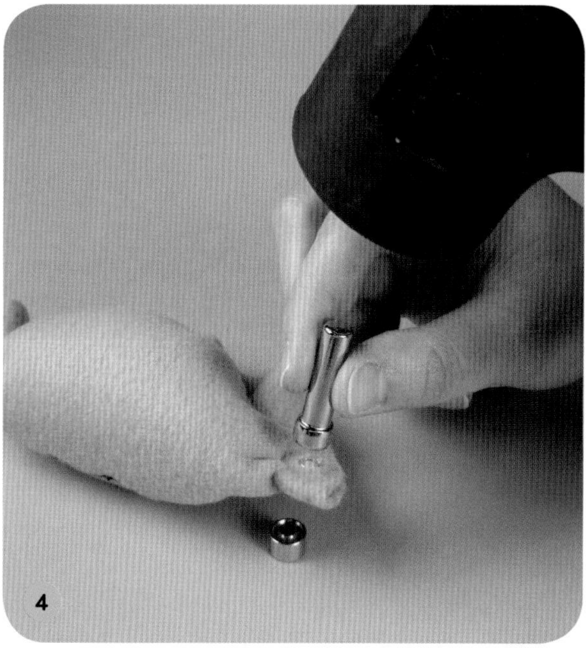

Insert an eyelet. Clip a small hole on one end of the Dumpling as indicated by the pattern. Follow the manufacturer instructions to insert an eyelet here. Attach a lariat or lanyard to the eyelet, using a key ring in between if necessary.

Strawberry Key Chain Plush

Difficulty: Very Easy

This strawberry is another great example of how a few small details and stitches can transform a little bit of fabric into a friendly little guy with personality. Fleece or felt are great fabrics to use in this project because the raw edges won't unravel and make your key chain fall apart. The white seed beads make the transition complete, so only the smiling face will let you know your strawberry isn't real!

Patterns on page 144.

Materials

- 6" x 6" (150 x 150mm) square of red fleece or felt
- 3" x 3" (75 x 75mm) square of green fleece or felt
- White seed beads
- Ribbon to match main fleece color
- Fabric for appliqué
- Thread to match Strawberry body
- Thread to match leaves
- Thread to match appliqué fabric
- Batting
- Fusible web
- Stabilizer

Tools

- Fabric scissors
- Fabric marker
- Fabric pins
- Hand-sewing needle
- Key chain or strap

This top view shows the ribbon, cinching, and leaf details.

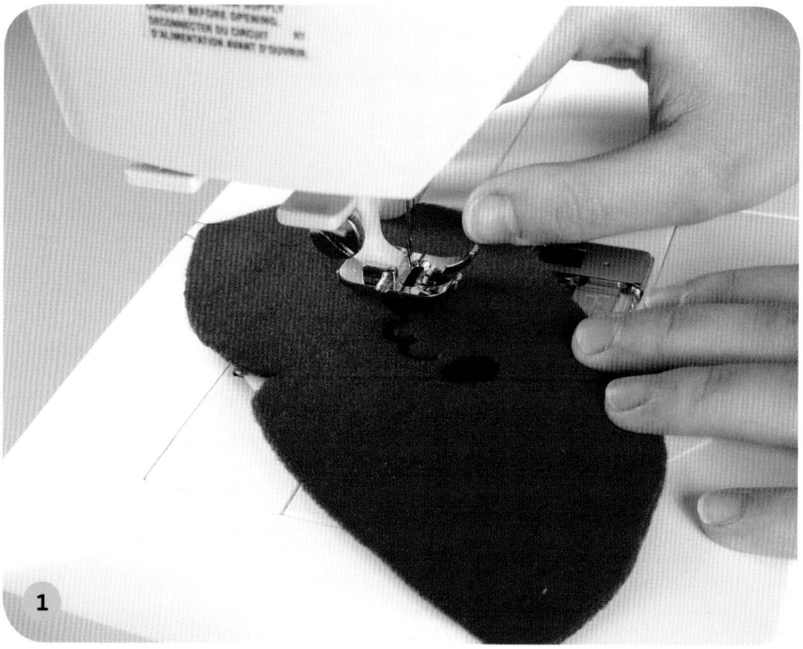

Appliqué. Cut the pattern pieces from your fabric and make all applicable markings. Apply fusible web to the appliqué pieces. Iron the appliqué pieces to the main fabric according to the pattern guidelines. Sew along the appliqué edges and along the pattern guideline to form the mouth.

Sew the side. Cut a 1" (25mm) piece of ribbon, fold it in half, and pin it inside the side seam of the Strawberry where indicated by the pattern. Sew the side seam, leaving the top edge open for stuffing.

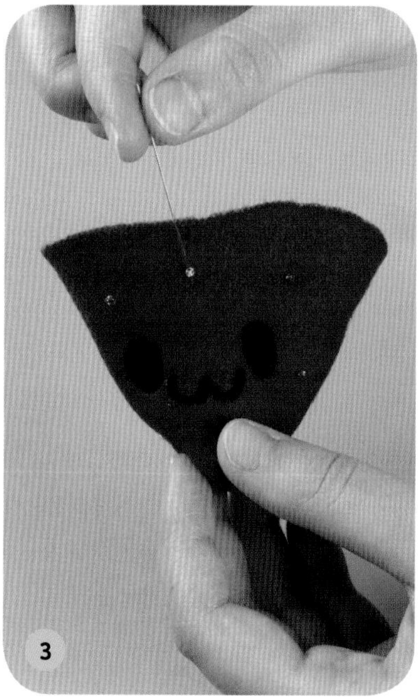

Apply the beads. Hand-sew the white seed beads to the Strawberry according to the pattern.

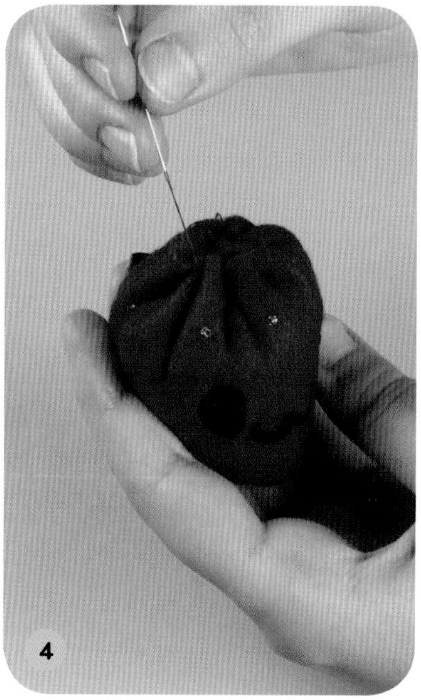

Stuff and sew closed. Stuff the Strawberry semi-firmly with batting. Run a gathering stitch along the top of the strawberry and cinch it closed, encasing the stuffing. Hold the thread tight while making several knots to secure it.

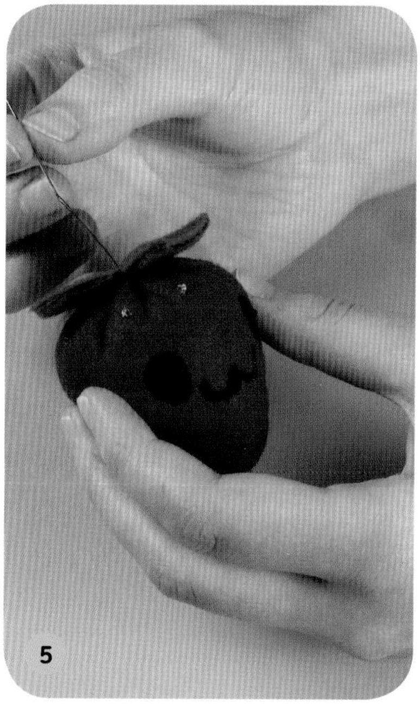

Sew the leaves. Sew the center of the leaves to the top center of the Strawberry.

Layer Cake Key Chain Plush

Difficulty: Easy

This cake-shaped plush has several pieces and is a bit more complicated than the previous two projects. However, all the different pieces make customizing your cake to any color combination very easy. Fleece or felt are good fabrics to choose for this project, though fleece gets my highest recommendation. Matching corners and edges is the challenge—if you find your edges don't match up by a few millimeters, don't hesitate to stretch your fleece a little bit to make them match. Fleece is very accommodating this way, and if you stretch it only a little, you won't notice any mistakes when your cake is done!

Materials

- 6" x 7" (150 x 180mm) square of main cake color fleece or felt
- 9" x 9" (230 x 230mm) square of frosting color fleece or felt
- Ribbon to match main cake color
- Fabric for appliqué
- Thread to match main cake color
- Thread to match frosting color
- Thread to match appliqué fabric
- Batting
- Fusible web
- Stabilizer

Tools

- Fabric scissors
- Fabric pins
- Fabric marker
- Hand-sewing needle
- Key chain or strap

Patterns on page 144.

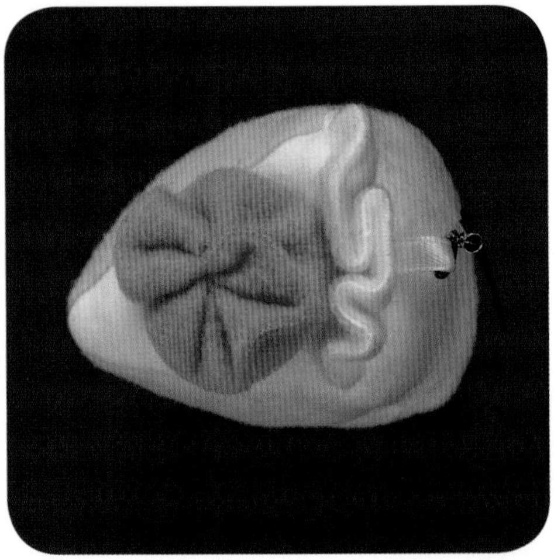

This top view shows the rosette and ruffle details.

Cake: ケーキ
Keiki (KAY-kee)

Learn to Speak Japanese

Layer Cake Keychain Plush

Sew the layers. Cut the pattern pieces from your fabric and make all applicable markings. Apply fusible web to the appliqué pieces. Sew a cake layer to each long side of a frosting layer. You should have a frosting layer between two cake layers. Repeat this process for the other side, and finger-press the seams when finished.

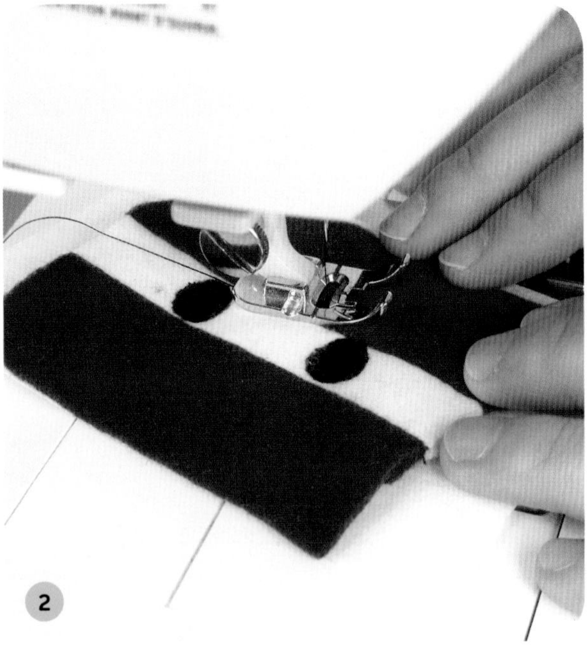

Appliqué. Iron the appliqué fabric to the cake's side. Sew the appliqué fabric down along the edges, and sew a line where indicated by the pattern for the mouth.

Sew the top and bottom. Sew one cake side along the long edge of the top piece, and another cake side to the other edge, meeting together at the point. Repeat this for the bottom piece.

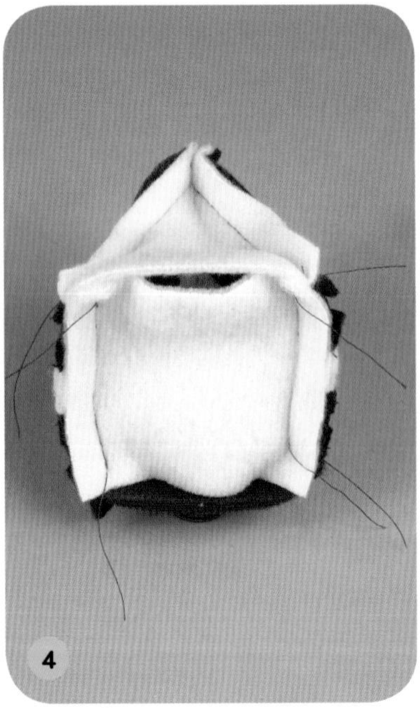

Sew the front and back. Sew the cake side edges to the back, leaving the top and bottom open. Also sew the cake sides together at the point of the cake, where they met in Step 3.

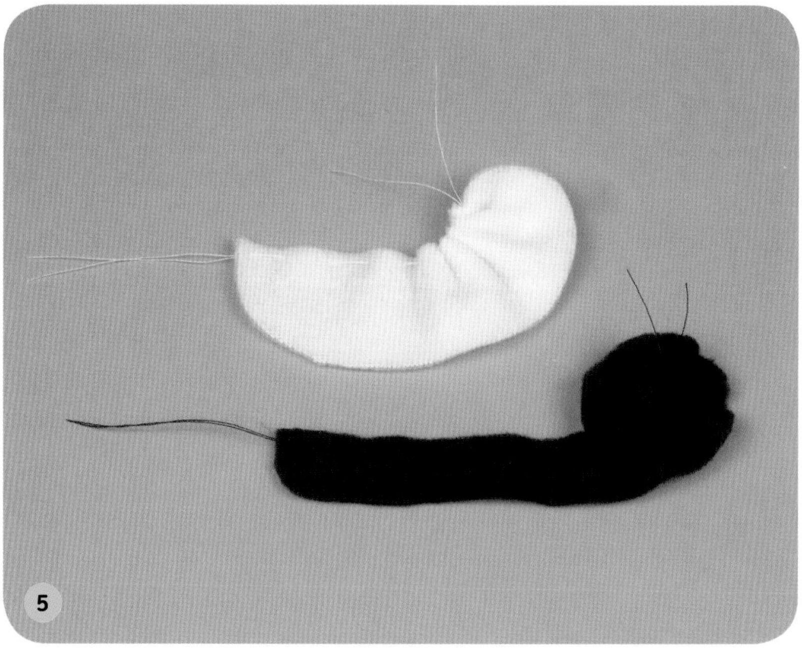

5

Gather the ruffles. Hand-sew a gathering stitch along the bottom of the ruffle and rosette pieces. Gather the ruffle piece small enough to fit inside the top edge of the cake that you left open in Step 4. Set the rosette aside for later.

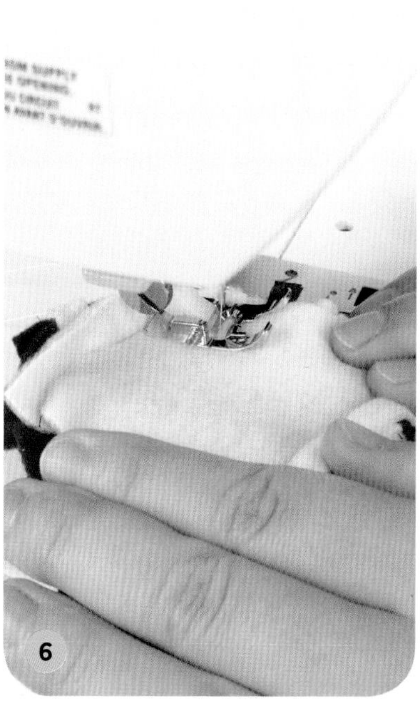

6

Sew the ruffle. Cut a 1" (25mm) piece of ribbon, fold it in half, and insert it into the top edge of the cake, centered beneath the ruffle, facing the back of the cake. Sew in place.

7

Turn and stuff. Turn the cake inside out and stuff it firmly with batting. Using the ladder stitch, hand-sew the bottom of the cake closed.

8

Attach rosette. Curl the rosette piece into a flower shape and hand-sew it to the top of the cake. Attach a key ring or lanyard to the ribbon to finish.

2

Storage Accessories

Why settle for a boring purse or pouch when it provides such an ample canvas for adorable appliqué? These projects are both cute and functional, giving you just enough room to hold your things, and making you smile at the same time. They range from the very simple electronics cases to the more complex cube purses. No matter what, they're worth the effort, serving as stylish bag and friend all in one!

Electronics Cases

Difficulty: Very Easy

These cases are perfect if you want a little extra protection for your laptop, handheld games, or cell phone. They'll prevent scratches and keep your gear looking adorable. Simple woven fabrics are best for this project, such as cotton, corduroy, or twill. If you would like a little extra security, a layer of thin fleece or quilt batting can be added between the lining and outside layers. The patterns provide guides to make a netbook case, handheld video game (such as Nintendo DS) case, and a cell phone (such as iPhone) case. If the patterns don't quite fit your electronic device, simply tweak the dimensions to fit.

Materials

- For netbook: ½ yd. (½m) woven fabric
- For netbook: ½ yd. (½m) lining fabric
- For video game or cell phone case: ¼ yd. (¼m) woven fabric
- For video game or cell phone case: ¼ yd. (¼m) lining fabric
- Hook-and-loop tape
- Fabric for appliqué
- Thread to match woven fabric
- Thread to match appliqué fabric
- Fusible web
- Stabilizer

Tools

- Fabric marker
- Fabric scissors
- Fabric pins
- Hand-sewing needle

Patterns on pages 145–146.

This view shows the lining and hook-and-loop tape details.

Like: 好き
Suki (sKEE) The "u" is pretty much silent here.

Learn to Speak Japanese

Electronics Cases

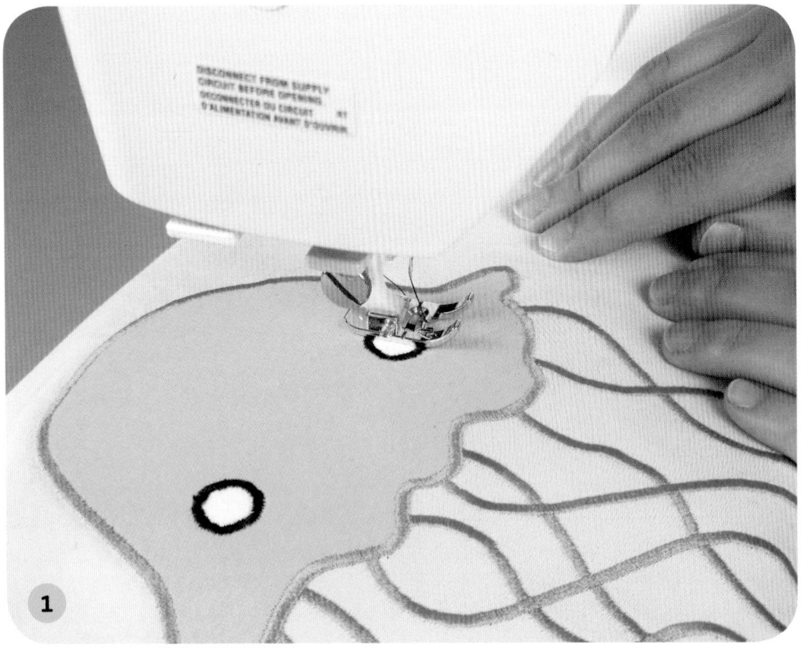

Appliqué. Cut the pattern pieces from your fabric and make all applicable markings. Apply fusible web to the appliqué pieces. Iron the appliqué fabric to the main pieces where the pattern indicates and sew along the edges. Also sew lines where the pattern indicates.

Apply the hook-and-loop tape. Sew the loop side of the tape on the outer fabric front piece, and the hook side on the lining fabric back piece.

Sew the front. Sew the front lining and outer pieces together at the top. Turn them over and iron them flat.

Sew the front to the back. Sandwich the front piece between the back and back lining. Do this with the lining fabrics facing each other. Sew along the perimeter, keeping the opening as indicated by the pattern to turn the pouch right side out.

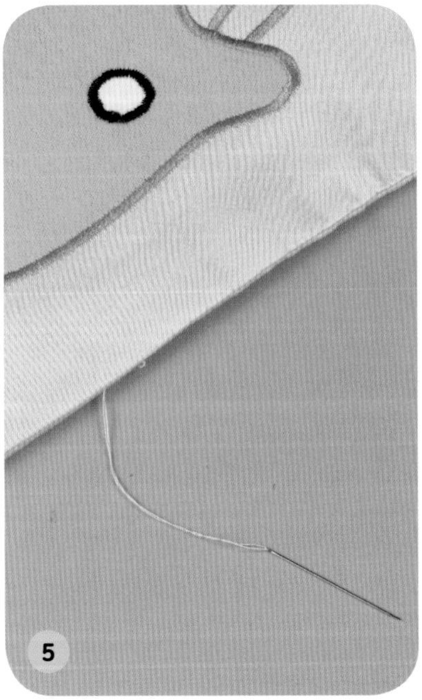

Finish. Turn the bag right side out and iron flat. Using the ladder stitch, sew the opening at the bottom closed.

Square Purse with Flap

☺ **Difficulty: Very Easy**

This simple and versatile purse is great for storing lots of things. You can easily whip one up in no time, so it won't be hard to make them in as many colors and characters as you like! This purse will work out best with a light- or medium-weight woven material, such as corduroy, cotton, or twill. The patterns provide guides to make a Bird, Seal, or Platypus.

Patterns on page 147.

Materials

- ½ yd. (½m) woven fabric for main purse
- ⅓ yd. (⅓m) lining fabric
- For Platypus: ⅛ yd. (⅛m) contrasting fabric for feet and bill
- Fabric for appliqué
- Thread to match woven fabric
- Thread to match appliqué fabric
- Fusible web
- Stabilizer

Tools

- Fabric marker
- Fabric scissors
- Fabric pins
- Hand-sewing needle
- Safety pin

This view shows the lining and back details.

Pieces without a pattern

For the purse strap, cut one 3¼" x 44" (85 x 1120mm) rectangle from the main fabric. Use a ⅝" (15mm) seam allowance.

Bird:鳥
Tori (toh-REE)

Learn to Speak Japanese

Square Purse with Flap

Appliqué. Cut the pattern pieces from your fabric and make all applicable markings. Apply fusible web to the appliqué pieces. Iron the appliqué pieces to the main fabric according to the guidelines. Sew the appliqué fabric along the edges and sew any lines according to the pattern.

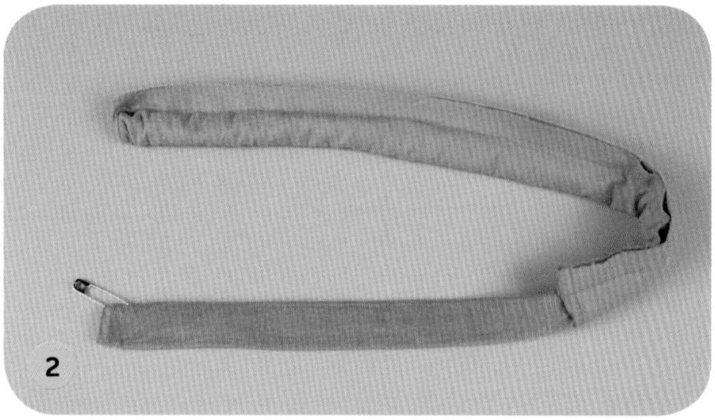

Sew the strap. Sew the strap piece in half using a ⅝" (15mm) seam allowance. Using a safety pin, turn it inside out and iron it flat.

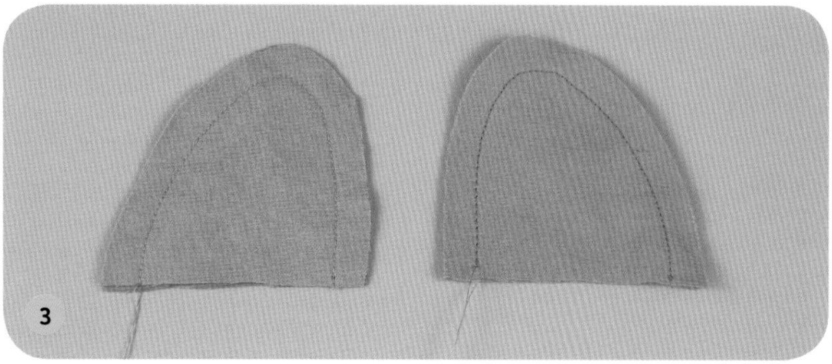

Sew the arms. Sew the flipper, foot, or wing pieces together, leaving the straight side edge open. Turn them inside out and iron them lightly. [For Platypus: Sew the bill pieces together, leaving the top edge open. Turn it right side out and hand-sew the opening closed.]

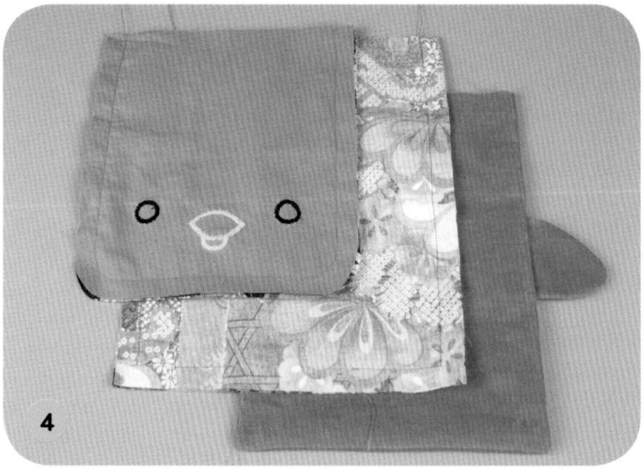

Sew the pouch and flap. Sew the main purse body pieces together, inserting the flipper, wing, or foot pieces in between according to the pattern. Leave the top edge open. Repeat this with the lining pieces (without the flippers/wings/feet) and leave an opening at the bottom as indicated by the pattern to turn right side out.

Sew the top and finish. Nestle the lining into the main pouch, aligning the upper edges. Insert the strap in between, lining each end up with the purse's side seam. Insert the flap on one side, making sure the appliqué faces the main fabric. Sew along the top. Turn the purse right side out and use the ladder stitch to sew the opening closed. [For Platypus: Topstitch the bill onto the edge of the flap.]

Jellyfish Purse

Difficulty: Experienced Beginner

The shape of a jellyfish really suits itself as a purse—the tentacles dangle sweetly as you carry him around! A medium-weight woven fabric is best for this project, such as corduroy or twill. Too heavy a fabric will make the tentacles and ruffles difficult to gather, while going too light will make the jellyfish lose its shape. The challenge in this project comes from inserting a zipper, which can be made a lot easier if you have a zipper foot for your sewing machine. To give yourself extra insurance, you can also baste the zipper to your fabric before sewing it, so it won't move around while you sew.

Patterns on page 148.

Materials

- ⅔ yd. (⅔m) woven fabric
- ¼ yd. (¼m) lining fabric
- 7" (180mm) zipper to match woven fabric
- Fabric for appliqué
- Thread to match woven fabric
- Thread to match appliqué fabric
- Fusible web
- Stabilizer

Tools

- Fabric marker
- Fabric scissors
- Fabric pins
- Hand-sewing needle
- Safety pin

This view shows the lining and interior of the Jellyfish purse.

Pieces without a pattern

For the purse strap, cut one 3¼" x 44" (85 x 1120mm) rectangle from the main fabric. Use a ⅝" (15mm) seam allowance.

Jellyfish:くらげ
Kurage (KOO-RAH-geh)

Learn to Speak Japanese

Jellyfish Purse

1

Sew the strap. Cut the pattern pieces from your fabric and make all applicable markings. Apply fusible web to the appliqué pieces. Sew the strap piece in half (use a ⅝" [15mm] seam allowance), and, using a safety pin, turn inside out.

2

Sew the front and back. Pin two of the Jellyfish body pieces together. Insert the strap between them where the pattern guidelines show. Sew along that one side, and repeat for the other side, making two halves. Repeat the same steps with the lining, but don't include the strap. Iron the seam open lightly.

3

Appliqué. Iron the appliqué pieces to the main fabric. Sew along the edges of the fabric and sew a line to form the mouth.

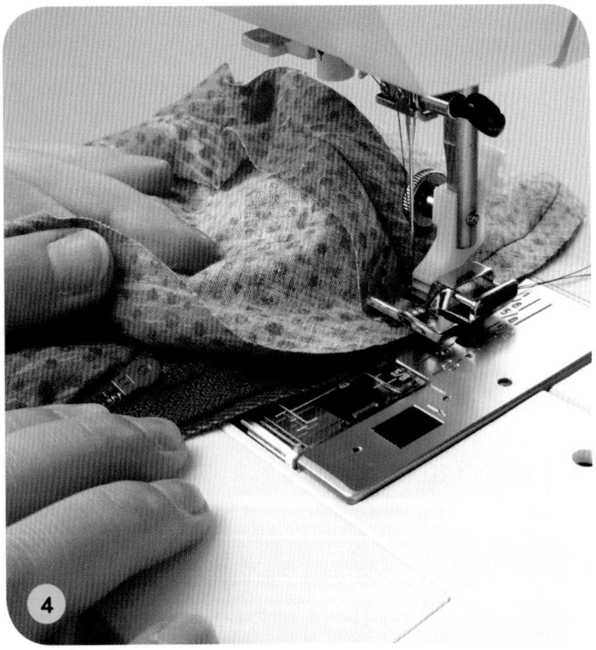

4

Sew the zipper. Sandwich the zipper between the outer Jellyfish fabric and the lining, matching the ends of the zipper with the circles indicated on the pattern. Sew as close to the zipper teeth as possible. Repeat this for the other side, being sure to keep the strap untwisted. This will leave the ends beyond the circle marking unattached to anything. Sew them together so that they, along with the zipper, make one continuous dome shape.

Tip: Working with Zippers

Zippers can be inserted into projects in a number of different ways. For the projects in this book, the process is kept very simple: the zipper is sewn into the project much like any other piece of fabric. To help you get used to inserting zippers, follow these steps whenever working with zippers is called for.

Zipper feet. Zipper feet are an attachment for your sewing machine that allow your needle to get as close to the zipper teeth as possible. The side of the foot rides up against the zipper teeth so the needle is properly placed at all times. Zipper feet are optional for the projects in this book, but can make maneuvering easier.

Pin the pieces in place. Pin the fabric to the zipper tape, right sides together, following any markings or guidelines as indicated on the pattern.

Sew around the zipper pull. When starting the seam, the zipper pull is the biggest obstacle. When you approach it, open the zipper slightly to move it down. After a few inches of sewing, lift the presser foot and move the pull back up, closing the zipper. If you have a particularly large zipper pull, you may have to lift the needle as well. Doing this will get the zipper pull out of your way while you continue sewing.

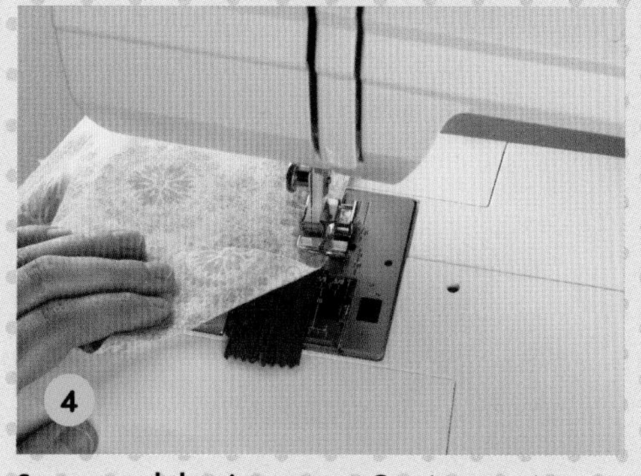

Sew around the zipper stop. Continue sewing along the zipper tape. This can be done while the zipper is open or closed, whichever allows better maneuverability with the fabric. You will likely have to curve slightly around the large zipper stop at the end. Be careful not to get too close, as hitting it with the needle can cause dangerous breakage.

Jellyfish Purse

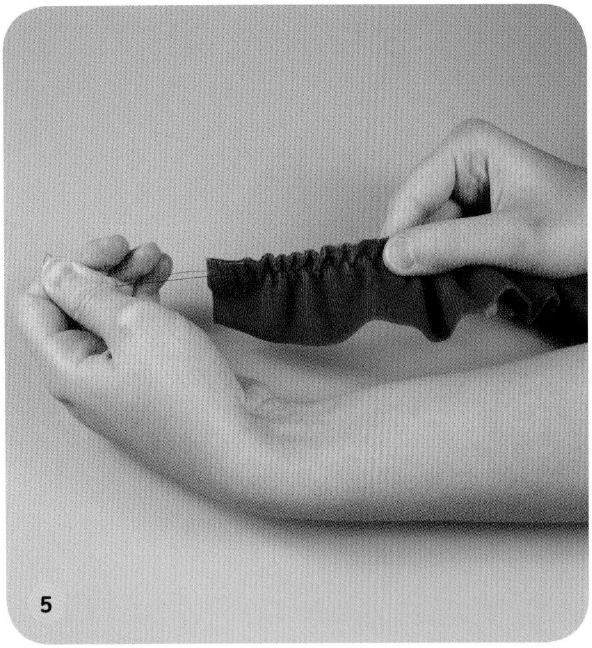

Gather the ruffle. Iron the ruffle piece in half widthwise and run a basting stitch along the raw edge. Gather it until it's worked down to about 21" (535mm).

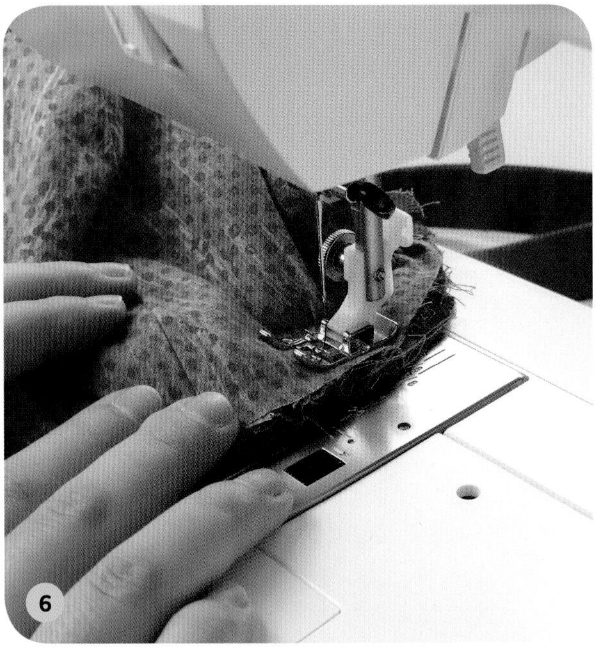

Sew the bottom. Pin the Jellyfish body to the bottom, inserting the ruffle between them, and aligning all raw edges. Tuck the ends of the ruffle inside the purse to avoid them showing on the outside. Sew along the bottom.

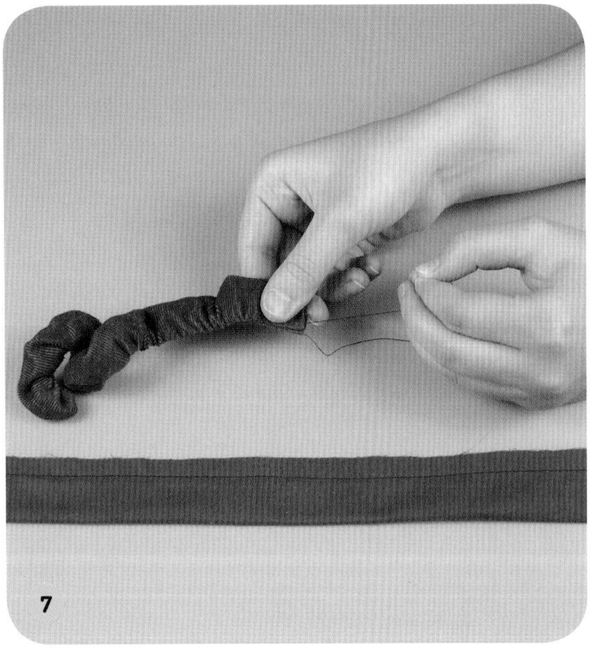

Sew the tentacles. Fold the tentacle pieces along the fold line. Leave a long beginning thread tail and sew along the long edge with a basting stitch. When you arrive at the curved end, return to a normal-length stitch. Turn the tentacles right side out, and using the beginning thread tail, gather the tentacles until they are about half their original length.

Attach the tentacles. Turn the raw edges of the tentacles inside and sew them onto the purse bottom, following the guidelines from the pattern.

Cube Purse

Difficulty: Intermediate

This design is what you get when you cross a super-cute plush with a tote. It can be made from woven fabric, but I prefer a plush fabric, such as minky; the finished purse is a real treat, and you'll have a cuddly buddy by your side all day! The challenges in this project include inserting zippers, making pivots around corners, and working with tricky lining pieces. Basting your seams before sewing them can be a real help here. Also, be sure extra pieces are kept away from your sewing area and nothing gets sewn down accidentally. The patterns provide guides to make a Fox, Bunny, or Tofu cube.

Patterns on page 149.

Materials

- ½ yd. (½m) minky or woven fabric
- ¼ yd. (¼m) lining fabric
- For Fox: ⅛ yd. (⅛m) black or contrast fabric for ear/foot/tail tips
- 7" (180mm) matching zipper
- For Bunny: Batting
- Fabric for appliqué
- Thread to match woven fabric
- Thread to match appliqué fabric
- Fusible web
- Stabilizer

Tools

- Fabric marker
- Fabric scissors
- Fabric pins
- Hand-sewing needle
- Safety pin

Pieces without a pattern

For the purse strap, cut one 3¼" x 44" (85 x 1120mm) rectangle from the main fabric. Use a ⅝" (15mm) seam allowance.

Fox: 狐
Kitsune (KIT-soo-neh)

Learn to Speak Japanese

Cube Purse

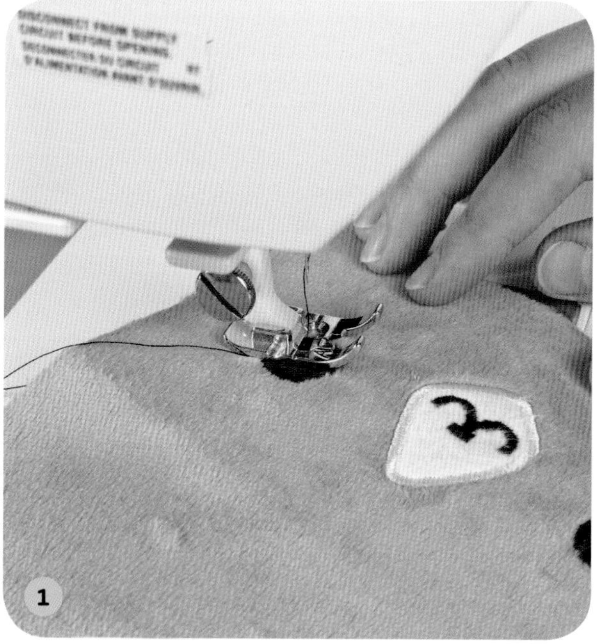

Appliqué. Cut the pattern pieces from your fabric and make all applicable markings. Apply fusible web to the appliqué pieces. Iron the appliqué pieces to the main fabric according to the pattern guidelines. Sew the appliqué fabric along the edges and sew along any lines indicated on the pattern.

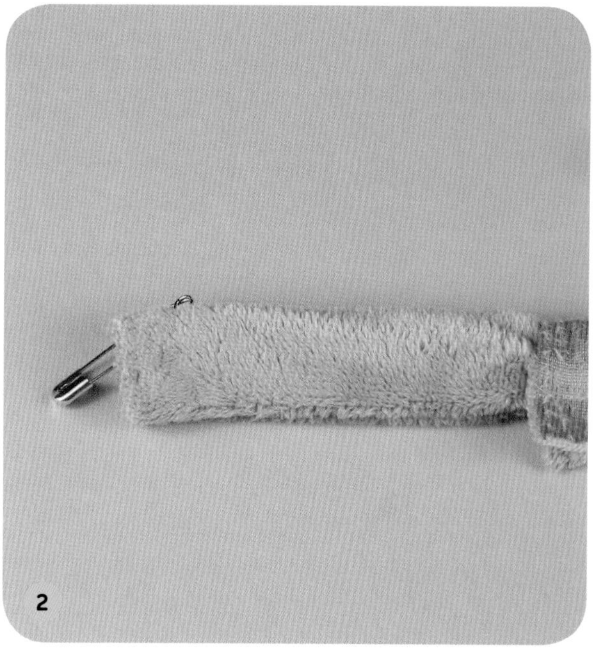

Sew the strap. Sew the strap piece in half (use a ⅝" [15mm] seam allowance), and, using a safety pin, turn it inside out.

Sew the appendages. [For Fox: Sew leg, ear, and tail tips to their corresponding base pieces. Finger press the pieces flat.] Sew the arm, leg, ear, and tail pieces together, leaving straight edges open to turn right side out. [For Bunny: Use a gathering stitch along the edges of the circle piece for the tail, stuff lightly with batting, and cinch closed.]

Sew the sides. Sew all four of the side pieces together in a circle. Repeat this for the lining pieces.

Tip: Sewing Corners

Sewing corners can be tricky, especially for a 3-D cube like this purse project. If you find that you want to get your corners lined up just right, or are simply having trouble with Step 6, follow these tips to be extra sure that the bottom of your cube purse is sewn to the sides perfectly. Getting the hang of this technique is indispensible for tougher garment sewing projects.

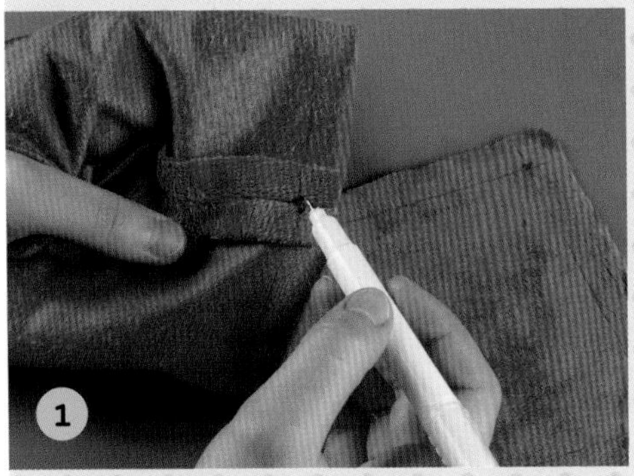

Mark the fabric. Use a washable fabric marker to mark where the seams should go, particularly where they intersect at the corners.

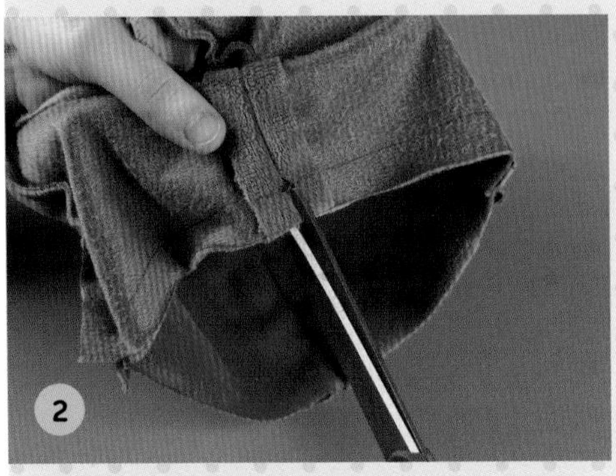

Clip the corners. Clip the corners of the sides very close to the intersecting seam lines, about ⅛" (3mm).

Pin the pieces in place. Pin the sides to the bottom piece, matching seam lines. Stretch the fabric lightly where necessary to make these marks match up.

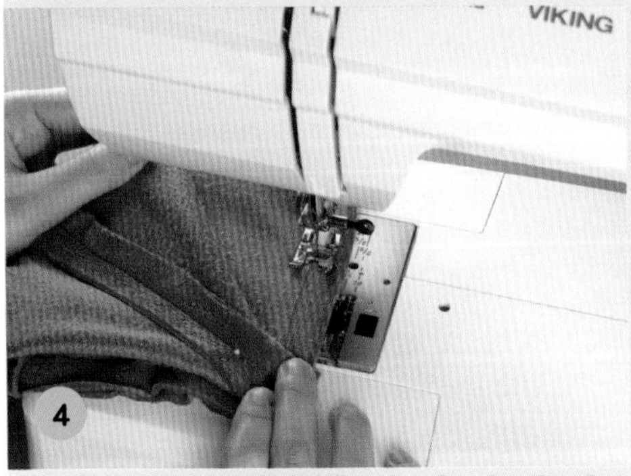

Sew along the seam lines. Sew along the seam lines indicated. Fold excess fabric away from you to keep your working area uncluttered, so you're less likely to accidentally sew fabric you don't mean to.

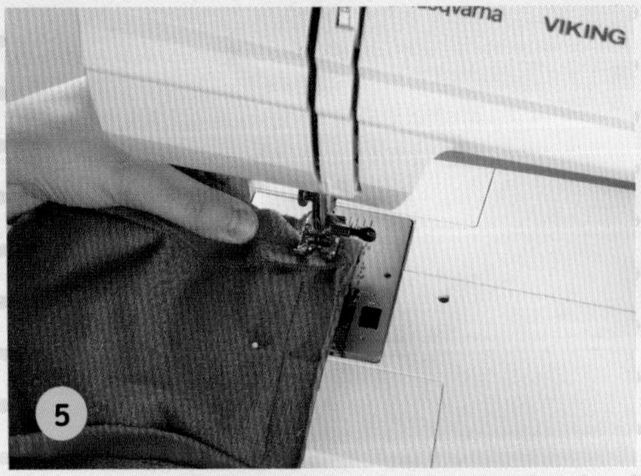

Sew the arms. When coming to a corner, stop the needle down exactly at the intersecting mark. Lift the presser foot and turn the work 90°. Before lowering the presser foot, make sure the fabric is shifted out of the needle's way so the next part of the seam is smooth and clear to sew.

Cube Purse

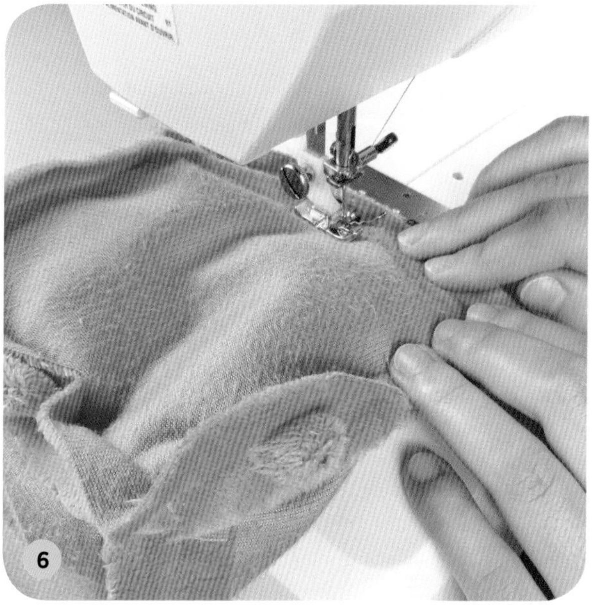

Sew the zipper. Sandwich the zipper between the top main fabric and lining pieces and sew as close to the zipper teeth as possible between the circles indicated on the pattern. Repeat this for the other side. Cut off any extra zipper that sticks out and sew a few new stitches at the bottom of the teeth to prevent losing the zipper pull. Note: Make sure your top piece is now a 5¾" (145mm) square. Inserting the zipper can throw this measurement off. If one side is longer, carefully trim it equally on each side to make it 5¾" (145mm).

Sew the bottom. Sew the bottom piece along the bottom edges of the cube, inserting the arms, legs, and tail where applicable. Match the corners and pivot 90° between the sides, making sure to move excess fabric out of the way so it doesn't get sewn accidentally. [For Bunny: Hand-sew the tail on the back.] Sew the bottom onto the lining in the same fashion, but leave a small space open for turning it right side out.

Sew the top. Sew the top to the rest of the purse, inserting the strap where indicated, and ears if applicable. Catch the zipper edges in the seam, but be sure to keep the lining separate. Repeat the same process for the lining.

Finishing. Turn the purse right side out and sew the lining closed. From the inside, hand-sew a few stitches of the corners of the lining to the main purse fabric to keep it in place.

3

Wearable Accessories

These projects are perfect for throwing on quickly to add a little extra to your outfit. You'll also find they are surprisingly warm and add brightness to what otherwise might be a cold and dreary day. You'll enjoy these characters so much you might even decide to work your entire outfit around them. All of these accessories are simple to make, so nothing should stop you from making these for your friends and family as well as for yourself!

Character Hats

Difficulty: Easy

You'll be surprised how easy it is to take such a plain hat and transform yourself into an adorable character instantly. I've found men and women of all ages love these hats, so feel confident in making your own designs. Ears for this hat can also be interchanged with those found for the Poncho and Character Hoodies in Chapter 5 (pages 110 and 102). Fleece is the best fabric for this hat, because it is soft and warm, and stretches enough to fit snugly around almost everyone's head. The only challenge in this hat will be in lining up ears and front and back seams correctly. Watch out for that and you'll be fine. The patterns provide guides to make a Broken Bunny long-eared aviator hat, Zombie Kitty aviator hat, Strawberry Kitty beanie, or Fox beanie.

Materials

- Fabric for appliqué
- Thread to match main fleece fabric
- Thread to match appliqué fabric
- Fusible web
- Stabilizer

For Broken Bunny (long-eared aviator hat):

- ½ yd. (½m) white fleece
- ¼ yd. (¼m) pink fleece
- ½ yd. (½m) linen

For Zombie Kitty (aviator hat):

- ⅓ yd. (⅓m) olive fleece
- ⅛ yd. (⅛m) black fleece

For Fox (beanie):

- ¼ yd. (¼m) orange fleece
- ⅛ yd. (⅛m) black fleece
- ⅛ yd. (⅛m) white fleece

For Strawberry Kitty (beanie):

- ¼ yd. (¼m) red fleece
- ⅛ yd. (⅛m) white fleece
- ⅛ yd. (⅛m) green fleece

Tools

- Fabric marker
- Fabric scissors
- Fabric pins

Patterns on pages 150–151.

Hat: 帽子
Boushi (BOH-shee)

Learn to Speak Japanese

Hat Gallery

< Broken Bunny hat front detail.

^ Broken Bunny hat ear detail.

> Fox hat front detail.

> Zombie Kitty front detail.

< Zombie Kitty ear flap detail.

Character Hats

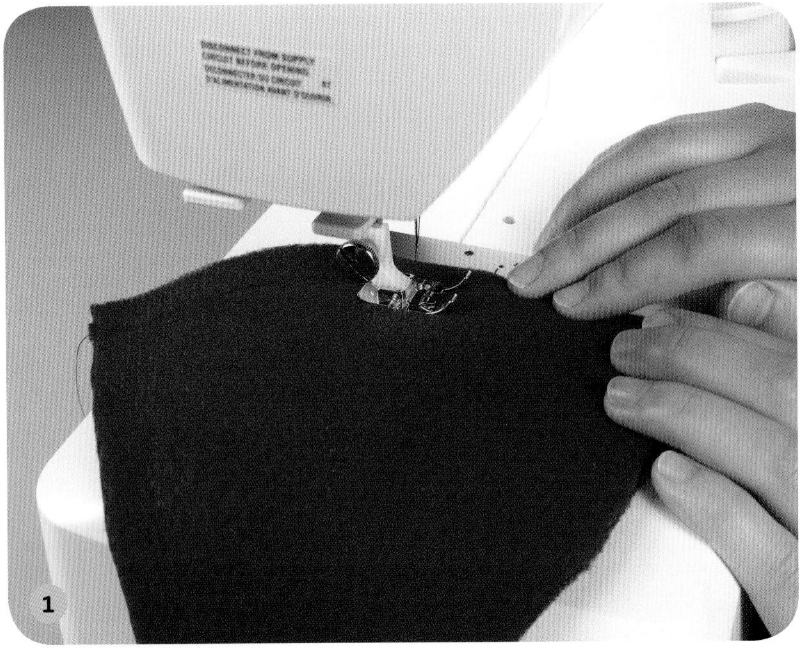

Sew the front, back, and band. Cut the pattern pieces from your fabric and make all applicable markings. Apply fusible web to the appliqué pieces. Sew both pairs of the crown pieces together along one side, creating two halves. Also sew the back seam of the hat band. For the standard hat band, fold it along the fold line and press lightly. For the aviator hat band (Bunny and Zombie Kitty), see Step 3.

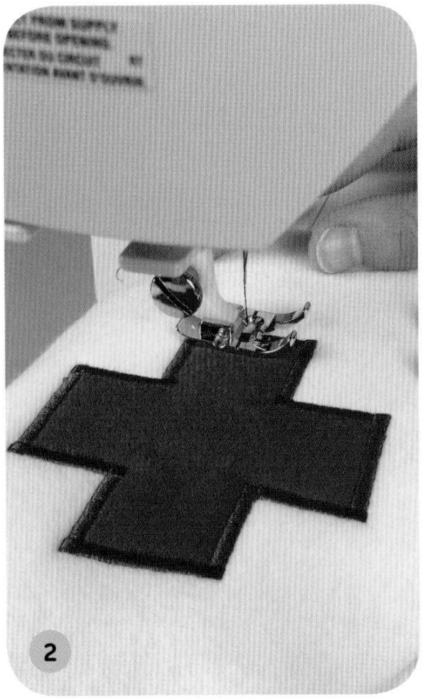

Appliqué. For Bunny and Zombie Kitty: Iron the appliqué pieces to the ear flaps and sew along the edges.

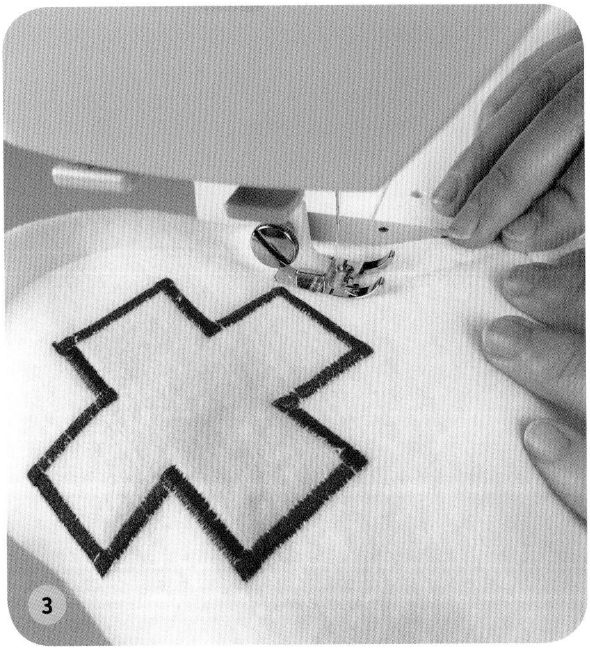

Sew the aviator band. For Bunny and Zombie Kitty: Sew the aviator band pieces together along the bottom curved edge. Leave the top straight edge open. Turn the band right side out and press lightly.

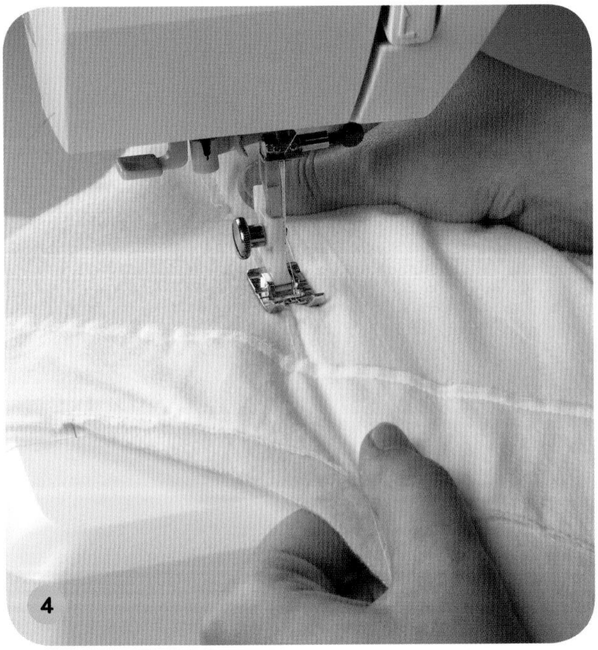

Attach the linen. For Bunny: Rip the linen fabric with the grain into strips of various widths between 1" and 3" (25 and 75mm). Pin these at various angles on the inner bunny ear pieces to resemble bandages. Use a straight stitch along the edges to sew them down, and leave the edges raw to complete the bandaged effect. Trim any excess linen sticking out beyond the ear pieces.

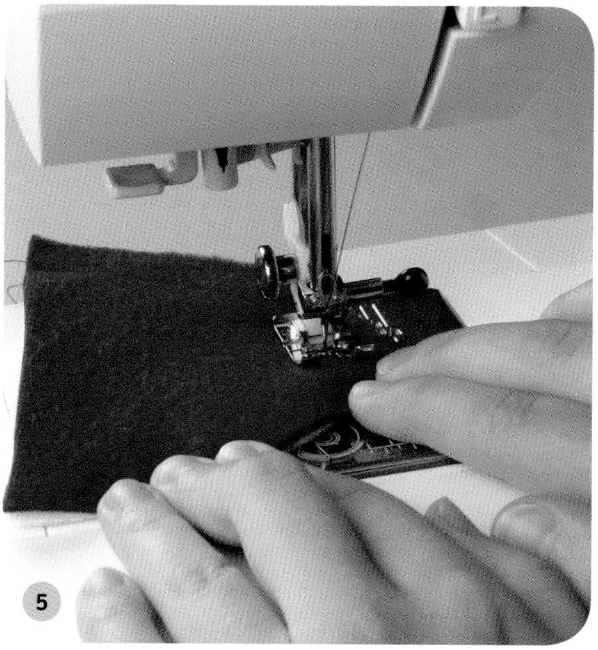

5

Sew the ears. [For Fox: Sew the ear tips to the main ear pieces and press them flat.] Sew the inside ear pieces to the outside ear pieces, leaving the bottom edge open. [For Strawberry Kitty: Also sew the stem pieces together.] Turn them all right side out and press.

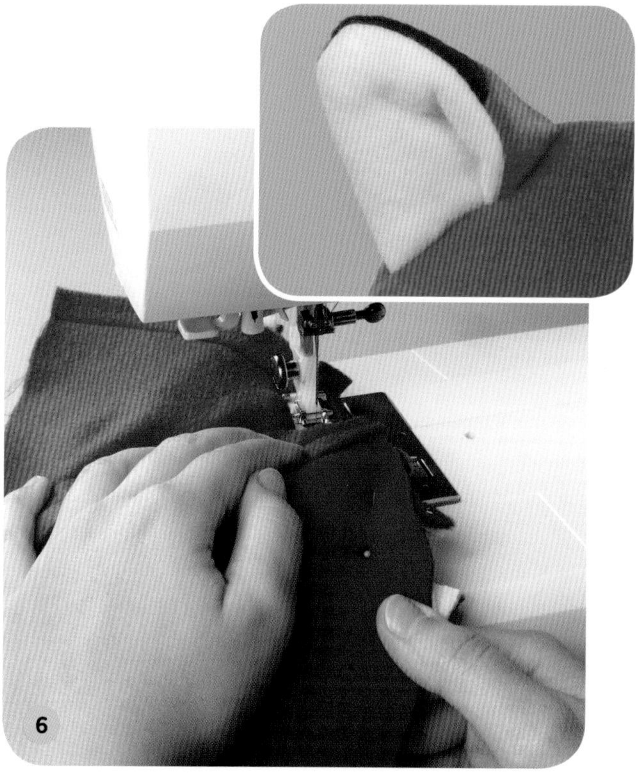

6

Sew the front to the back. Pin the front of the crown to the back, inserting ears between them where the pattern indicates. If using kitty or fox ears, fold over ⅓ of the ear away from the center seam for a bit of depth (see inset). Sew along the top curved edge, leaving the bottom open.

7

Sew the crown to the band. Sew the band around the crown of the hat. Match the center back and front of the band with the center back and front crown seams. Stretch the fabric a bit if necessary to match up the lengths. Press the seam open when finished.

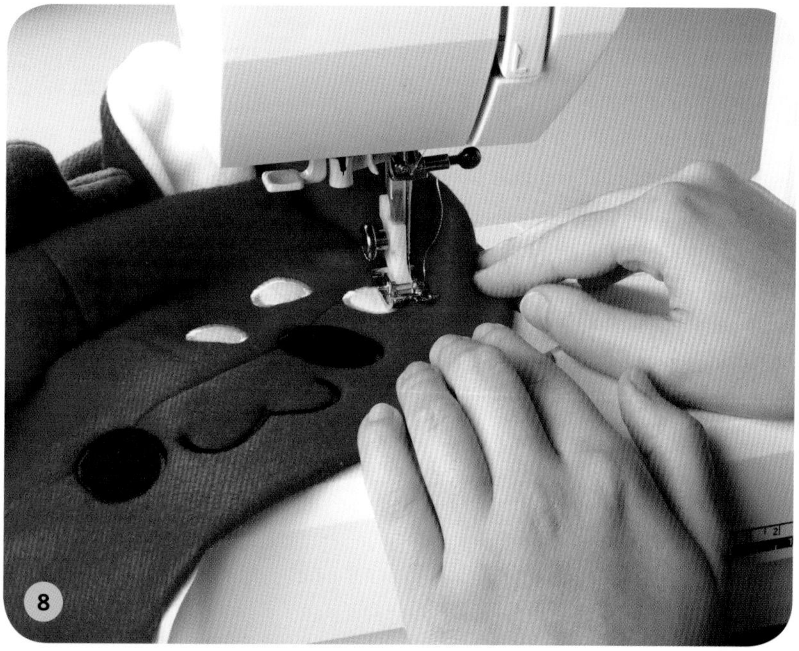

8

Appliqué the face. Iron the features onto the front of the hat. Sew along the edges of the fabric and along any lines indicated by the pattern.

Arm & Leg Warmers

Difficulty: Easy

These arm and leg warmers are great for heating you up, but also for using all kinds of crazy colors and trims. You might see them as part of some fun Japanese fashion styles. Just about any fabric works well for this project, except for anything very heavy. With this project, you'll also be able to do a fancy corset-style design, without all the mess of steel eyelets. The only challenge in this project comes from adding the optional trim. Making sure the trim is consistently straight and even is the trick to getting the perfect result. Marking, pinning, or even taping your trim in place can work wonders! The pattern provides guides to make either arm or leg warmers, and several appliqué motifs.

Materials

- ½" (13mm) elastic
- Fabric for appliqué
- Thread to match main fabric
- Thread to match appliqué fabric
- Fusible web
- Stabilizer

For leg warmers:

- ⅔ yd. (⅔m) fabric
- 1½ yds. (1½m) ribbon or lace trim (optional)
- For corset variation: 2 yds. (2m) crocheted lace with holes for ribbon
- For corset variation: 3 yds. (3m) ribbon

For arm warmers:

- ½ yd. (½m) fabric
- 1 yd. (1m) ribbon or lace trim (optional)
- For corset variation: 1½ yds. (1½m) crocheted lace with holes for ribbon
- For corset variation: 2½ yds. (2½m) ribbon

For angel wing, devil wing, star, or strawberry appliqué:

- ⅛ yd. (⅛m) appliqué fabric
- 6" x 6" (150 x 150mm) scrap for strawberry stem

For tiger stripes:

- ⅓ yd. (⅓m) appliqué fabric

Tools

- Fabric marker
- Fabric scissors
- Fabric pins

Arm: 手 Te (TEH)
Leg: 足 Ashi (ah-SHEE)

Learn to Speak Japanese

Patterns on pages 152–153.

Warmer Gallery

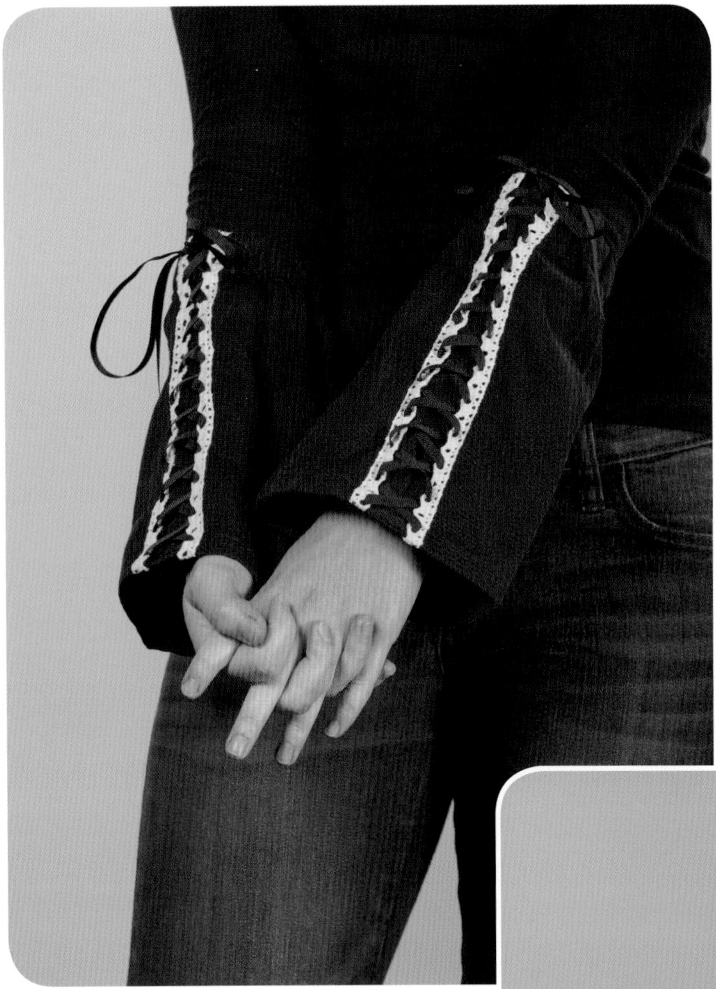

^ Detail on the corset-style arm warmers.

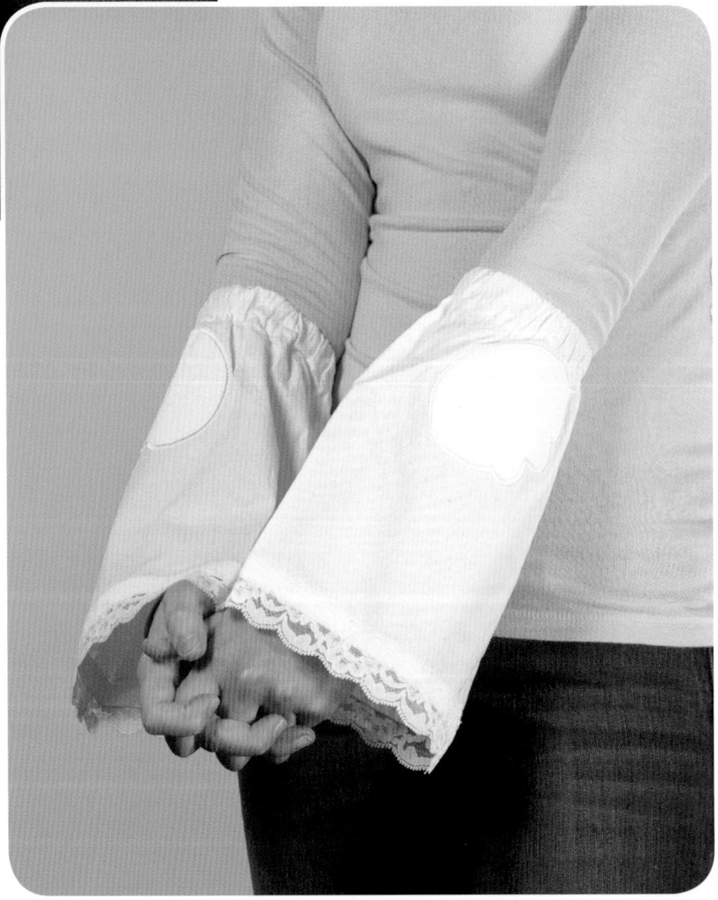

> These arm warmers feature lace and angel wings.

> Tiger stripes are a fun design for leg warmers.

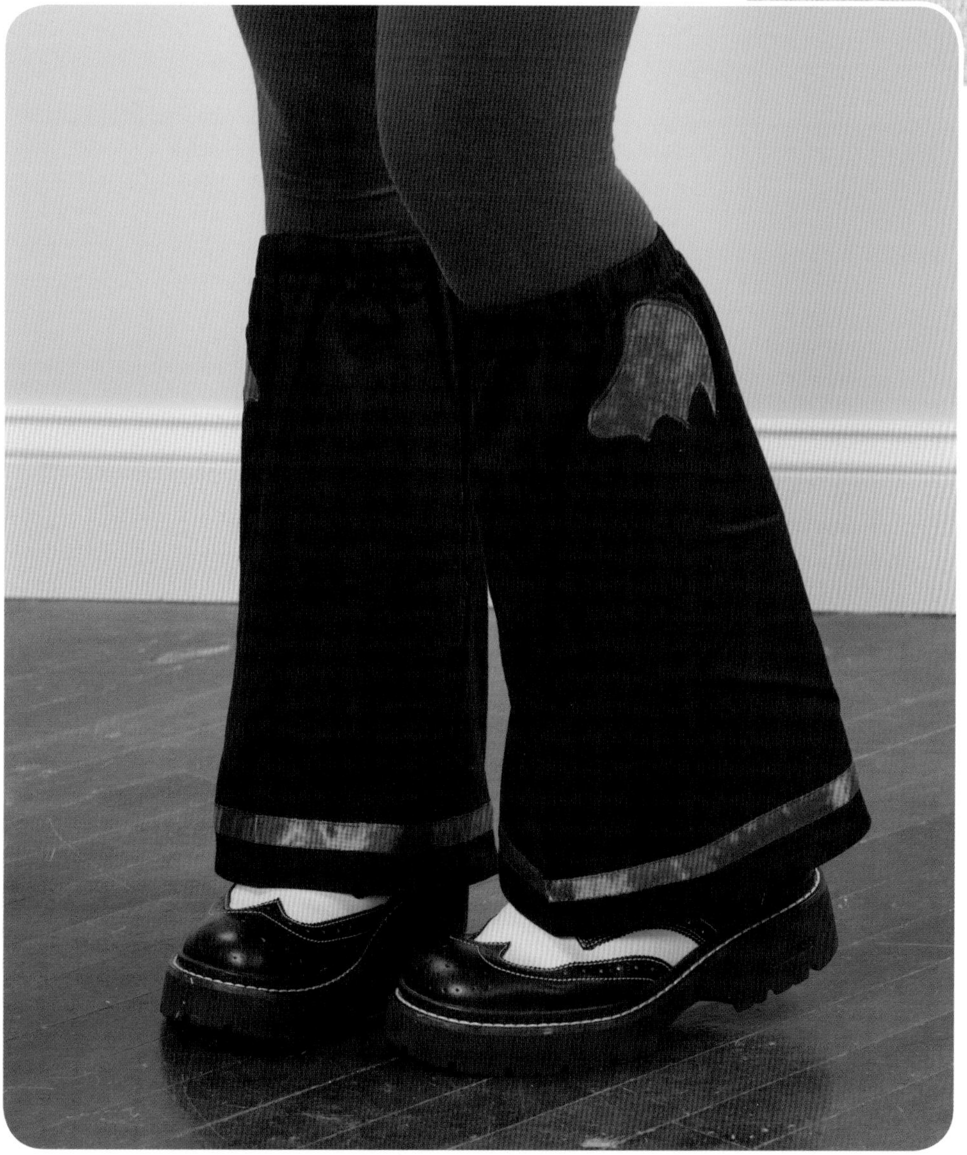

< A shiny satin ribbon that matches the appliqué fabric makes a great accent.

Arm & Leg Warmers

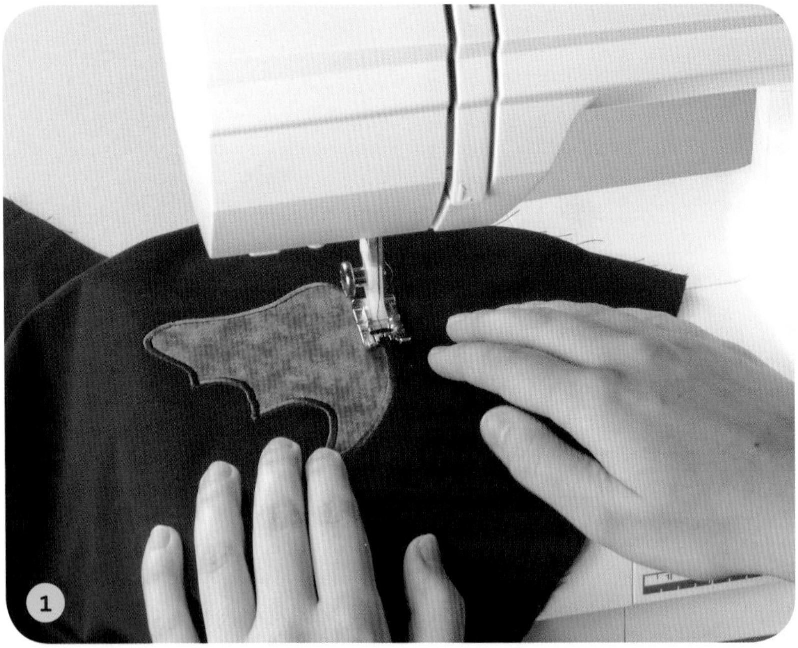

Appliqué. Cut the pattern pieces from your fabric and make all applicable markings. Apply fusible web to the appliqué pieces. Iron the appliqué pieces to the main fabric according to the guidelines. Sew along the edges of the fabric and along any lines as indicated.

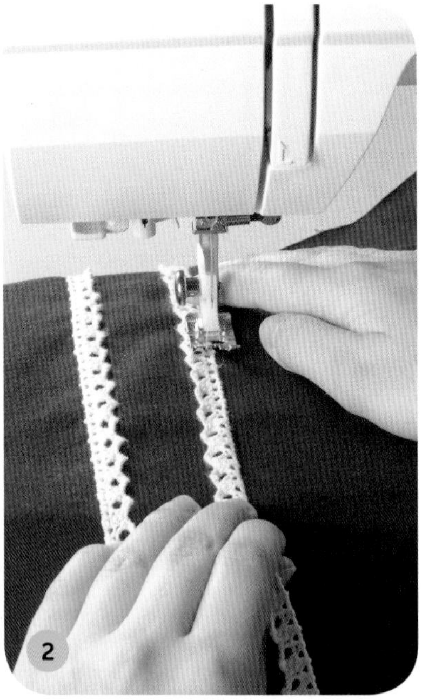

Apply lace to the sides. For corset variation: Sew the lace along the sides of the arm or leg warmer as indicated by the pattern.

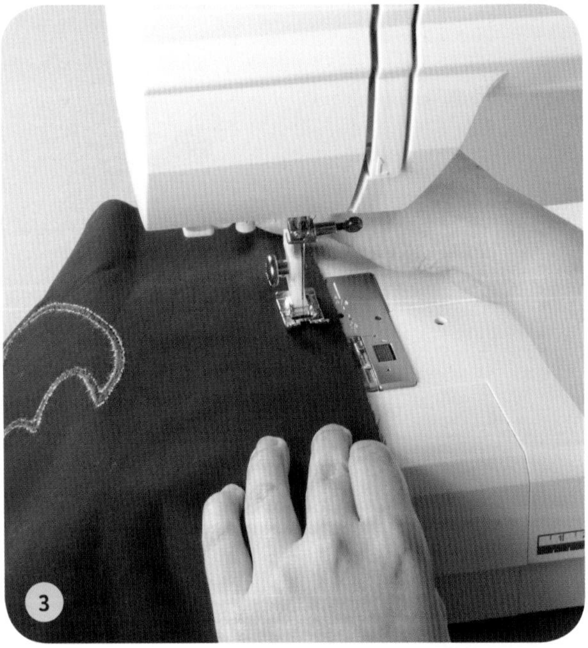

Sew the back seam. Sew the back seam of the arm or leg warmer.

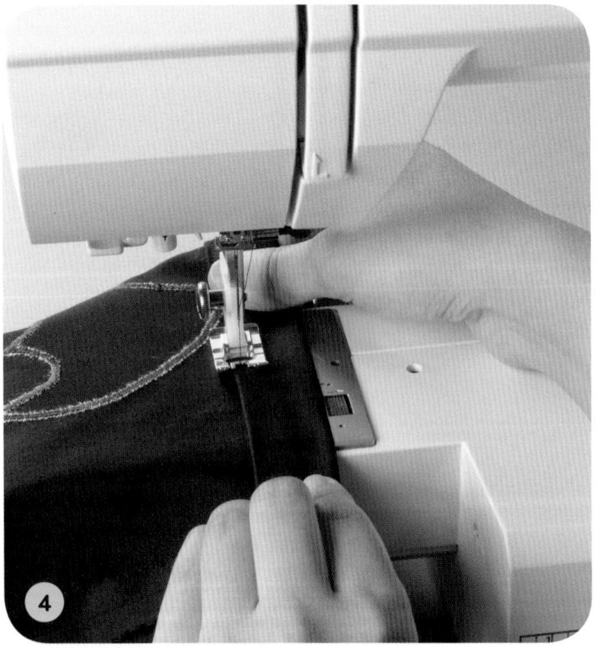

Hem the bottom and top. Turn under ⅜" (10mm) of the bottom and iron it flat. Turn under ⅝" (15mm) more and iron it flat. Sew along the edge to hem. Repeat this same process for the top, but leave a 1" (25mm) opening for inserting elastic.

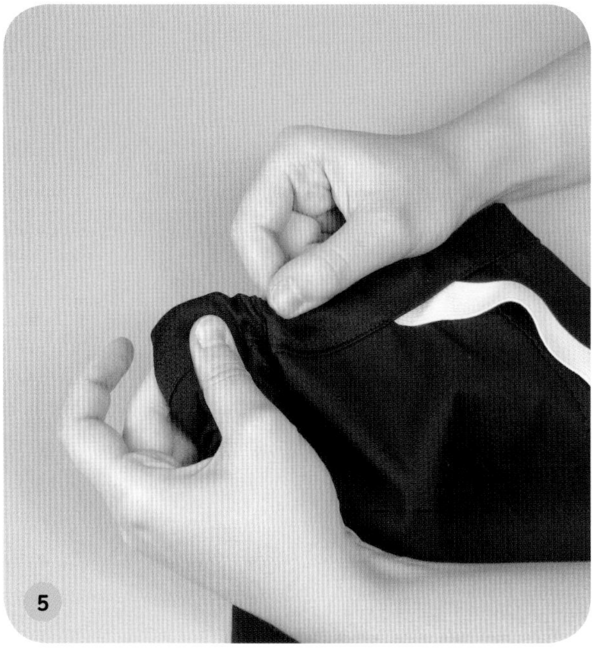

Insert the elastic. Hold the elastic against the top of your calf or below your elbow (depending whether you are making a leg or arm warmer). Stretch the elastic lightly until it is comfortable, and cut the elastic to that length plus ½" (15mm). Thread the elastic through the top of the warmer with a safety pin.

Close the elastic. Bring the elastic all through the top casing, making sure that it doesn't get twisted along the way. Bring the ends together and sew them using a few layers of zigzag stitching.

Add trim. Sew any trim you wish along the edge of the warmer. Fold over and overlap the remaining ribbon edge to make a neat finish.

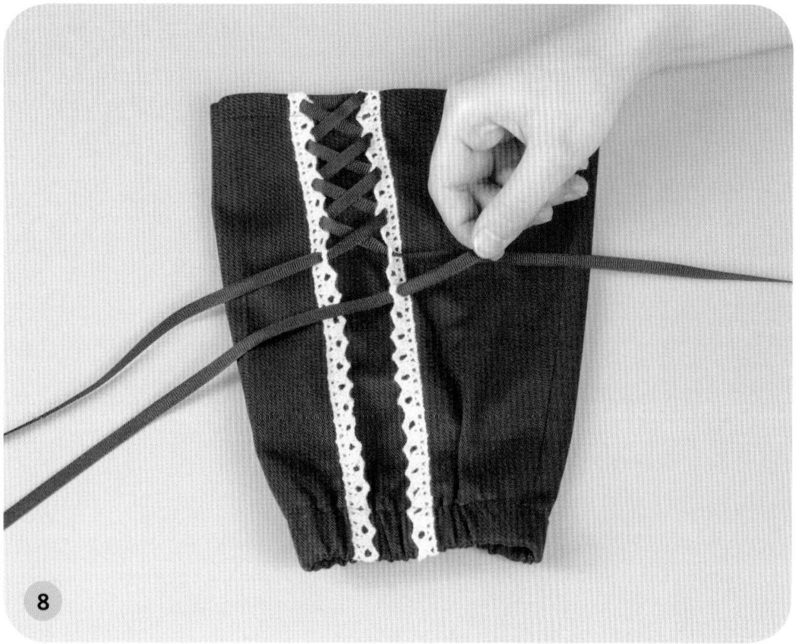

Weave the ribbon. For corset variation: Weave the ribbon through the holes of the lace in a criss-crossed pattern, like a corset. Tie the ends into a bow.

Animal Scarf

Difficulty: Easy

This scarf is just like your favorite knitted muffler, but ten times cuter. The plush head and tail add a wonderful touch that brings the scarf to life. This project is best made with plush knitted fabric because the stretchiness will help the head and tail look smooth. The only challenges in this project can be found in the bit of hand sewing for the head and tail. Read carefully about the ladder stitch (page 24), however, and your work can be nearly invisible! The pattern provides guides to make a Vampire Bunny, Panda, or Kitty.

Patterns on page 154.

Materials

- ½ yd. (½m) plush fabric
- For Panda: ⅛ yd. (⅛m) black or contrasting plush fabric
- Batting
- Fabric for appliqué
- Thread to match main fabric
- Thread to match appliqué fabric
- Fusible web
- Stabilizer

Tools

- Fabric marker
- Fabric scissors
- Fabric pins
- Hand-sewing needle

Cat: 猫
Neko (NEH-koh)

Learn to Speak Japanese

Animal Scarf Gallery

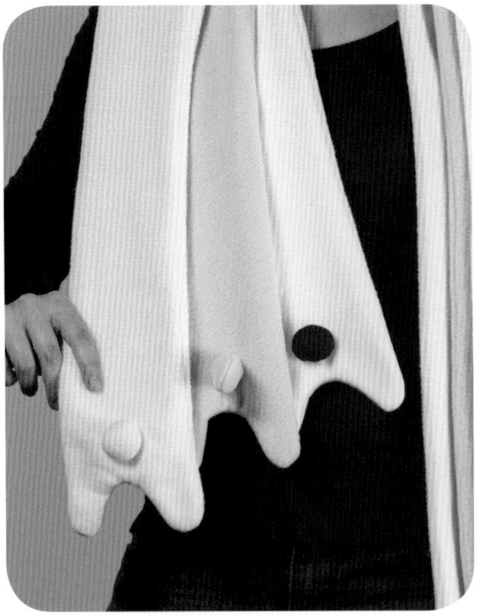

< Tail detail.

> Panda scarf.

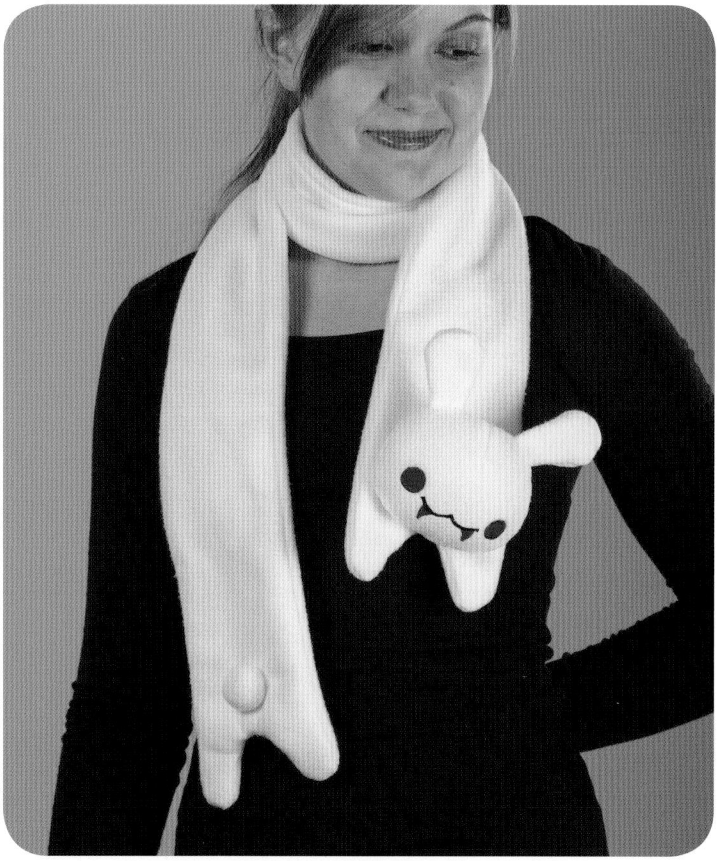

Vampire Bunny scarf.

Kitty scarf.

Animal Scarf

Sew the dart. Cut the pattern pieces from your fabric and make all applicable markings. Apply fusible web to the appliqué pieces. Sew the dart in the front face piece.

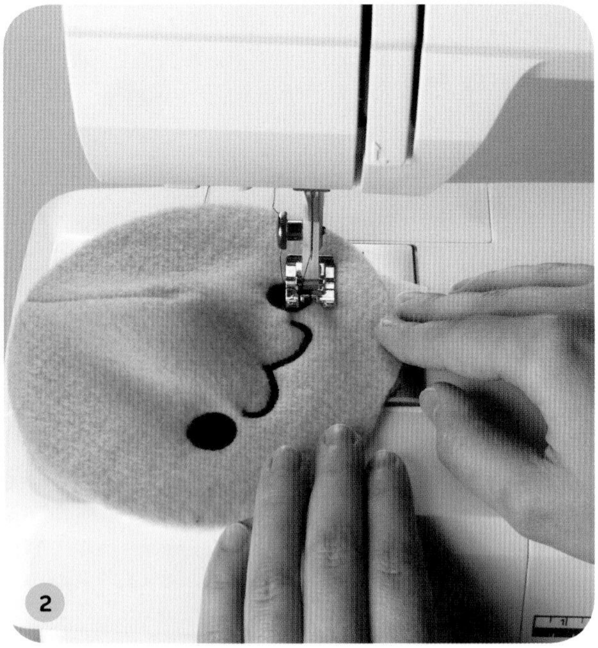

Appliqué. Iron on the appliqué pieces and sew along the edges and along any lines where the pattern indicates.

Sew the ears and tail. Sew the ear and tail pieces together, leaving the bottom edge open, and turn them right side out. [For Bunny and Panda tail: Run a short gathering stitch around the circle, lightly stuff the tail, and cinch it closed.]

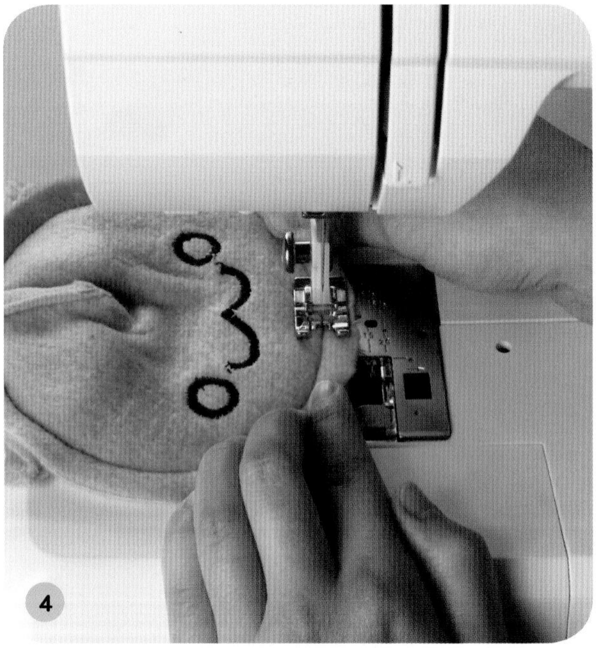

Sew the head pieces. Pin the front of the head to the back, inserting ear pieces between them as indicated by the pattern. Sew the halves together completely the whole way around. Turn the head right side out by cutting a small slit in the back of the head.

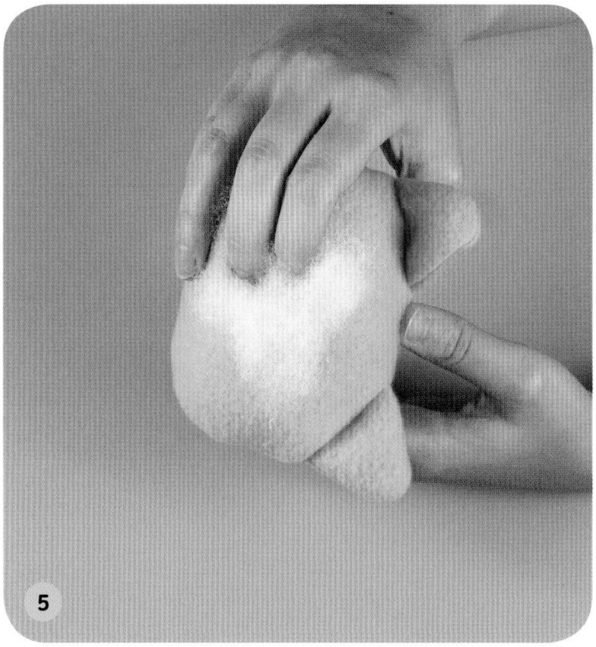

Stuff the head. Stuff the head firmly with batting and hand-sew it closed, using a whip stitch or ladder stitch.

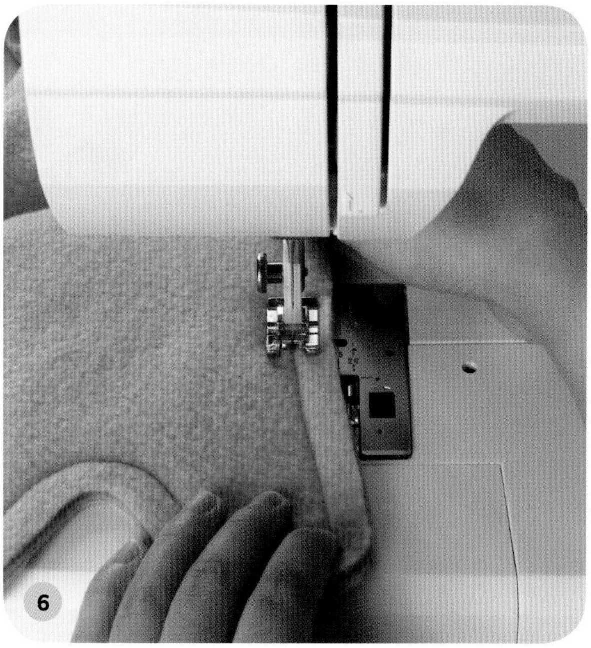

Sew the body. Sew the body pieces together, leaving an opening where indicated by the pattern. Turn right side out and press lightly if desired.

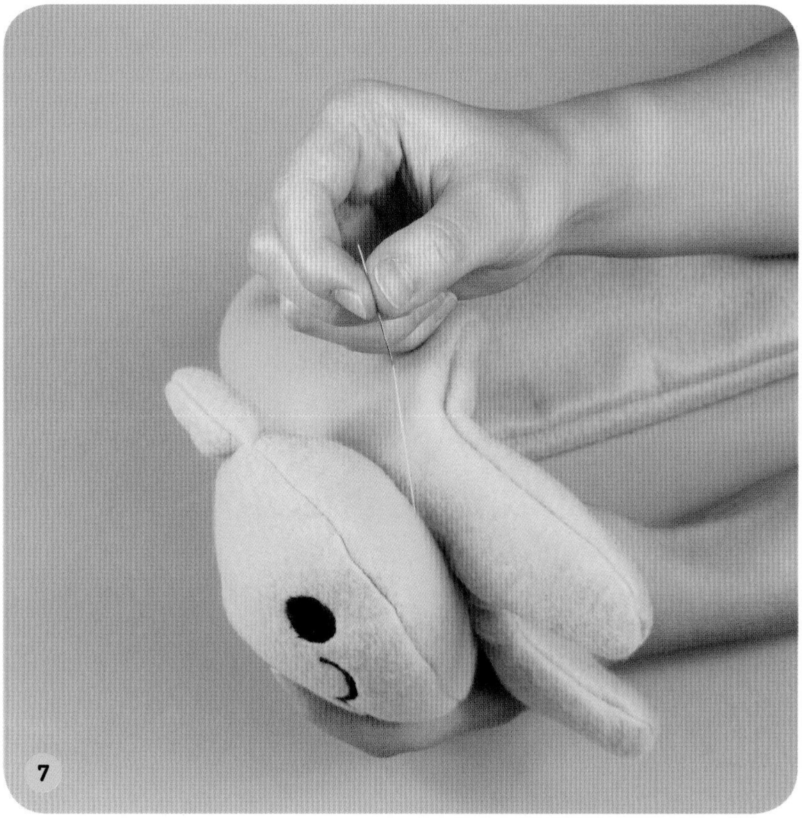

Finish. Hand-sew the head and tail to the body where indicated and sew the opening in the body closed.

4

Plushies

You might think that owning an adorable plush is possible only if you buy one. Not so! This chapter will show you how to make very kawaii, customizable, and super-soft plushies that are quite a step above the flat rag dolls one usually associates with handmade toys. This chapter starts with the very simple and moves on to the more complex, so you can work your way up through all the interesting projects. In every case, making the plush will be kept as straightforward as possible, with minimal hand sewing or awkward steps. Inside, you'll find classic cuties, such as cats and rabbits, but also some genuinely underrated friends, such as platypi—you'll never look at stuffed animals the same way again.

Blob Plush

Difficulty: Easy

Patterns on page 155.

This plush has a very simple but irresistible design. It's ready to plop anywhere, from your nightstand to your desk. These are great for filling with batting, but micro beads and pellets provide extra squishiness. A plush knit fabric is ideal for this project because of its stretchiness. However, for the ultimate effect, try stretchy spandex material. It is particularly pliable and can really mush around and then come back to shape. If the spandex gives you trouble, tips for working with knits can be found in the Jellyfish Dress project on page 121. The challenges in this project will come from aligning your pieces properly and sewing the nori (edible seaweed) band if you make the Onigiri (a Japanese rice ball snack). The patterns provide guides to create a Kitty, Bunny, or Onigiri.

Materials

- ¼ yd. (¼m) knit or plush fabric
- Fabric for appliqué
- For Onigiri: ⅛ yd. (⅛m) dark green appliqué fabric
- Batting, micro beads, or micro pellets
- Thread to match plush fabric
- Thread to match appliqué
- Fusible web
- Stabilizer

Tools

- Fabric marker
- Fabric scissors
- Fabric pins
- Hand-sewing needle

Rabbit: 兎
Usagi (oo-SAH-gee)

Learn to Speak Japanese

Blob Plush

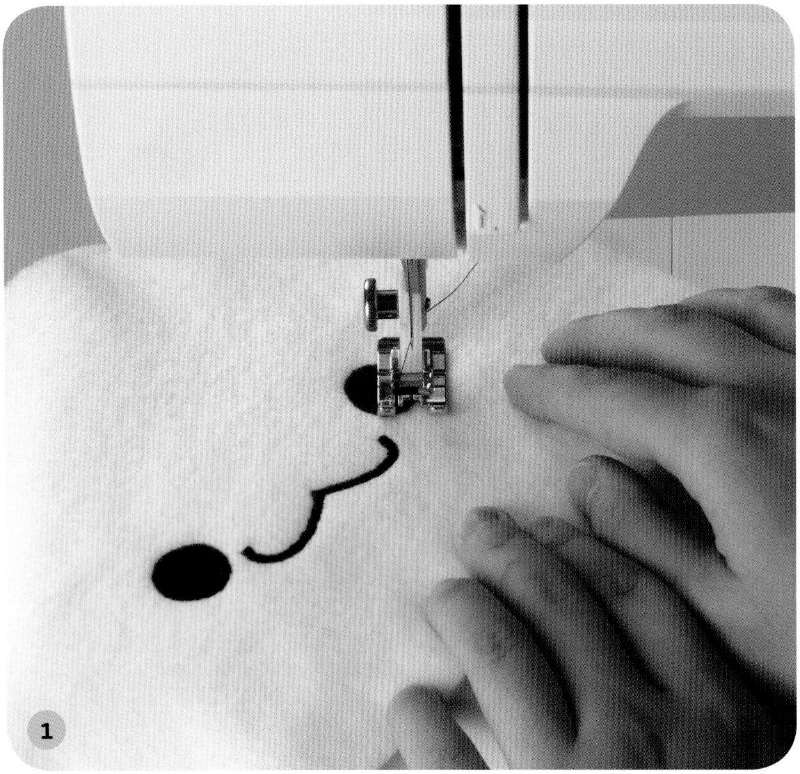

Appliqué. Cut the pattern pieces from your fabric and make all applicable markings. Apply fusible web to the appliqué pieces. Iron the appliqué pieces to the front of the plush, following the pattern guidelines. Sew along the edges of the fabric and along any lines as indicated.

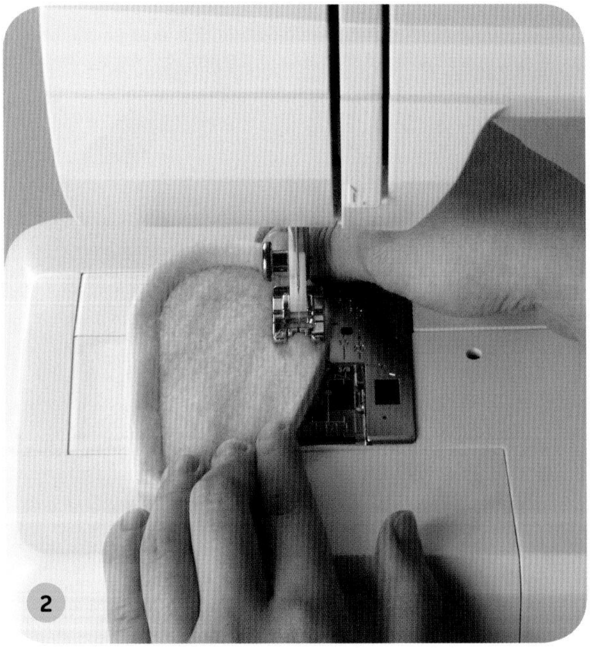

Sew the ears and tail. For Bunny and Kitty: Sew the ear and tail pieces together, leaving bottom edge open. Turn right side out. [For Bunny tail: Sew a short gathering stitch along outer edge of circle.] Stuff the tail and cinch closed.

Sew the front to the back. Sew the front to the back at the top curved seam, inserting any ears you may have as indicated by the pattern. Leave an opening, as the pattern shows, to turn it right side out.

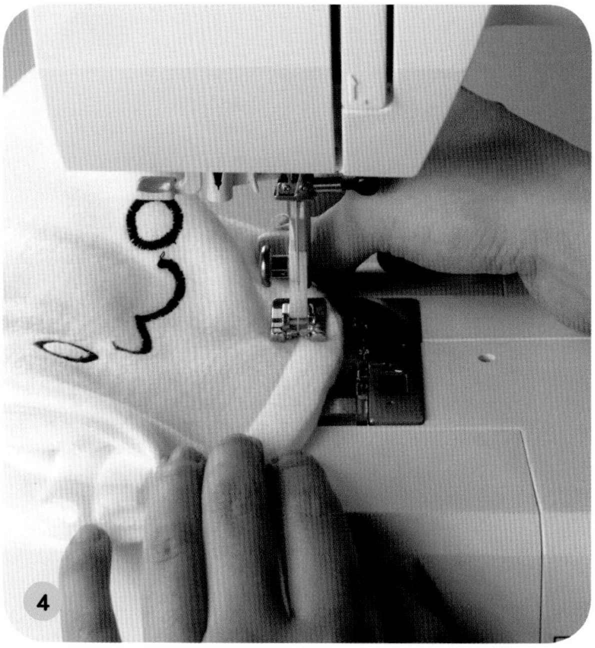

Sew the bottom. Sew the bottom piece to the top along the bottom of the dome shape made by the body. [For Kitty: Include the tail, according to the pattern guidelines.]

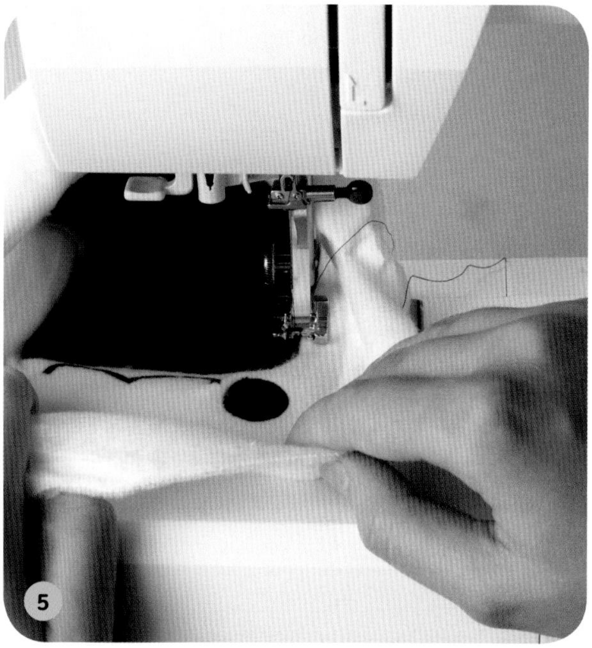

Appliqué the nori. For Onigiri: Iron the nori band to the bottom of the plush, following the pattern guidelines. Using the opening in the side, carefully sew along the edges of the fabric. Note: If this becomes difficult, don't hesitate to rip out some of the top seam stitches to give you more room to work. You can always go back and resew the top.

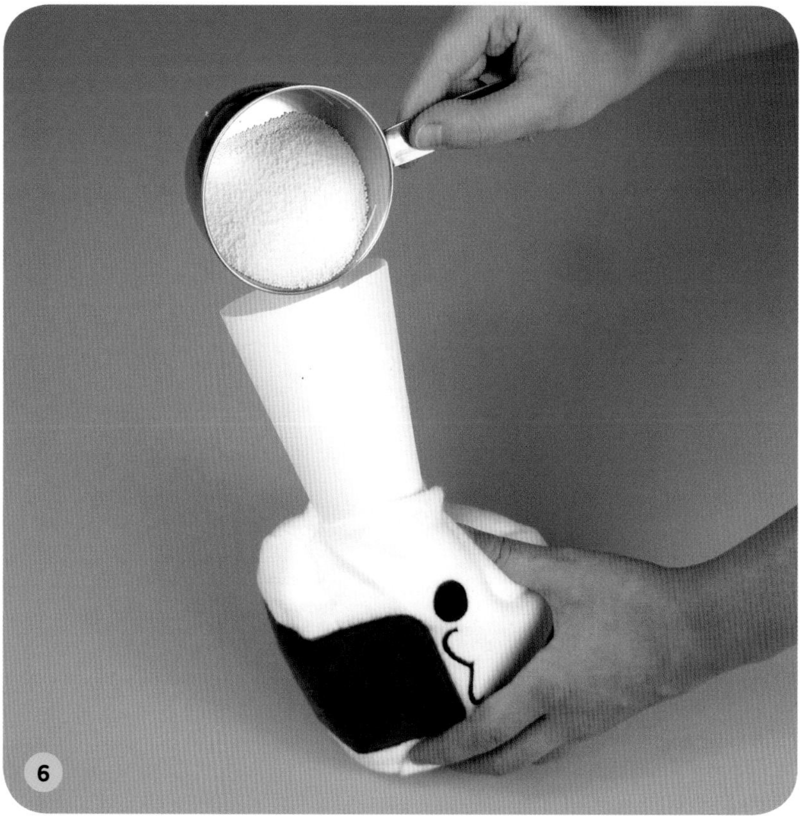

Stuff and finish. Stuff or fill the plush with your desired filling. Roll up a piece of paper to use as a funnel for micro beads or pellets. Use the ladder stitch to hand-sew the opening closed. [For Bunny: Hand-sew the tail to the back.]

Octopus Plush

Difficulty: Experienced Beginner

Patterns on page 156.

Octopi are very popular cute characters in Japan, so let's help start the trend to make them famous all over the globe! Show off your Latin skills by making a Pentapus (5 legs) or Septopus (7 legs) instead. This plush is best made with minky or other stretchy plush fabric. He can be filled entirely with batting, or to give him some heft, his legs can be filled with micro pellets. The challenges in this project come from the octopus needing a little more hand sewing than most of the other projects. With all of his legs, there are also more little bits to keep track of. But if you stay focused and patient, you can tackle this cephalopod!

Materials

- ⅓ yd. (⅓m) plush fabric
- Batting
- Fabric for appliqué
- Thread to match plush fabric
- Thread to match appliqué fabric
- Fusible web
- Stabilizer
- Micro pellets (optional)

Tools

- Fabric marker
- Fabric scissors
- Fabric pins
- Hand-sewing needle

Octopus: 蛸
Tako (TAH-koh)

Learn to Speak Japanese

Octopus Plush

This top view shows the Octopus leg placement.

This top view shows the Sentapus leg placement.

This top view shows the Pentapus leg placement.

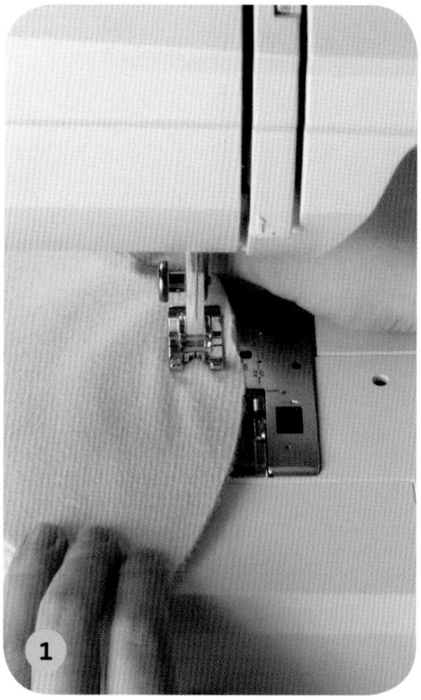

Sew the front, back, and mouth. Cut the pattern pieces from your fabric and make all applicable markings. Apply fusible web to the appliqué pieces. Sew both pairs of the octopus head along one side, creating two halves. Fold the mouth piece in half shortways and sew along the side.

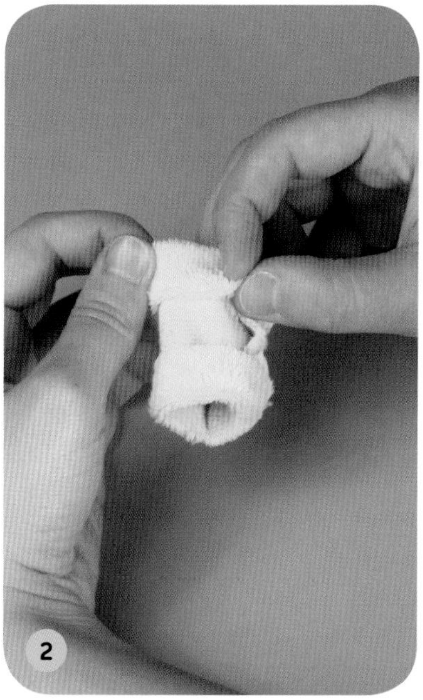

Form the mouth. Fold over ⅝" (16mm) on each side of the raw edges of the mouth piece. Then, fold the whole piece in half. Finger press it or iron it lightly to hold it in place.

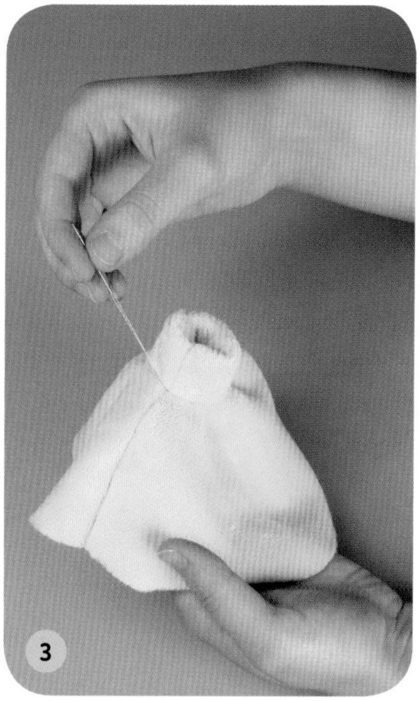

Attach the mouth. Hand-sew the mouth to the front of the face, following the guidelines from the pattern.

Appliqué. Iron on the appliqué pieces and sew along the edge of the fabric.

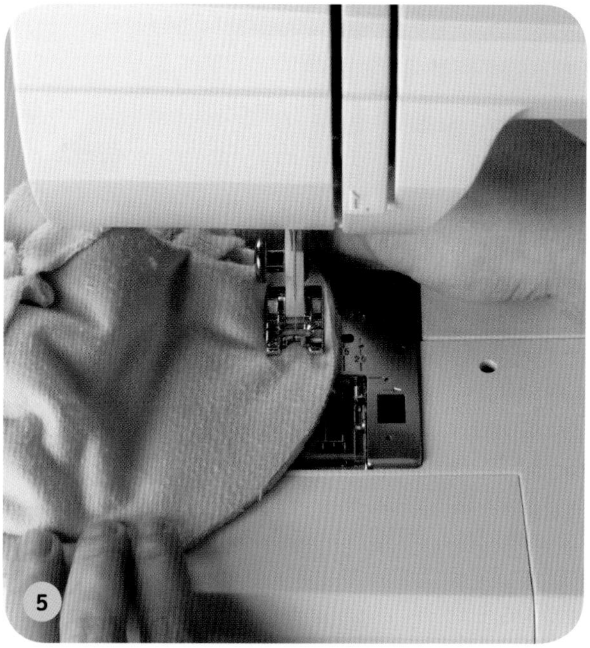

Sew the front to the back. Sew the front head half to the back head half, leaving a small opening, as indicated by the pattern, for turning it right side out.

Octopus Plush

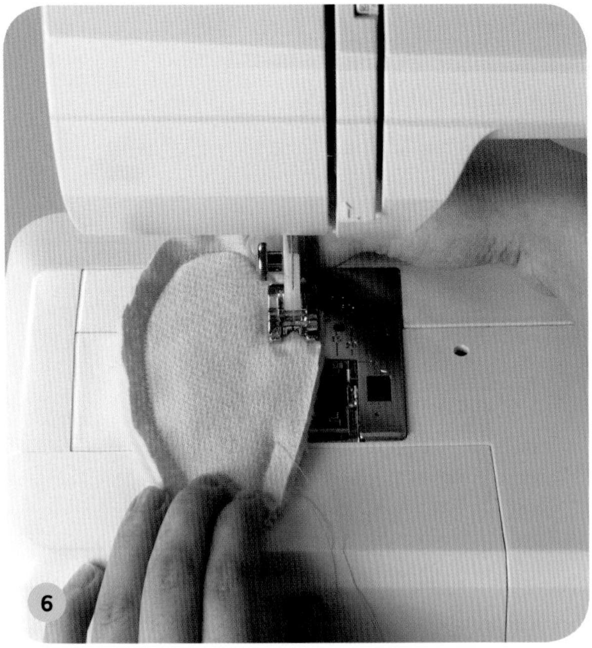

Sew the legs. Sew the leg pieces together, leaving a small opening, as indicated by the pattern, for turning them right side out.

Stuff and finish the legs. Stuff or fill the legs and hand-sew each opening closed using the ladder stitch.

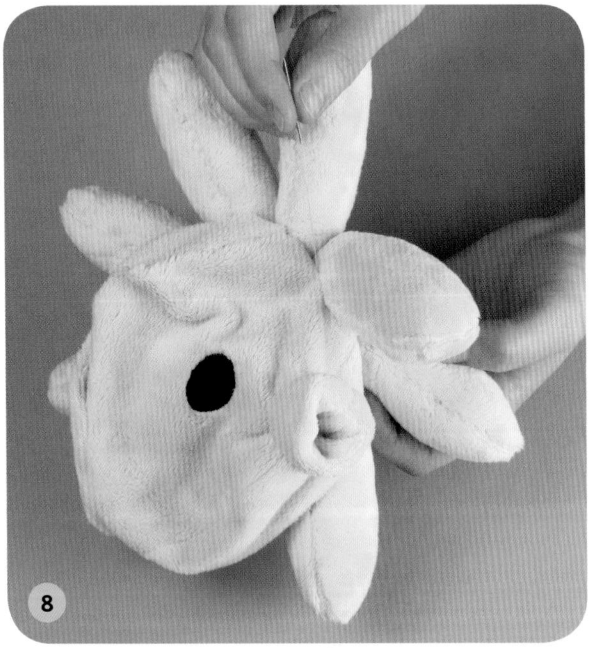

Attach the legs. Using the opening left in the Octopus head, attach the legs to the bottom. Space them evenly apart in a radial pattern.

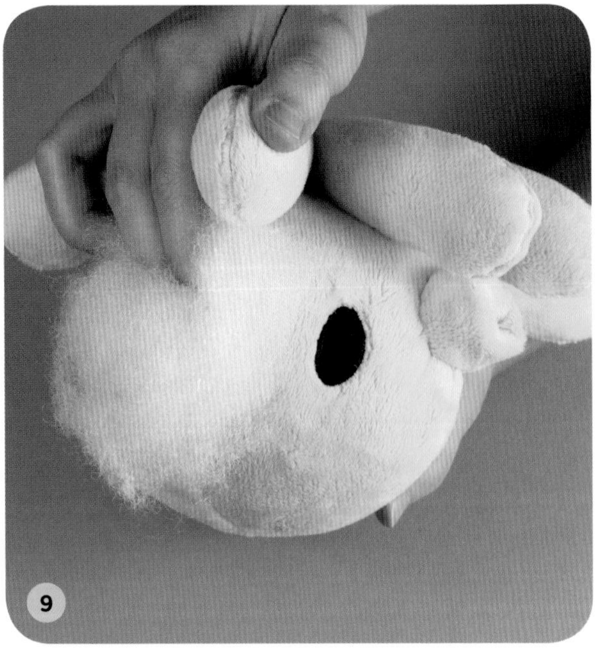

Finish the body. Stuff the body firmly and hand-sew the opening closed.

Platypus Plush

Difficulty: Experienced Beginner

Platypi are yet another underrated animal. They may look funny, but that's definitely what makes them so cute! Minky or another knit plush fabric is best for this project—it will look nice and smooth. Any kind of filling can be used, however, as that won't bother his weight distribution. The challenges in this project come from the tight curves found in the Platypus's body, and the need to line up the edges just right to achieve the correct shape. So work slowly through those curves and remember to clip your seam allowances, and you can master this monotreme.

Materials

- ½ yd. (½m) plush fabric
- ⅛ yd. (⅛m) contrasting plush fabric for bill, tail, and feet
- Batting
- Fabric for appliqué
- Thread to match main plush fabric
- Thread to match contrasting plush fabric
- Thread to match appliqué fabric
- Fusible web
- Stabilizer

Tools

- Fabric marker
- Fabric scissors
- Fabric pins
- Hand-sewing needle

Patterns on page 157.

Platypus: かものはし
Kamonohashi (KAH-moh-noh-HA-shee)

Learn to Speak Japanese

Platypus Plush

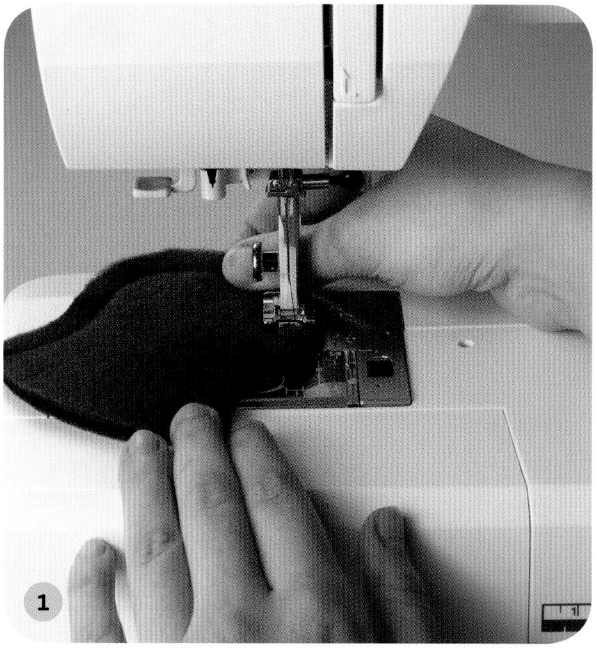

Sew the feet, bill, and tail. Cut the pattern pieces from your fabric and make all applicable markings. Apply fusible web to the appliqué pieces. Sew the feet, bill, and tail pieces together, leaving the bottom edges open for turning them inside out. Stuff the bill and tail lightly with batting.

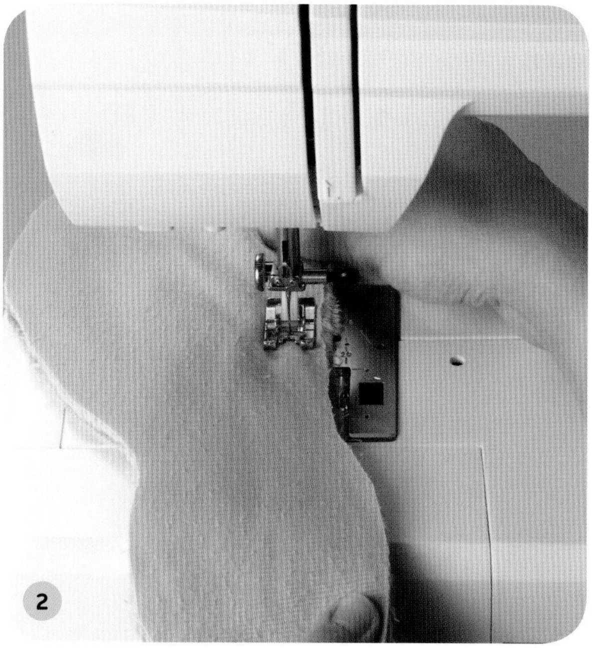

Sew the top seam. Sew the top pieces together along the single notched edge.

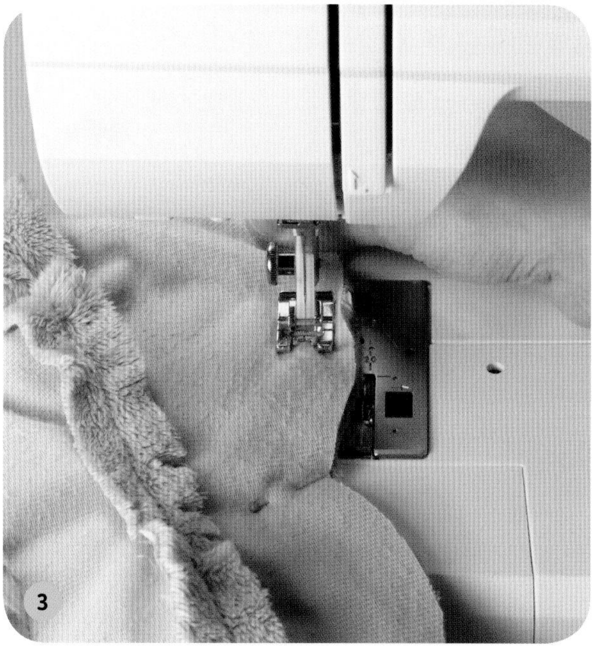

Sew the sides to the top. Sew the side pieces to the top piece along the double-notched edges.

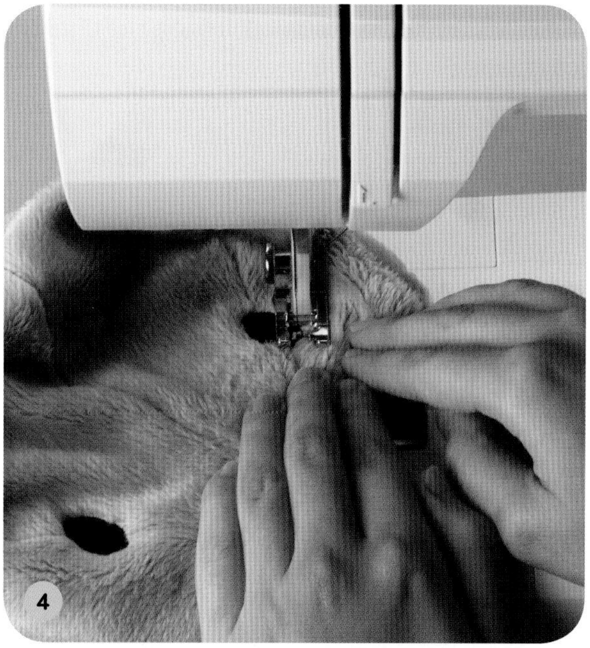

Appliqué the eyes. Iron down the appliqué fabric where indicated by the pattern. Sew along the edges of the fabric.

Platypus Plush

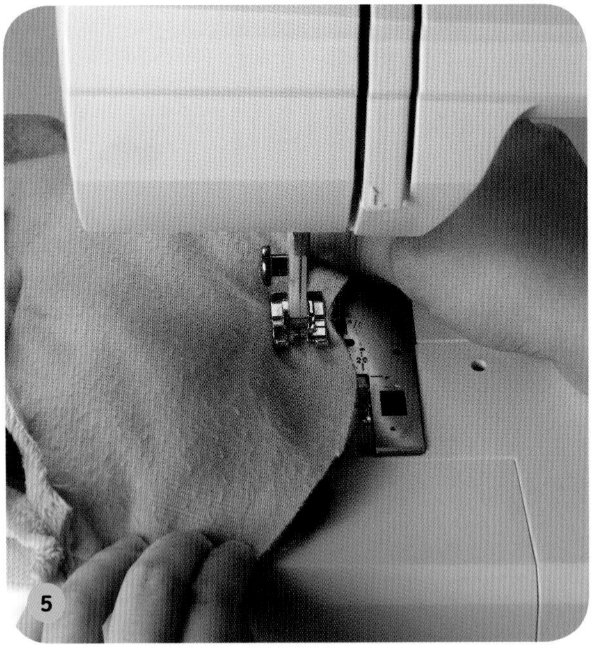

5

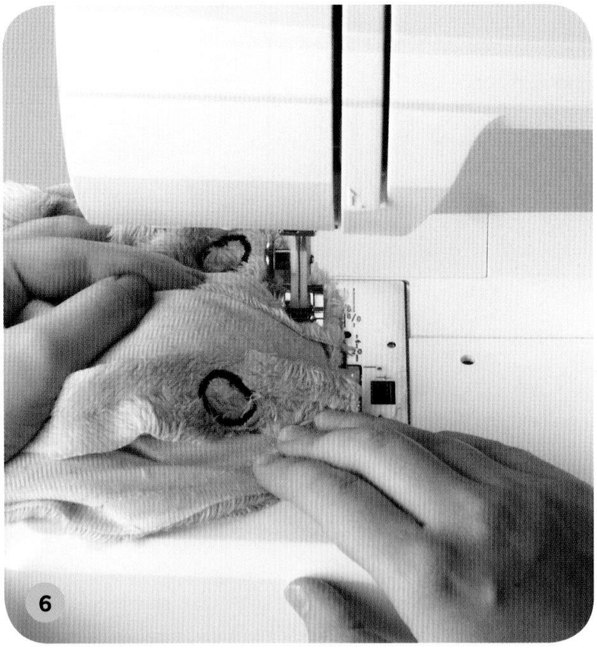

6

Sew the top to the bottom. Pin the top portion to the bottom piece along the triple-notched edges. Insert the foot pieces between them, where it's indicated by the pattern. Sew both sides, leaving an opening where the pattern indicates to turn the plush right side out.

Sew the bill and tail. Sew the bill into the opening in the front, and the tail in the opening in the back.

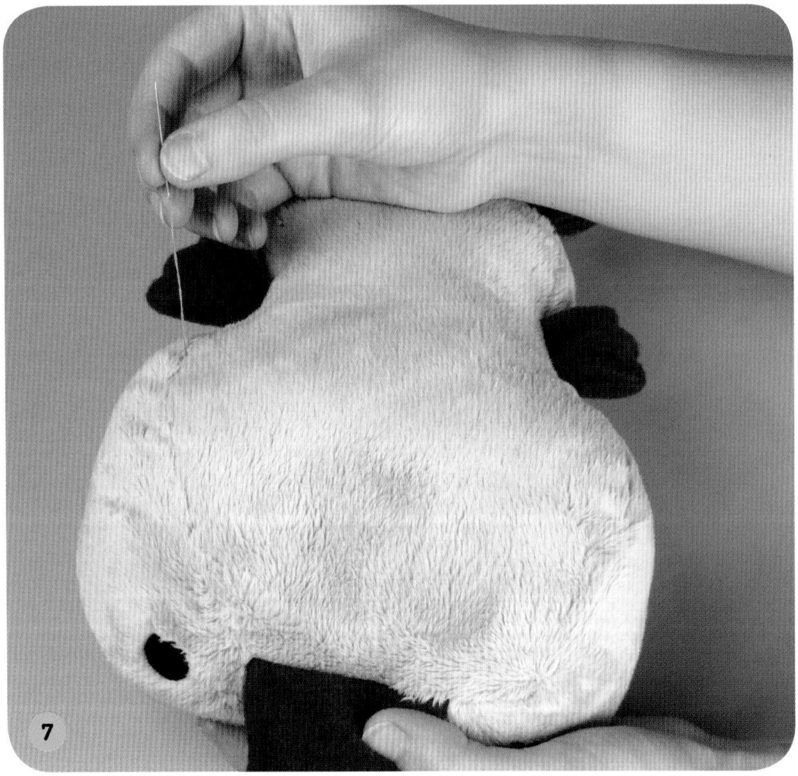

7

Stuff and finish. Stuff the entire body firmly and hand-sew the opening closed.

Sitting Plush

Difficulty: Experienced Beginner

Here we have all the classic animals that everyone likes to see: cats, bunnies, and bears—though an elephant still managed to sneak in! This is a very versatile pattern, and if you're adventurous, you can try making it into your own favorite animal. Minky or knit plush fabric is best for this project, due to its stretchiness. Also, I highly recommend filling the body with micro pellets to keep the plush sitting upright. The challenges in this project come from working with some of the tinier pieces and seams. Basting the fabric before sewing your seam is a great way to make this easier. The patterns provide guides for making a Kitty, Bunny, Panda, and Elephant.

Materials

- For Elephant: ½ yd. (½m) plush fabric
- For Panda: ⅓ yd. (⅓m) main plush fabric, ⅛ yd. (⅛m) contrasting plush fabric
- For Kitty and Bunny: ⅓ yd. (⅓m) plush fabric
- Batting
- Micro pellets
- Fabric for appliqué
- Thread to match plush fabric
- Thread to match appliqué fabric
- For Panda: Thread to match contrasting plush fabric
- Fusible web
- Stabilizer

Tools

- Fabric marker
- Fabric scissors
- Fabric pins
- Hand-sewing needle

Patterns on page 158.

Elephant: 象
Zou (ZOH)

Learn to Speak Japanese

Sitting Plush

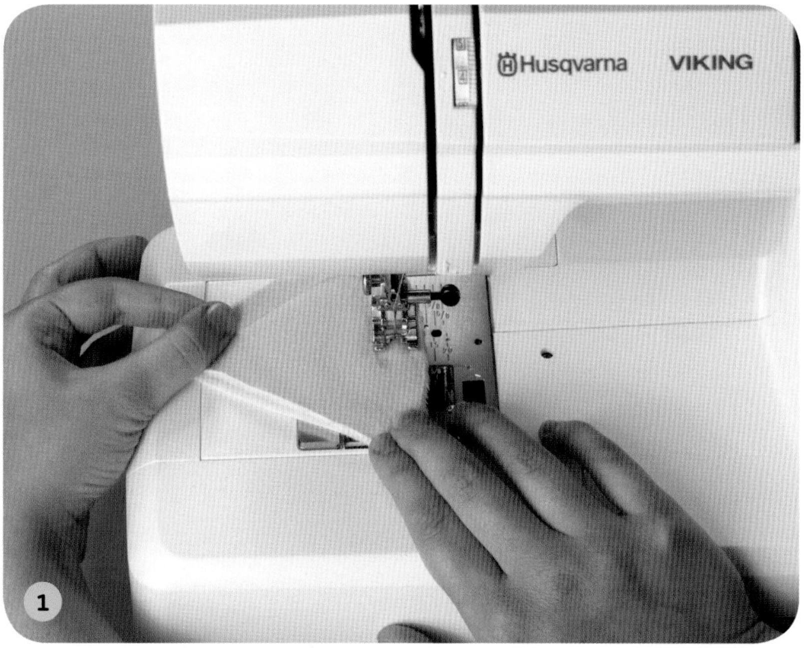

Sew the appendages. Cut the pattern pieces from your fabric and make all applicable markings. Apply fusible web to the appliqué pieces. Sew the feet, tail, and ear pieces together, leaving the bottom side open. Turn them right side out and stuff lightly. [For Panda and Bunny tail: Run a short gathering stitch around the circle, stuff lightly, and cinch closed.] [For Elephant: Sew the trunk piece in half along the long seam line.]

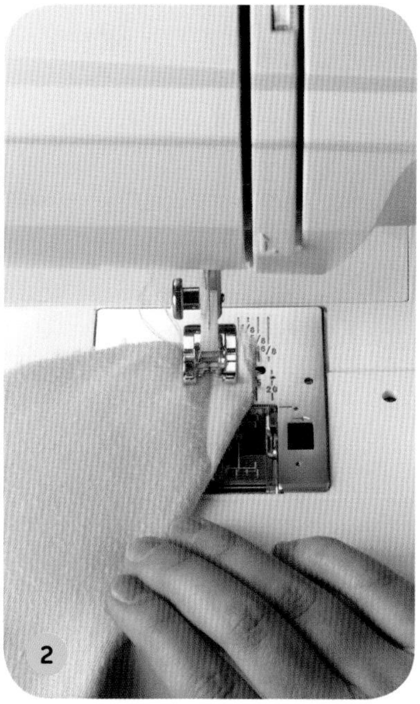

Sew the darts. Sew the darts indicated in the front and back head pieces. Cut the larger darts open and finger press them flat.

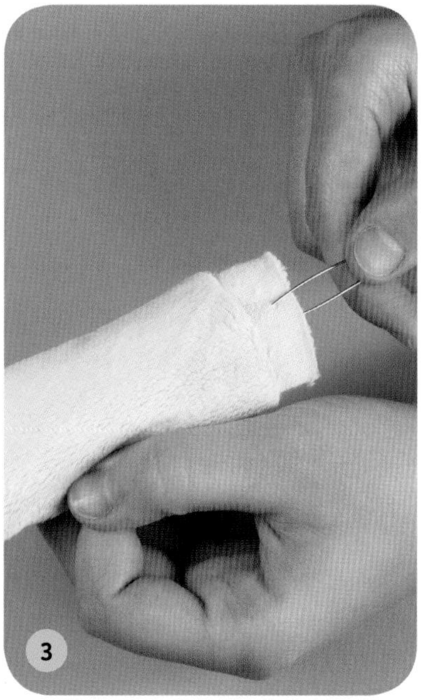

Form the trunk. For the Elephant: Turn the trunk right side out using a safety pin. Then, bring the safety pin back again as if turning the trunk inside out, but stop halfway when the two raw edges meet. Fold under those raw edges by ⅝" (16mm) and finger press or iron lightly to hold the folds in place.

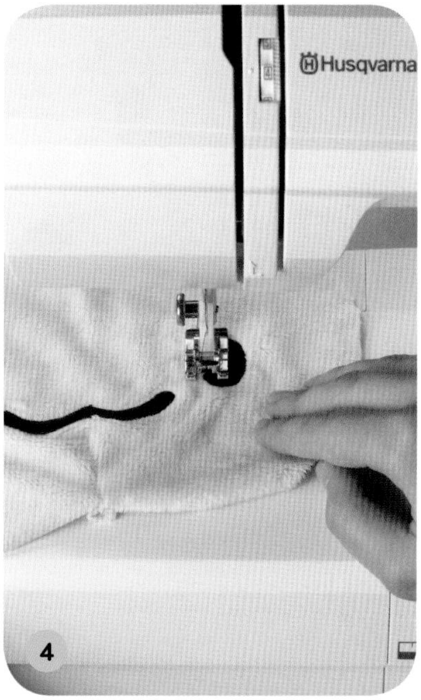

Appliqué. Iron the appliqué pieces to the front face piece following the pattern guidelines. Sew along the edges of the fabric. [For Elephant: Hand-sew the trunk in place.]

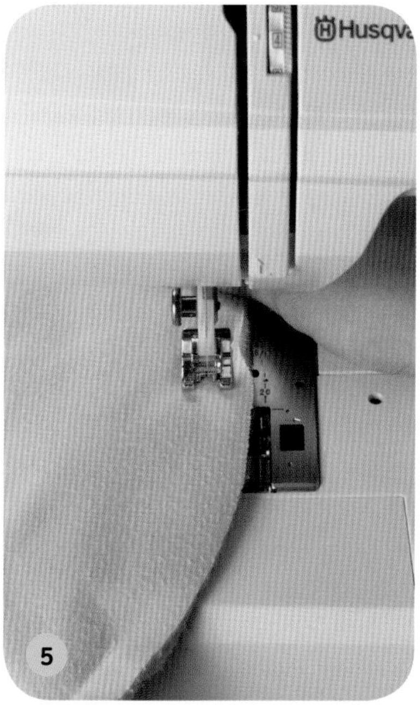

Sew the back of the head. Sew the center back seam of the head, leaving an opening where indicated by the pattern for turning it right side out.

Sitting Plush

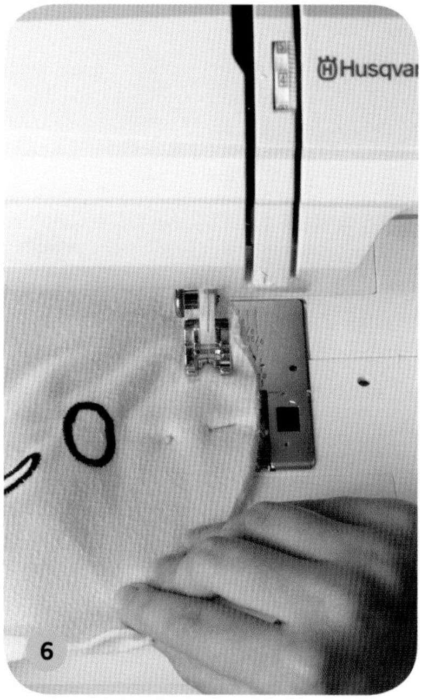

Sew the head's front to back. Pin the front of the head to the back along the curved top seam. Insert the ears where indicated by the pattern. Sew it all in place, leaving the neck open.

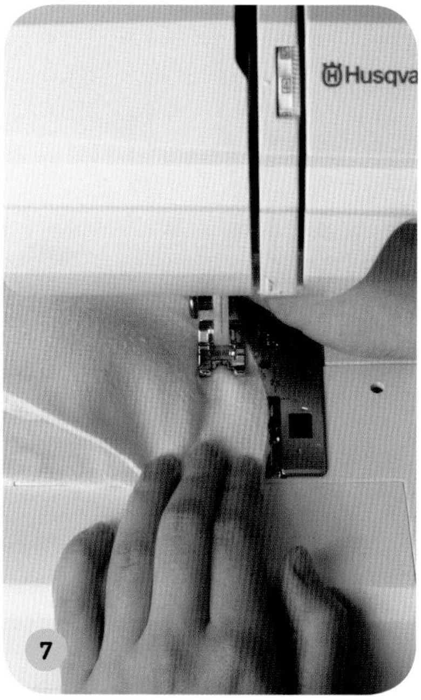

Sew the body's front to back. Pin the body front to the body back along the side seams, inserting the arms where indicated on the pattern. Sew the side seams, leaving the neck and bottom open.

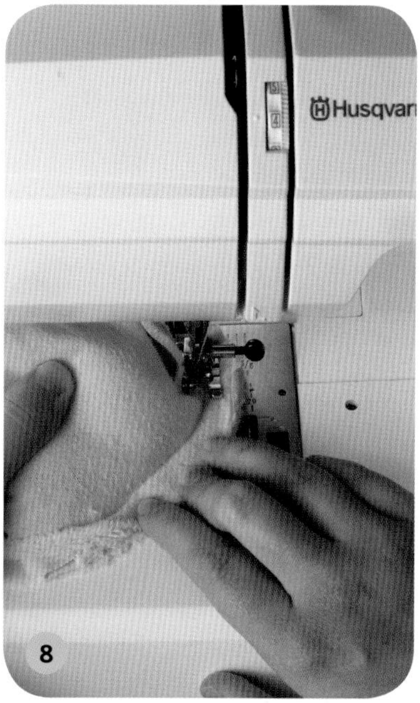

Sew the body to the bottom. Pin the body to the bottom. Flatten the legs, bringing the top and bottom seams together, and insert them between the body and bottom where the pattern indicates. [For Bunny and Panda: Hand-sew the tail to the back.]

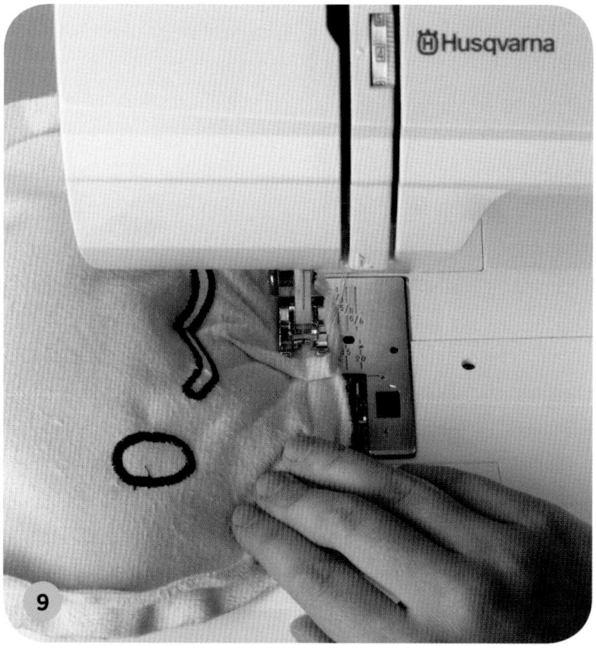

Sew the neck to the body. Sew the neck opening to the body opening, matching front and back center marks.

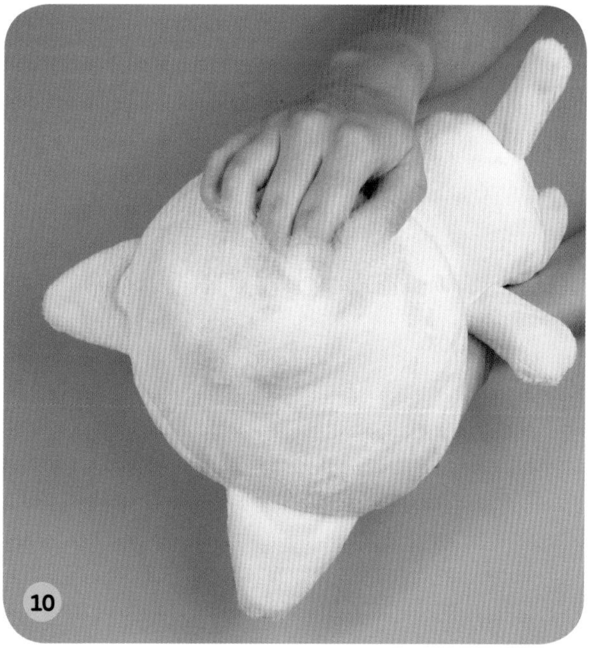

Stuff and finish. Fill the body with micro pellets and the rest with batting. Hand-sew the opening closed.

Llama Plush

Difficulty: Intermediate

Here is another plush featuring a much-underrated animal. If you're able to find a fluffier minky fabric that contrasts with a smoother one, your llama will look much more realistic. You'll also need micro pellets for his feet in order to keep him standing upright, rather than falling flat. The challenges you might face here are not only the small pieces and seams, but also difficult curves around the face, neck, and underside. Basting your seams before sewing them can help make this easier if you run into problems (see page 24).

Patterns on page 159.

Materials

- $\frac{1}{4}$ yd. ($\frac{1}{4}$m) smooth minky, main
- $\frac{1}{3}$ yd. ($\frac{1}{3}$m) fluffy minky, contrast
- Batting
- Micro pellets
- Fabric for appliqué
- Thread to match fluffy minky
- Thread to match appliqué fabric
- Fusible web
- Stabilizer

Tools

- Fabric marker
- Fabric scissors
- Fabric pins
- Hand-sewing needle

Llama: ラマ
Rama (RAH-mah)

Learn to Speak Japanese

Llama Plush

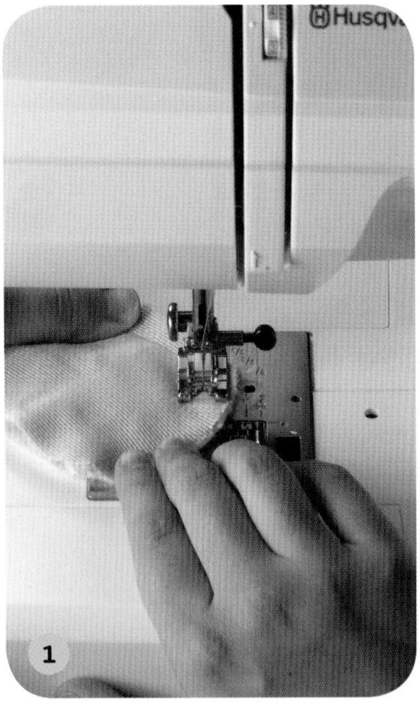

Sew the feet, tail, and ears. Cut the pattern pieces from your fabric and make all applicable markings. Apply fusible web to the appliqué pieces. Sew the feet, tail, and ear pieces together, leaving the straight sides open. Turn them right side out.

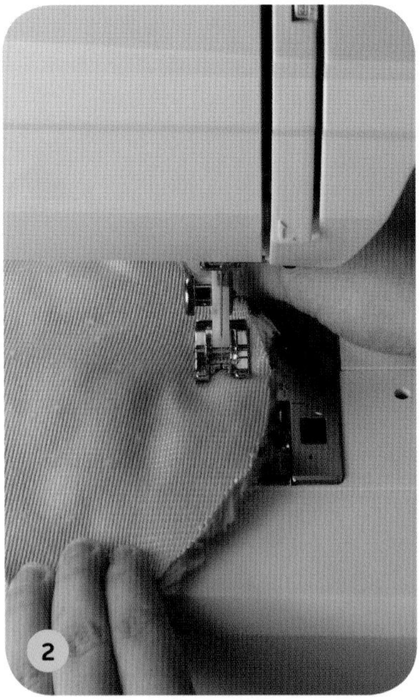

Sew the neck and underside. Sew the neck seam along the side, leaving the bottom and top open. Sew the long edge of the underside pieces, leaving an opening where indicated by the pattern for eventually stuffing the llama.

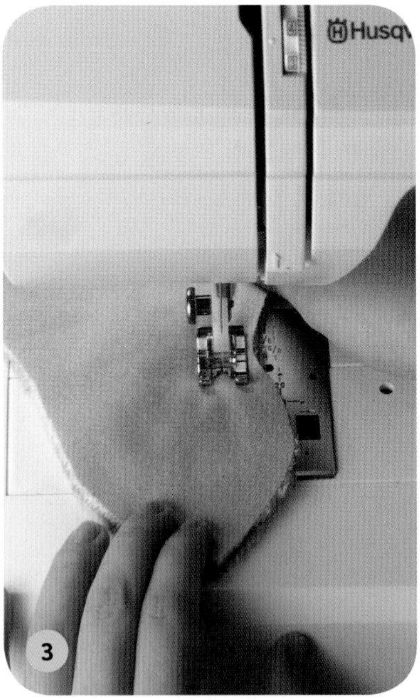

Sew the head halves. Sew the bottom and top quarter pieces to each other along the edges without notches.

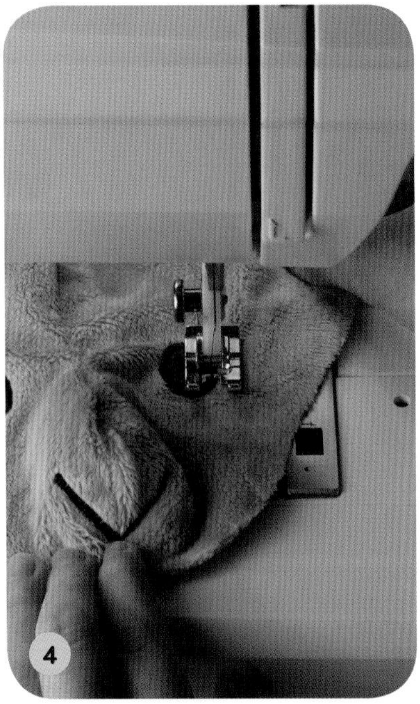

Appliqué. Iron on the appliqué pieces using the pattern guidelines. Sew down the fabric along the edges and along the lines as the pattern indicates for the nose.

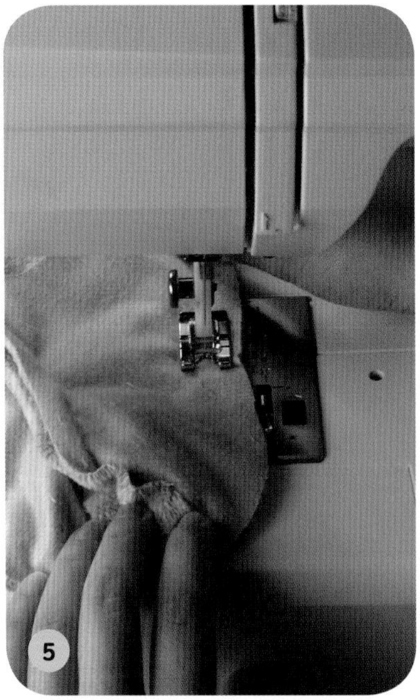

Sew the head top to the bottom. Sew the top half of the head to the bottom half, matching the single notches found along the side.

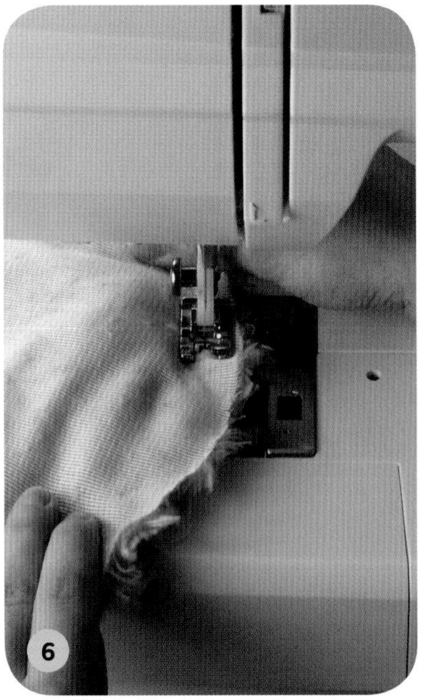

Sew the body halves. Pin the two halves of the body together along the upper side. Insert the tail where indicated by the pattern. Sew the body together, ending at the circle where the pattern indicates.

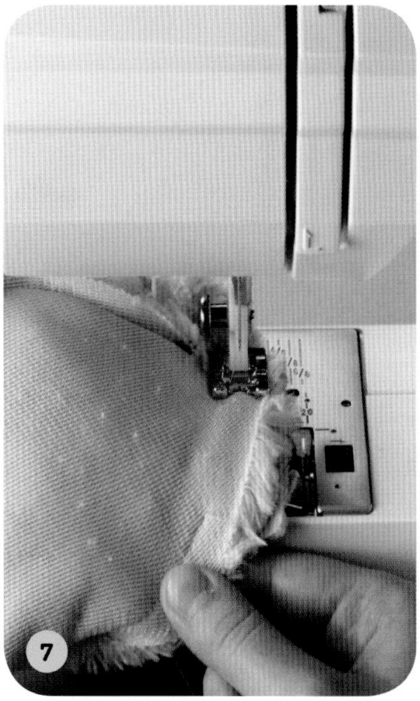

Sew the head to the neck. Pin the opening in the head to the top of the neck. Pinch the ears a bit to give them shape and insert them between the fabrics. Sew around the neck.

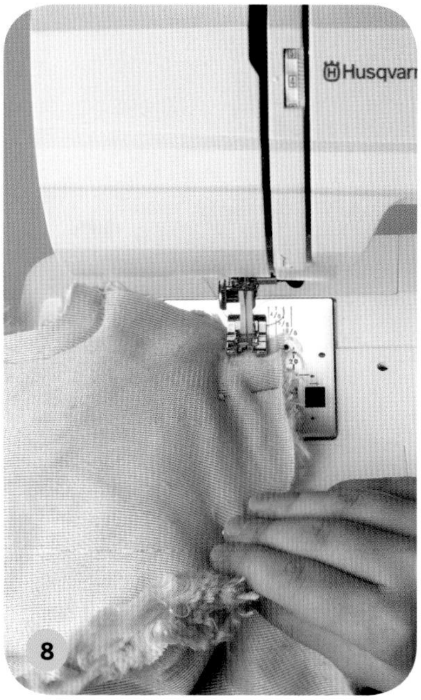

Sew the underside to the body. Open up the underside piece and body piece. Sew them together, matching up the curves for the neck, leaving openings for the feet, and pivoting when you reach the backside.

Attach the feet. Attach the feet to each leg using a short backstitch around the opening.

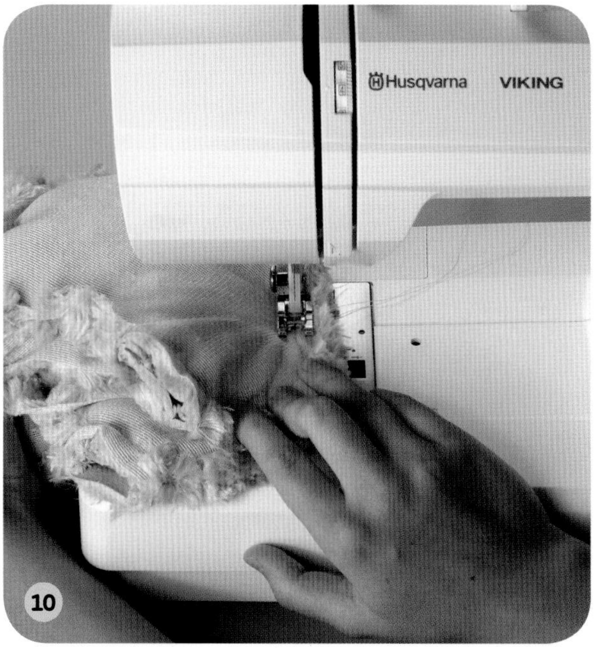

Sew the neck to the body. Sew the neck opening to the body opening, matching the front and back seams.

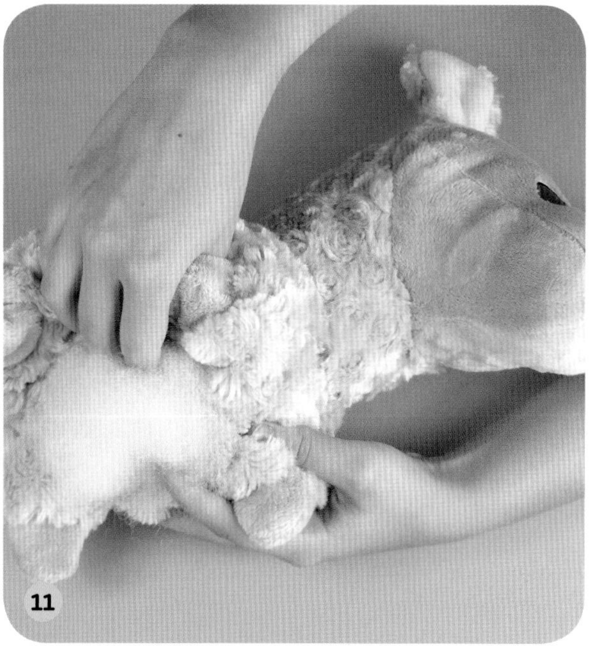

Stuff and finish. Fill the feet with micro pellets and the rest of the body with batting. Hand-sew the opening in the bottom closed using a ladder stitch.

5

Clothing

Adorable characters don't have to stop at accessories! This chapter will show you how to make cute clothing that's simpler than you might think. These hoodies, ponchos, and dresses are cute, but are also wearable pieces of clothing. There aren't any difficult steps to follow, so you can easily jump right in. Fool all your friends and family into thinking you've created just a nice well-made poncho, when in fact, you have a fluffy panda bear outfit!

Character Hoodie

Difficulty: Easy

For this project, you'll be adjusting a purchased hoodie with whatever additions you like, including ears, faces, tails, claws, and wings. Create the additions out of fleece or another knit fabric similar to your hoodie so they'll blend in to the feel of your jacket. Mix and match the elements to make any hoodie you want. The challenges in this project come from the little pieces you'll need to align just right so your design looks clean and symmetrical. A great way to help with this is to try your hoodie on many times before you sew anything down, and always measure twice and cut once! Included are patterns for kitty ears, bunny ears, fox ears, bunny tail, fox tail, claws, and mittens. You can also use the ear and wing patterns from the poncho and hat projects interchangeably to create a unique look!

Patterns on page 160.

Materials

- Purchased hoodie (relaxed fit, and preferably made from fleece, cotton, or polyester knit)
- Fabric for appliqué
- Fusible web
- Stabilizer
- Thread to match hoodie
- Thread to match appliqué fabric
- Thread to match detail fleece

For wings:

- ⅓ yd. (⅓m) fleece

For ears, mitts, or tails:

- ¼ yd. (¼m) fleece or knit

For claws:

- ¼ yd. (¼m) fleece
- Batting

Tools

- Fabric marker
- Fabric scissors
- Fabric pins
- Hand-sewing needle

Tail: しっぽ
Shippo (SHEE-poh)

Learn to Speak Japanese

Character Hoodie Gallery

< Bear hoodie detail.

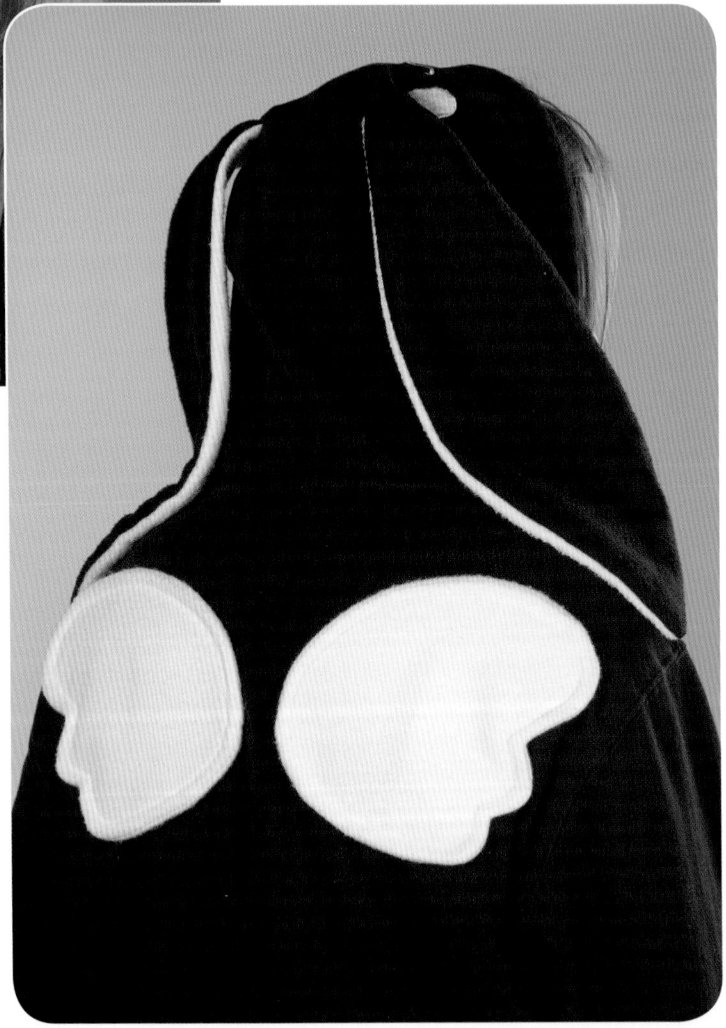

> Rear view of Bunny hoodie, showing wings and ears.

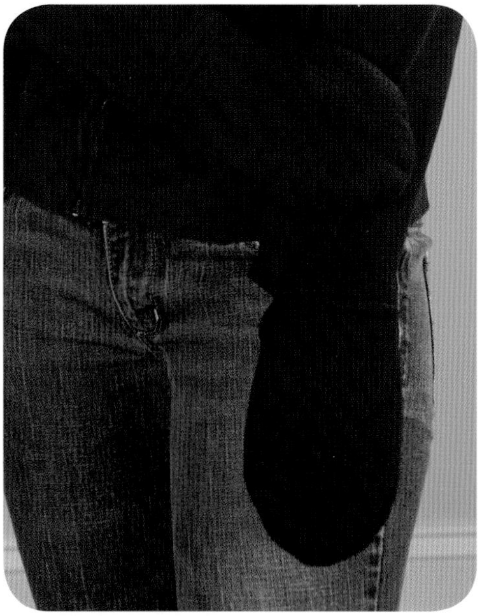

∧ Closeup of Bunny hoodie, showing mitten detail.

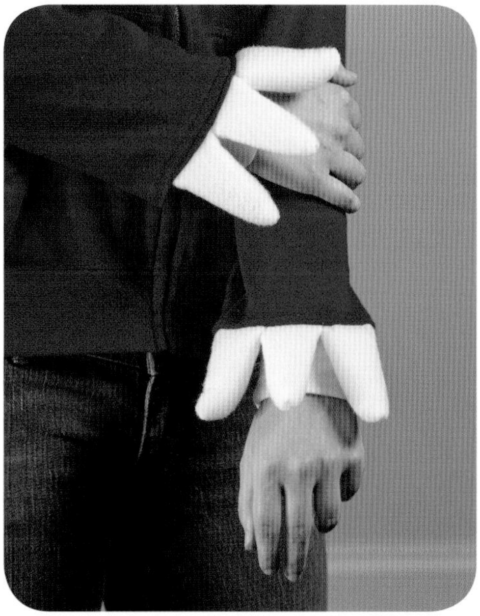

∧ Closeup of Devil Kitty hoodie, showing claw detail.

∧ Rear view of Devil Kitty hoodie, showing tail, wings, and ears.

Character Hoodie

For faces:

Appliqué. Pick the detail parts you want. Cut the pattern pieces from your fabric and make all applicable markings. Apply fusible web to the appliqué pieces. Use a combination of eyes and mouths from the pattern section to create a face for the hood. Position it about 1 to 2" (25 to 50mm) from the hood edge and 6 to 7" (150 to 180mm) wide, centered on the middle seam. Iron the pieces in place and sew around the edges of the fabric and along any lines as necessary from the pattern.

For ears:

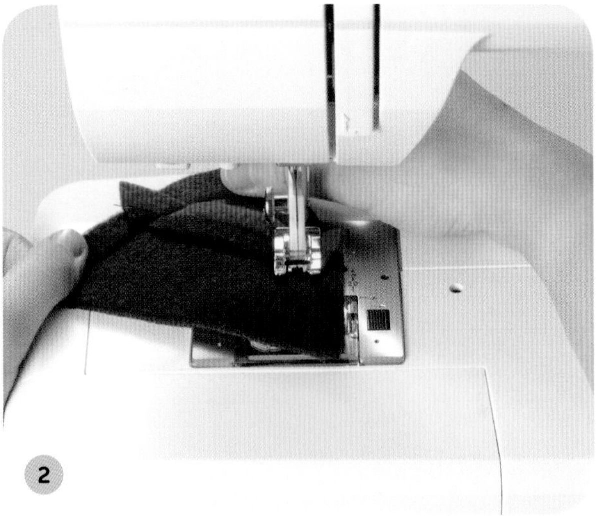

Sew the ears. [For Fox: Sew the ear tips to the ear base and press flat.] Sew the outer ear to the inner ear pieces, leaving the bottom straight edge open for turning right side out. Turn right side out and press.

Cut slits in the hood. Mark the areas for the hoodie ears to be placed. Measure about 5" (125mm) from the edge of the hood and 1½" (40mm) from the center. Cut 2½" (65mm) slits to make room for the ears.

Sew the ears to the hood. [For Kitty ears: Fold 1½" (38mm) of the ears down in order to make a more realistic, 3-D shape. Make sure the folds point towards the center of the hood.] Tuck the ears inside the slots you've cut. Sew the layers together using a ½" (15mm) seam allowance.

For tail:

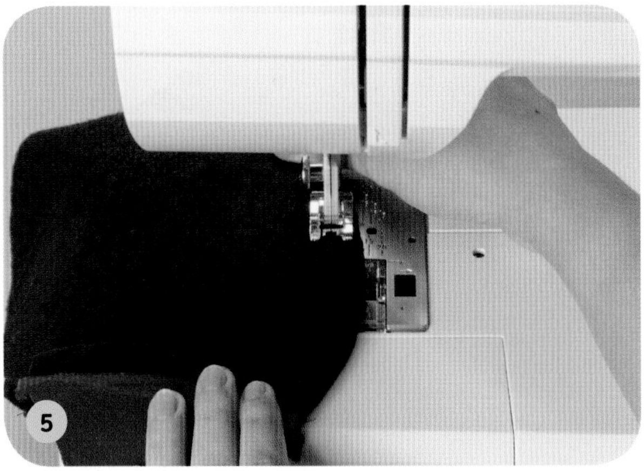

Sew the tail. [For Fox: Sew the tail tip to the tail base and press flat.] Sew the tail pieces together, leaving the top edge open to turn it right side out. Turn the tail right side out and press flat.

Attach the tail. Turn in ⅝" (15mm) from the opening in the top of the tail. Sew the tail to the inside bottom center of the back of the hoodie.

For mitts:

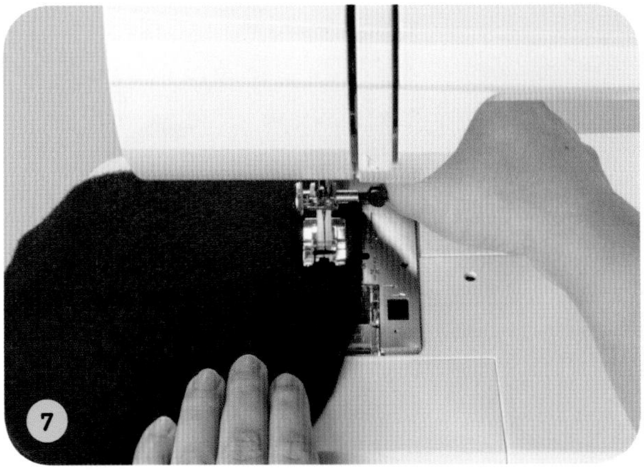

Sew the mitts. Sew the mitt pieces together along the curved edge. Leave the top edge open. Turn right side out and press lightly.

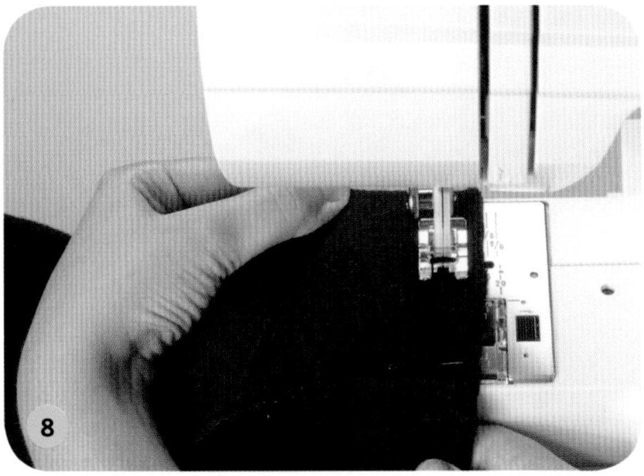

Sew the mitts to the sleeves. Pin the mitt to the edge of the sleeve, matching the seams found on the side. Sew them together, but only on the top half of the sleeve, starting at the seam on one end of the mitt and ending at the other seam.

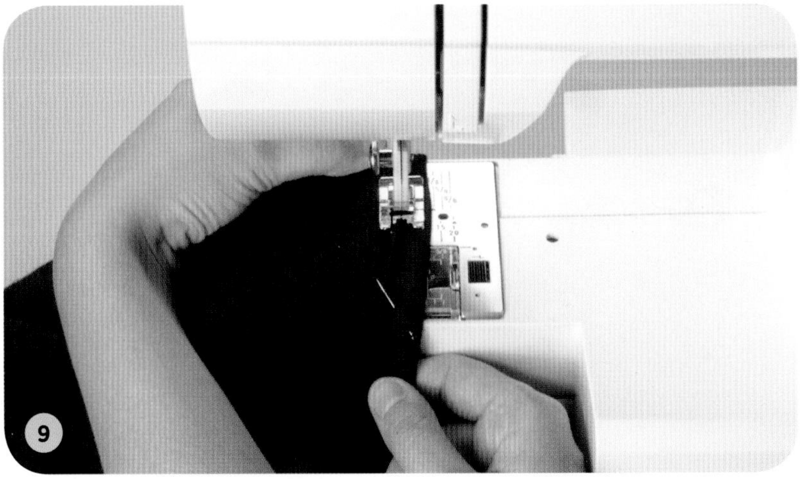

Finish the edges. Fold back the seam allowances for the sleeve and the mitt. Iron them flat and sew around the edge to hem them.

Character Hoodie

For claws:

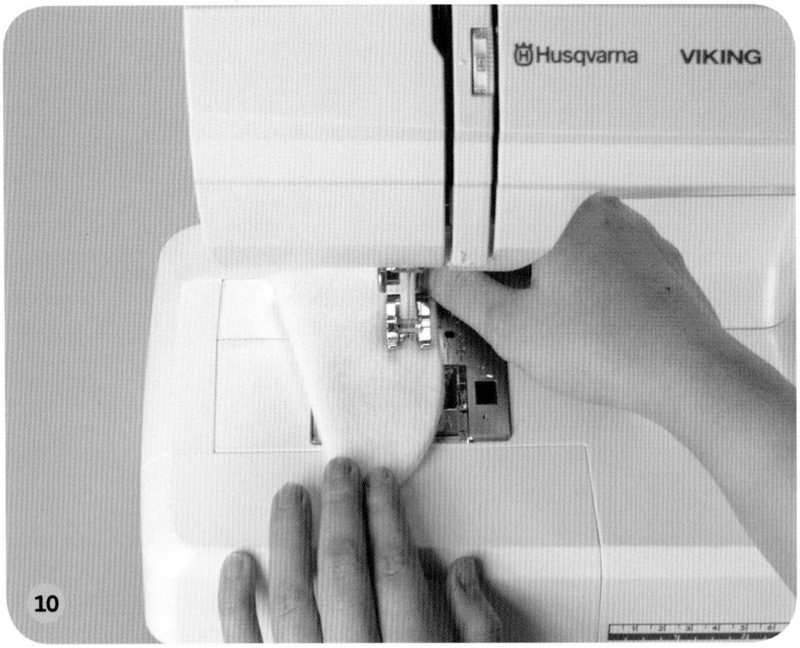

Sew the claws. Fold the claw pieces in half and sew along the side seam, leaving the top edge open. Turn the claw right side out.

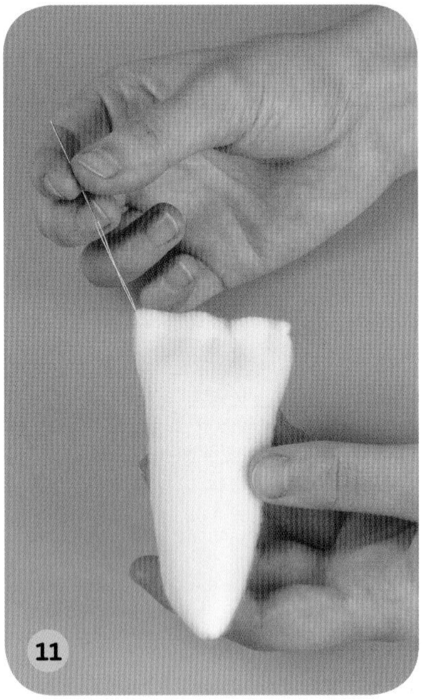

Stuff the claws. Stuff the claw lightly with batting and baste along the upper edge of the claw to keep the top closed.

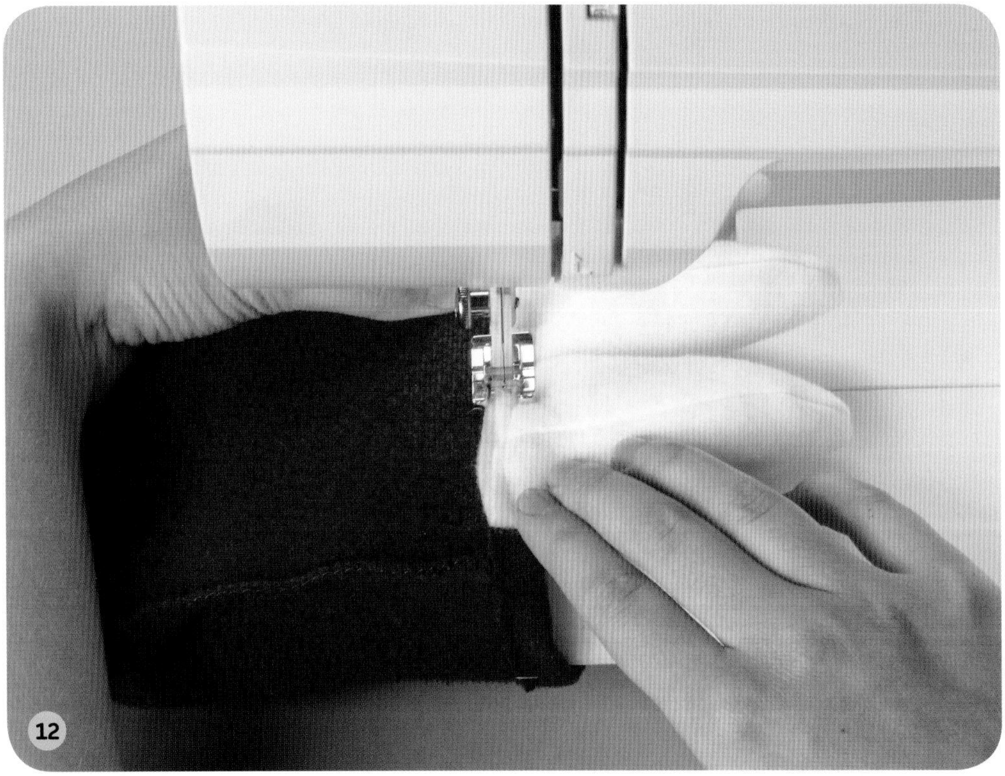

Attach the claws. Pin three claws along the upper edge of each hoodie sleeve. Sew them in place.

For wings:

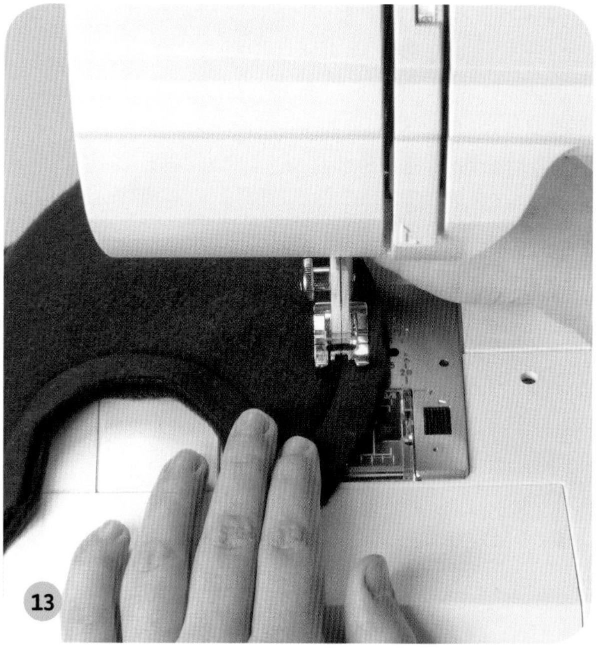

Sew the wings. Sew the wing pieces together around the entire perimeter. Cut a small hole in the back of the wing to turn it right side out.

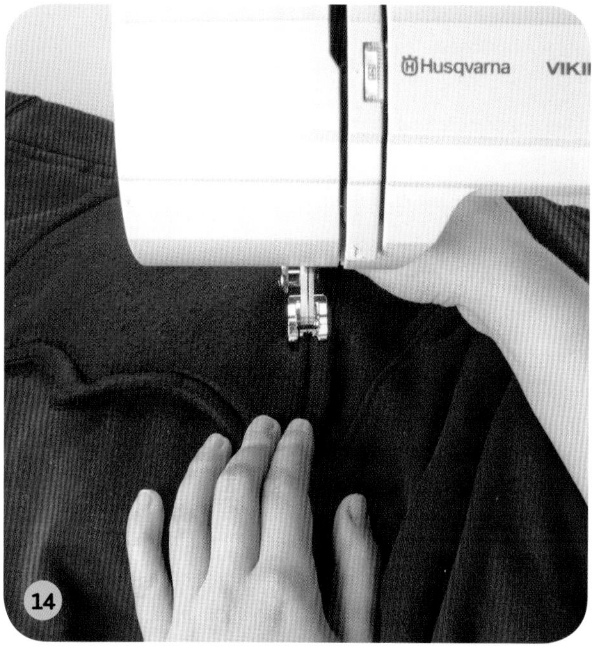

Attach the wings. Pin the wings to the back of the hoodie around the shoulder blade area. When you achieve the right positioning, sew them in place ⅝" (15mm) from the edge of the wings.

Extra Challenge: Hoodie from Scratch

If you have already mastered altering a purchased hoodie and know your way around making a garment, you might try your hand at making a hoodie from scratch. This way you can choose your own colors and fabrics to make sure all your pieces coordinate. Fleece is a great fabric to use when starting out, but you can also use interlock knits and sweatshirt knits, which are more like the fabrics you'll find in store-bought hoodies.

Start with a pattern, such as Burda 8042 or Simplicity 5362—any type of pattern that has simple straight lines and pieces. Avoid patterns with extra seams in the front or the hood. The hood should have one seam going down the center of the head for the most simplicity. Whether you choose a hoodie that needs a zipper is up to you. Inserting zippers in fleece or knits can be tricky, but the tips in the Jellyfish Purse project (page 49) will help with this.

To add ears to your hoodie, you'll want to cut your hood pattern into a front and back piece so that you might add your ears in between.

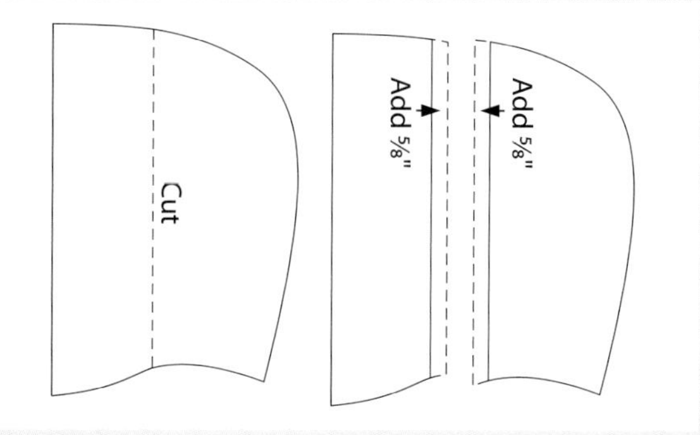

Measure about halfway through the hood piece and cut it in half vertically from top to bottom. This will be your new ear line. Add a ⅝" (15mm) seam allowance to each cut edge.

The original hood pattern will now be in two pieces, making four fabric pieces when you cut them out. When putting it all together, you'll need to sew the center seam of each separately. Appliqué your desired face to the front, and before sewing it to the back, insert the ears.

Poncho

Difficulty: Easy

This is possibly one of the best garments to start with if you're new to sewing your own clothing. Of course, you could start by making some plain pajama pants or a skirt, but who could pass up something this adorable? There's no need to worry about exact fit, because the poncho drapes like a soft and fuzzy cape. This project uses fleece, which is great as a warm fabric, though it can be switched out for any other medium-weight fabric as well. Any challenges in this project will come from lining up the wing and ear pieces, as well as lining up the trims properly. If you try on your poncho occasionally while working on it, you can catch any errors before they are sewn in. The patterns provide guides to create an Angel Bunny, Devil Kitty, and Panda Bear in XS-S, M-L, and L-XL sizes.

Materials

- 2½ yds. (2½m) medium-weight fabric
- ⅓ yd. (⅓m) contrast fabric for wings (optional)
- ⅛ yd. (⅛m) contrast or matching fabric for kitty, panda, or bunny ears
- ½ yd. (½m) minky or plush fabric for trim
- ⅔ yd. (⅔m) cording
- ½" (15mm) eyelets (2)
- Fabric for appliqué
- Thread to match medium-weight fabric
- Thread to match contrast fabric
- Thread to match trim fabric
- Thread to match appliqué fabric
- Fusible web
- Stabilizer

Tools

- Fabric marker
- Fabric scissors
- Fabric pins
- Safety pin
- Eyelet setting tools
- Hand-sewing needle

Patterns on pages 161–164.

Pieces without a pattern

For the bottom trim, cut two rectangles from the minky fabric, according to the size poncho you are making. Use a ⅝" (15mm) seam allowance.

(XS-S)	43¼" x 7¼" (1100 x 185mm)
(M-L)	47¼" x 7¼" (1200 x 185mm)
(L-XL)	51¼" x 7¼" (1300 x 185mm)

Angel: 天使
Tenshi (TEN-shee)

Learn to Speak Japanese

Poncho Gallery

∧ Face detail on Angel Bunny.

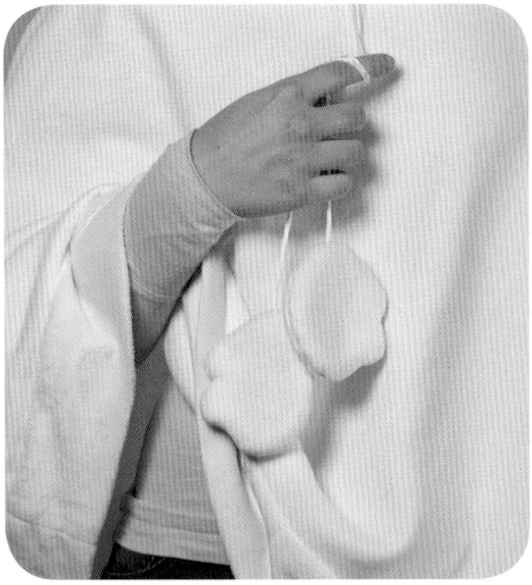

∧ Toggle and hem detail on Angel Bunny.

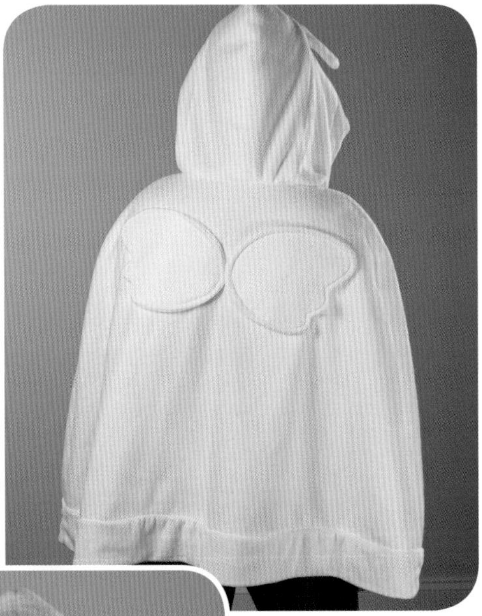

> Wing detail on Angel Bunny.

∧ Panda Bear poncho.

< Face detail on Panda Bear.

^ Toggle and hem detail on Devil Kitty.

^ Wing detail on Devil Kitty.

^ Devil Kitty poncho.

Poncho

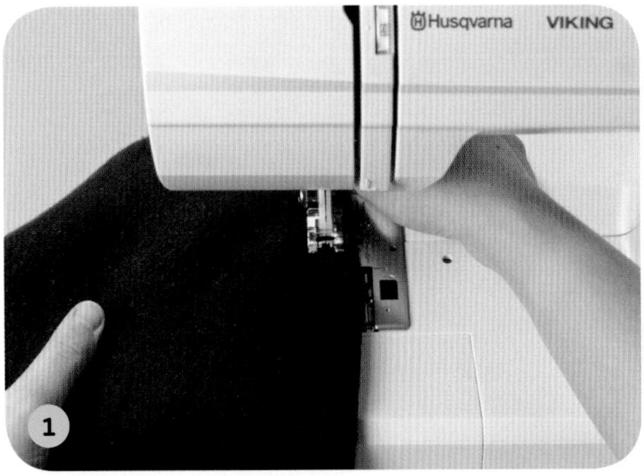

Sew the hood center seam. Cut the pattern pieces from your fabric and make all applicable markings. Apply fusible web to the appliqué pieces. Sew the top seam along the hood front and back.

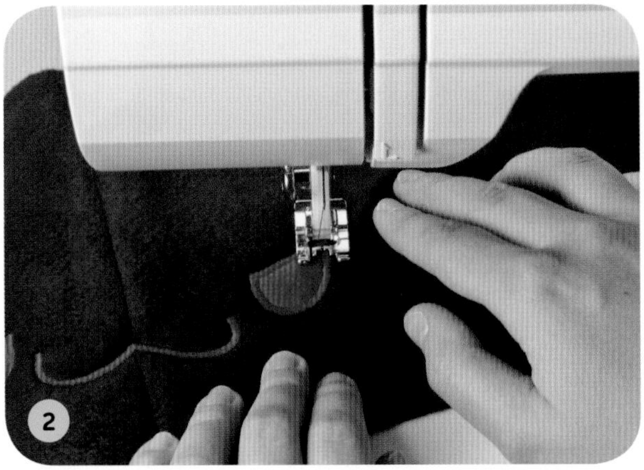

Appliqué. Iron the appliqué pieces to the hood front, following the guidelines. Sew along the edges of the fabric and along any lines to form the mouth.

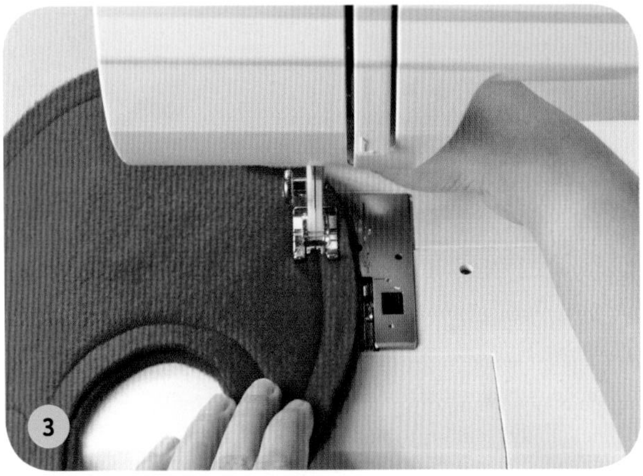

Sew the ears and wings. Sew the ear, wing, and cord toggle pieces together. Leave the bottom edges of the ears open and turn them right side out. Leave openings for the cord toggles where the pattern indicates and turn right side out. For the wings, cut a small slit in the back of the wing to turn them right side out.

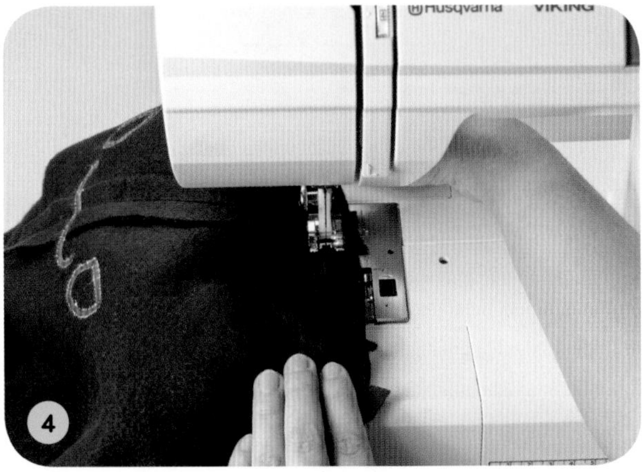

Sew the hood front to the hood back. Pin the hood front to the hood back. Insert the ears where the pattern indicates [For Kitty ears: Fold over the inside ⅓ of the ear away from the center of the hood to give the ear dimension]. Sew the two halves together.

Sew the poncho and trim. Sew the two poncho body pieces together along the side seams. Also, sew the bottom trim pieces together to form a circle.

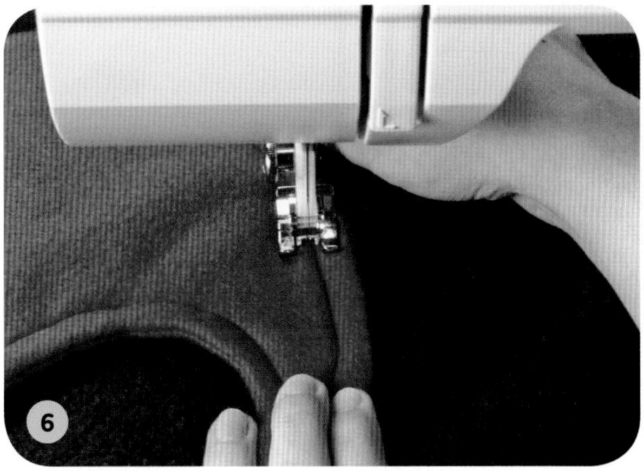

Attach the wings. Position the wings on the back of the poncho near the shoulder blades. Try on the poncho to get the best adjustment and sew them down ⅝" (15mm) from the edge of the wings.

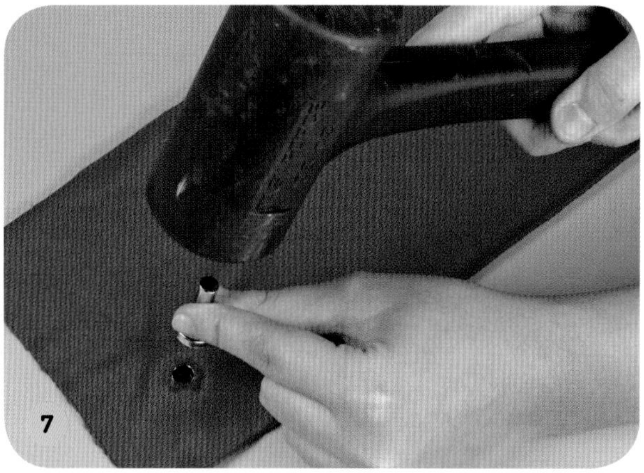

Place the eyelets. Clip two small holes in each end of the trim for the hood according to the pattern guidelines. Set the ½" (15mm) eyelets there, according to the package instructions.

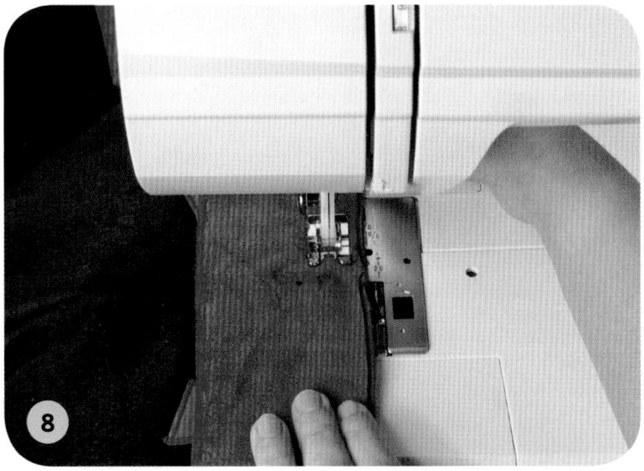

Sew the trim. Fold both the hood trim and bottom trim in half. Sew the hood trim to the hood edge and the bottom trim to the bottom edge. On the bottom, make sure the side seams of both the poncho body and the trim match up.

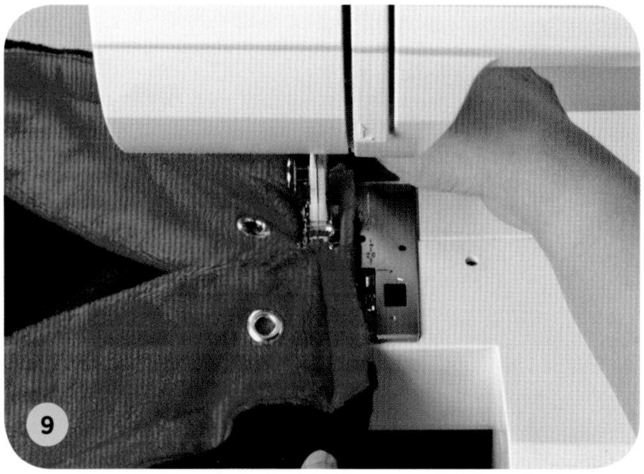

Sew the hood to the body. Pin the hood to the poncho body, matching the center back markings and overlapping the edges of the hood at the center front. Sew the hood in place, stretching the fabric slightly if necessary.

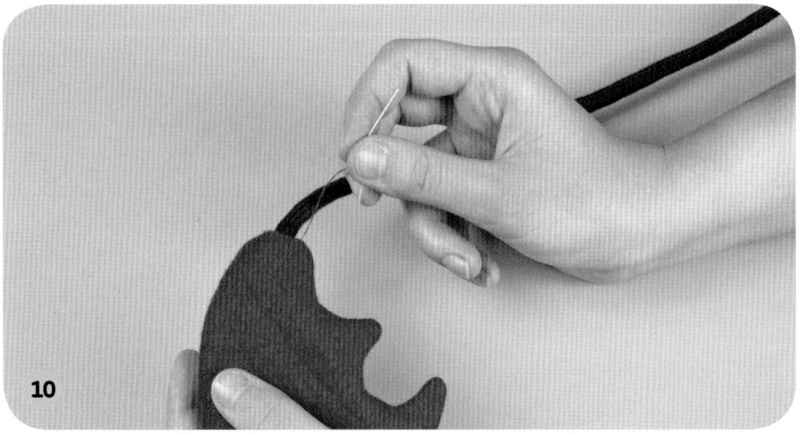

Thread the cording. Thread the cording through the eyelets in the hood trim using a safety pin. Hand-sew the cording detail pieces around the ends of the cord using the ladder stitch.

Jellyfish Dress

Difficulty: Experienced Beginner

This dress takes the classic bubble dress idea and runs with it in the form of an adorable jellyfish. You can go all out and add ribbons for the tentacles, or stay subtle and just keep the eyes. This design is best when made out of a thin slinky knit fabric that creates a beautiful drape. Another option is to make it out of terry cloth and have the cutest cover-up at the beach! Challenges from this project come from working with thin and slinky knits and making long and consistent straight lines on such a stretchy fabric. Check out the tips on working with knits if you run into any problems, and you might find your issues can be easily solved (page 121)! The patterns provide guides to make the dress in sizes XS-S, M-L, and L-XL.

Materials

- Jersey knit or terry cloth: 1½ yds. (1½m) (XS-S); 1¾ yds. (1¾m) (M-L); 2 yds. (2m) (L-XL)
- 2" (50mm) novelty buttons (2)
- 1½ yds. (1½m) ¾" (20mm) elastic
- 3 yds. (3m) ¼" (5mm) elastic
- Thread to match fabric
- Thread to match button color
- 3 yds. (3m) ribbon to match fabric (optional)

Tools

- Fabric marker
- Fabric scissors
- Fabric pins
- Hand-sewing needle
- Safety pin

Pieces without a pattern

For the dress, cut one rectangle on the fold from the main fabric, according to the size dress you are making. Use a ⅝" (15mm) seam allowance. See illustration on page 118 for more details.

(XS-S)	25" x 42" (635 x 1065mm)
(M-L)	30" x 43½" (760 x 1105mm)
(L-XL)	35" x 45" (890 x 1145mm)

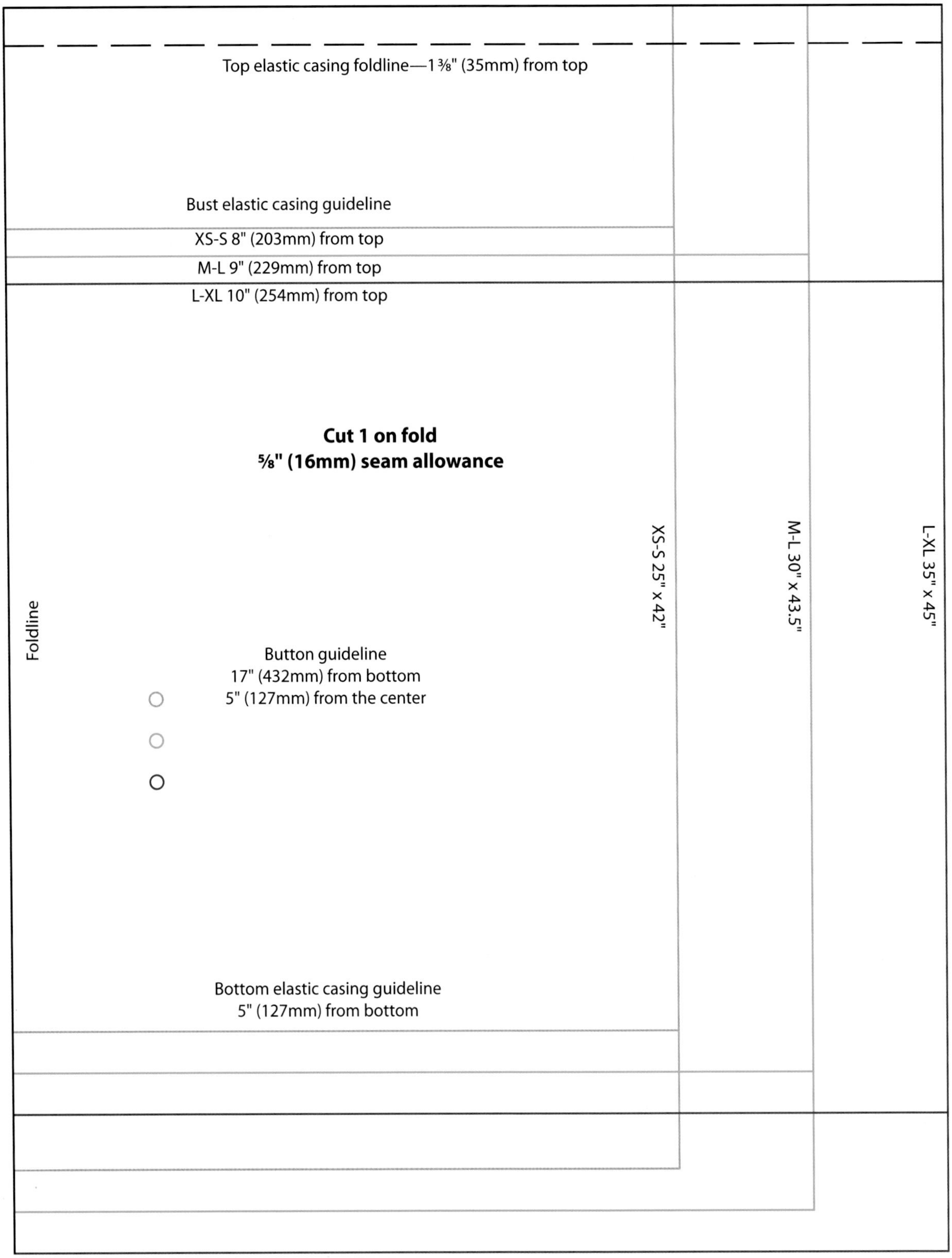
Top elastic casing foldline—1 3⁄8" (35mm) from top
Bust elastic casing guideline
XS-S 8" (203mm) from top
M-L 9" (229mm) from top
L-XL 10" (254mm) from top
Cut 1 on fold
5⁄8" (16mm) seam allowance
XS-S 25" x 42"
M-L 30" x 43.5"
L-XL 35" x 45"
Foldline
Button guideline
17" (432mm) from bottom
5" (127mm) from the center
Bottom elastic casing guideline
5" (127mm) from bottom

Jellyfish Dress

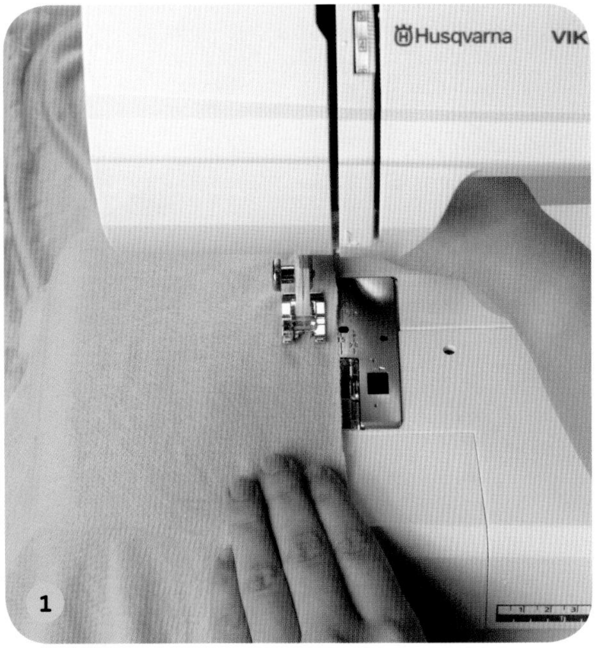

Sew the back seam. Cut the pattern pieces from your fabric and make all applicable markings. Fold the dress in half and sew down the back seam.

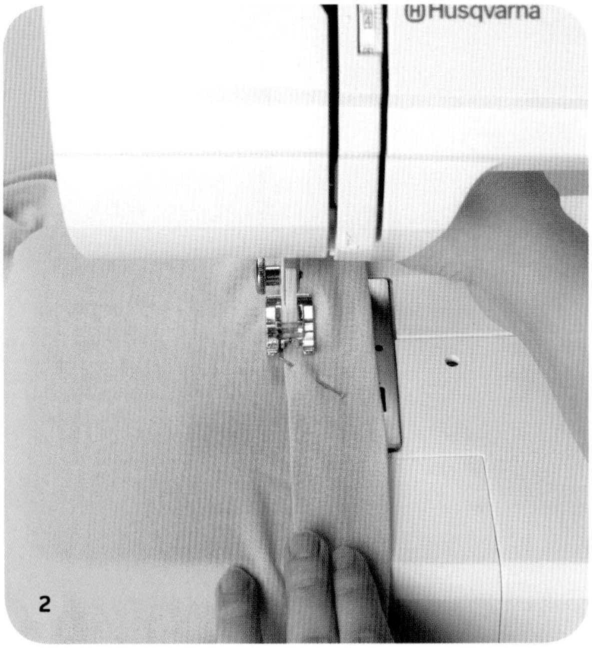

Hem the top and bottom. Fold over ⅜" (10mm) from the top and iron it flat, then fold over 1" (25mm) and iron flat. Sew along the edge to hem it, leaving a small opening to insert the elastic. For the bottom, fold over ⅜" (10mm) and iron flat, then ⅝" (15mm) and iron flat. Sew along the edge to hem it.

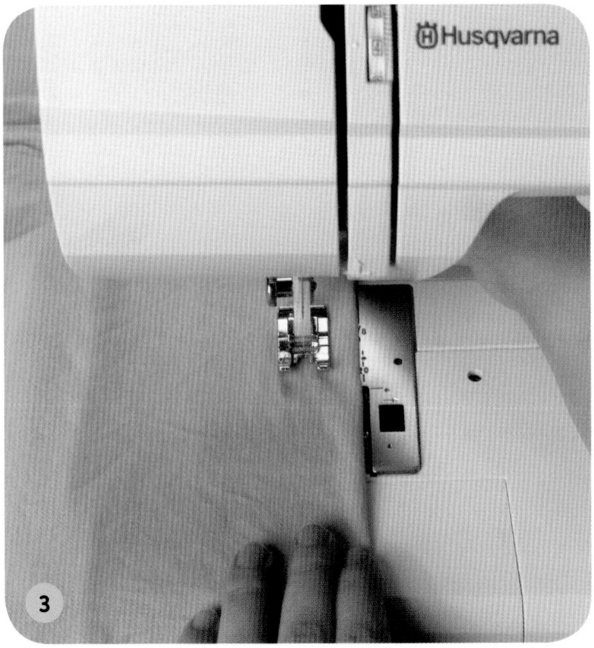

Sew the elastic casings. From the wrong side of the fabric, fold the dress along the elastic casing guidelines and sew ¾" (20mm) away from the edge.

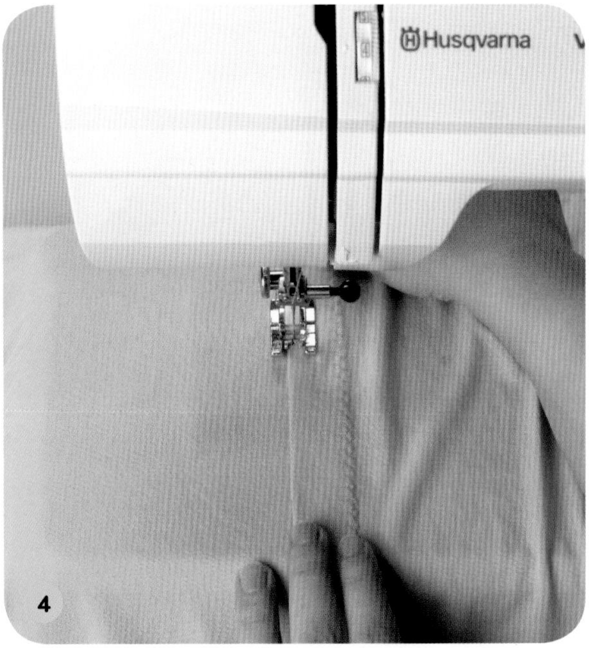

Finish the elastic casings. Doing this will make a small flap. Fold it downward along the seamline and iron it flat. Sew it to the body of the dress as close to the edge as possible, leaving a small opening to insert the elastic.

Jellyfish Dress

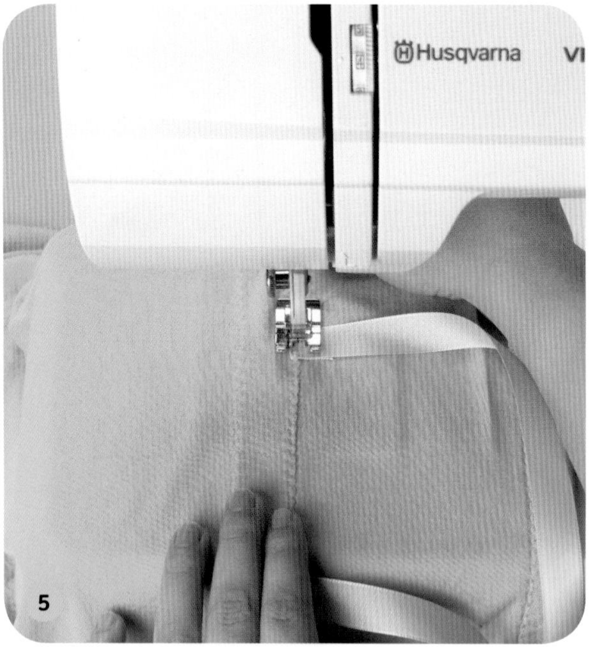

Attach the ribbon (optional). Cut 10 pieces of 14" (355mm) ribbon and sew them evenly around the edge of the elastic casing.

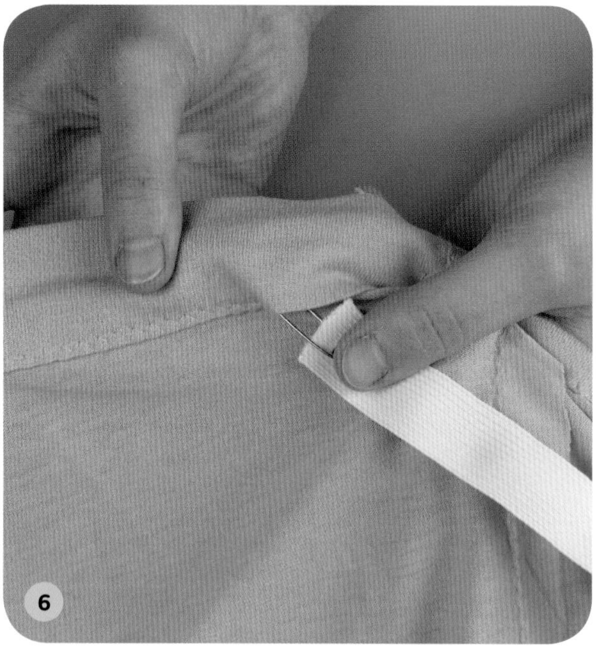

Insert the elastic. Hold the ¾" (20mm) elastic above your bust and stretch it slightly until it's comfortable. Cut the elastic at this length plus ½" (15mm) and insert it into the upper casing with a safety pin. Hold the ¼" (5mm) elastic below your bust and measure in the same manner. Insert this into the middle casing. Hold the last of the ¼" (5mm) elastic at your mid to upper thigh in the same manner. Insert this into the bottom casing.

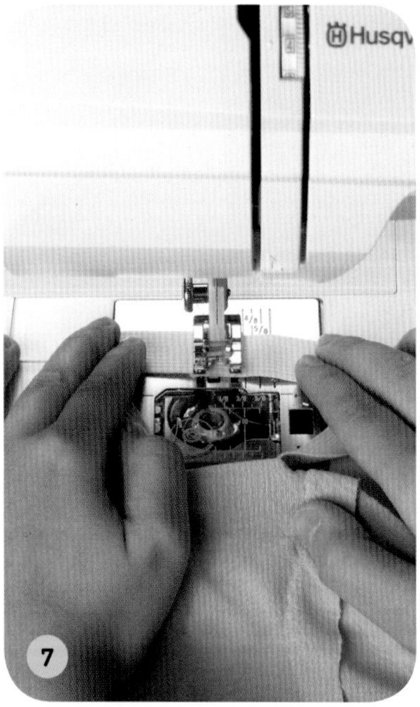

Close the casings. Using several rows of zigzag stitching, sew the ends of the elastic together and sew closed the openings in the casings.

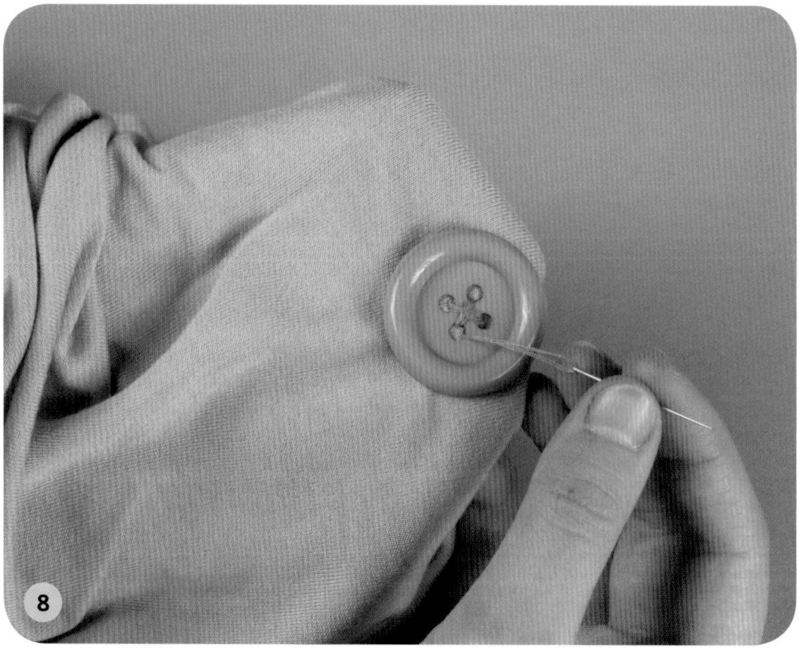

Sew on the eyes. Hand-sew the button eyes to the front using the pattern guidelines.

Technique: Sewing with Knits

Knits can be tricky to work with because of their stretchy quality. They tend to stretch and warp while you cut or sew them, and sometimes don't agree with standard sewing needles. If you encounter skipped or irregular stitches, your first step should be to use a sewing needle specifically for knits. If you encounter other problems, here are more tips on dealing with knit fabrics.

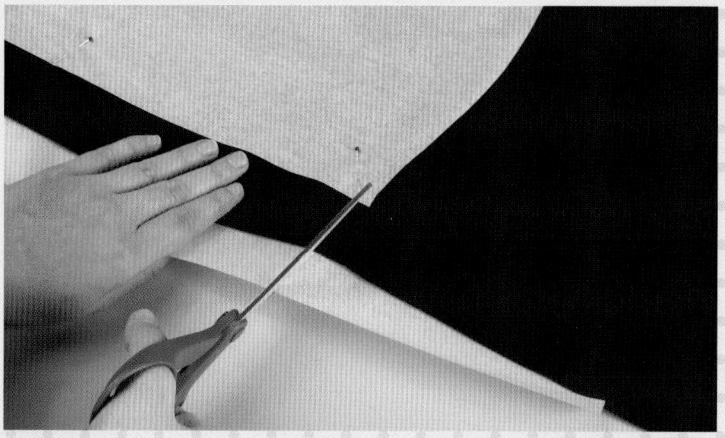

Cutting knits. Knits have a tendency to slink away and create inaccurate lines when being cut. To prevent this, place some newspaper or tissue paper beneath your fabric as you lay it out. When placing your paper pattern pieces, pin and cut through both the fabric and newspaper layer.

Stretch stitch. When sewing seams, a standard straight stitch will not stretch when it's finished. Switch to your machine's stretch stitch. If it does not have one, or causes your fabric to bunch up, a narrow zigzag is a good substitute.

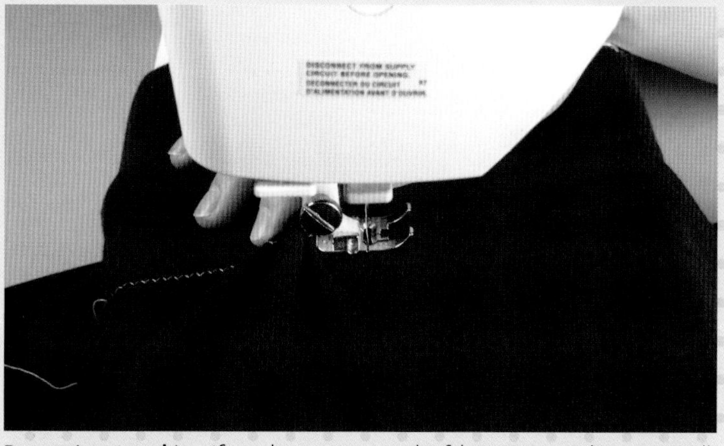

Preventing stretching. If you have very stretchy fabric, your machine may pull and warp the fabric while it sews. If your machine has the capability, lower your foot pressure adjustment. Another method is called easing. Hold your finger behind your sewing foot while it sews, causing the fabric to gather up between the foot and your finger. After about 5 seconds, when the sewing slows a bit, let go of the fabric and place your finger down again.

Stabilizing knits. If easing doesn't solve your problem or if your fabric is so thin it gets pulled down into the throat plate of the machine, stabilizing your fabric is a surefire solution. Use a very light-weight stabilizer or tissue paper beneath the fabric while you sew the seams. When the seam is done, gently pull the paper away from the fabric.

Extra Challenge: Making a Squid Dress

If you like the idea of a jellyfish dress, then you might like this squid dress idea. It goes along with the idea of a T-shirt dress and adapts it to yet another crazy aquatic creature. This dress was made from interlock knit, which is slightly more stable than jersey knit and less likely to sag and stretch out of shape with all the extra appendages we're giving the body.

Start with your favorite T-shirt pattern, such as Vogue 8536, and extend the length to make it closer to a mini dress. Modify the hood pattern from a separate project. Here it has been extended and cut in half along the middle to fit the squid fin in between. Lastly, create 8 strips at 2½" (65mm) wide to sew along the bottom for the tentacles.

Sew up the shirt as usual, but attach the hood to the neckline, overlapping the ends at the center front. Also attach the strips at equal intervals along the bottom of the dress. Here, they've been made just long enough to skim across the ground; any shorter and they would have created the optical illusion that the wearer has short legs. When you walk, they'll tend to flutter more than drag, so the extra length is worth it.

Hood detail.

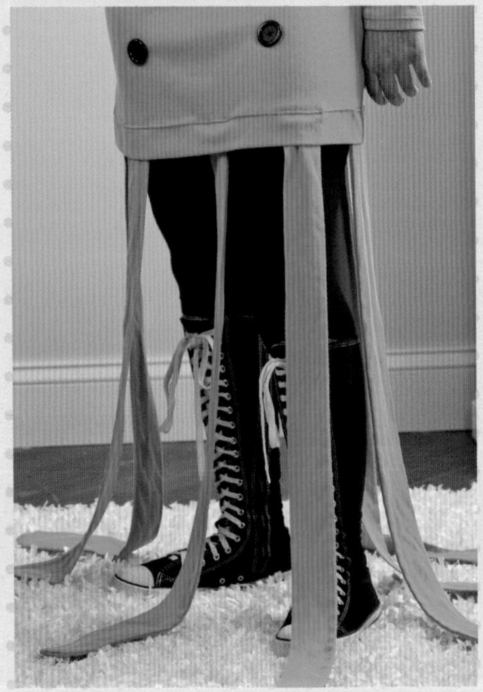

Tentacle detail.

Squid: いか
Ika (EE-kah)

Learn to Speak Japanese

6

Home Decorations

The projects in this chapter will help make your home a whole lot cozier. You'll be able to make all kinds and shapes of comfy pillows, and even a quilt. Now you can surround yourself with sweet characters—even as you sleep. As a plus, if you know somebody who is too tough to wear a bunny hat or kitty hoodie in public, make him or her a pillow for their bed. You can bet they won't be able to resist sleeping on a ridiculously soft minky fox, and you'll have them hooked!

Log Pillow

Difficulty: Easy

You might be surprised how comfortable it is to sleep on something so simple. Make this pillow with minky and you're in for a real treat! Other knit plush fabrics, such as fleece and faux fur, can work for this project as well. The only challenge in this project may come from going around the curves on each end of the log. If you line up your markings correctly and stretch the fabric lightly to make it around the curves, you will have no problem. The patterns provide guides to make a Pig, Fox, and Kitty pillow. The patterns and measurements are made for fabric that is 60" (1525mm) wide, the common width for fleece and minky.

Patterns on page 165.

Materials

- ½ yd. (½m) plush fabric
- For fox: ⅛" yd. (⅛m) contrast plush fabric for ear tips
- Fabric for appliqué
- Batting
- Thread to match plush fabric
- Thread to match appliqué fabric
- Fusible web
- Stabilizer

Tools

- Fabric marker
- Fabric scissors
- Fabric pins
- Hand-sewing needle

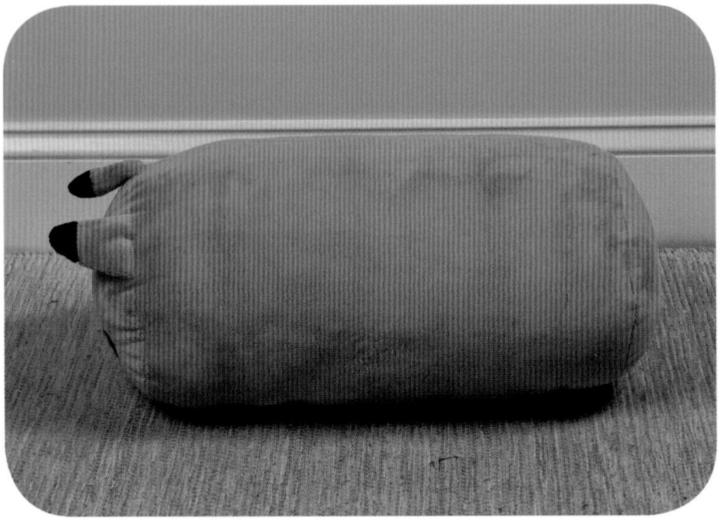

Side view of the Fox log pillow shows its dimensions.

Pig: 豚
Buta (boo-TAH)

Learn to Speak Japanese

Log Pillow

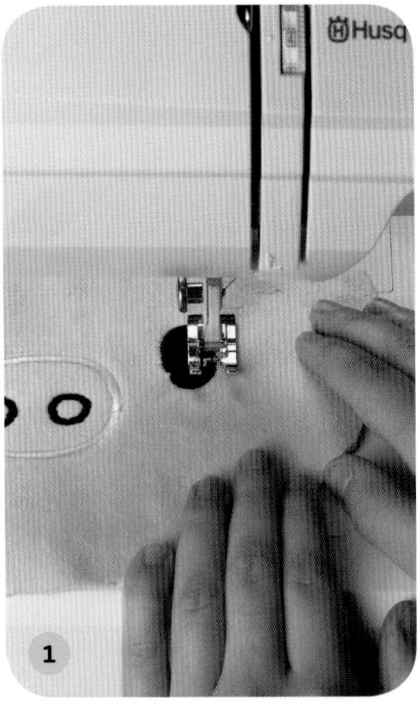

Appliqué. Cut the pattern pieces from your fabric and make all applicable markings. Apply fusible web to the appliqué pieces. Iron the appliqué pieces to the front of the pillow, following the pattern guidelines. Sew along the edges of the fabric and along any lines as indicated.

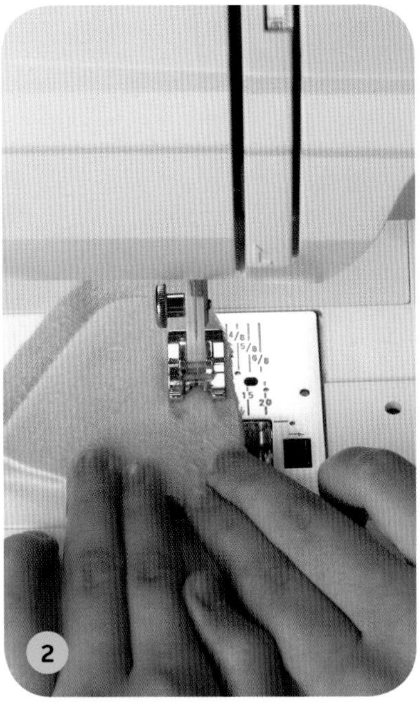

Sew the ears. [For Fox: Sew the ear base to the ear tip and finger press flat.] Sew the ear pieces together, leaving the bottom edge open. Turn them right side out.

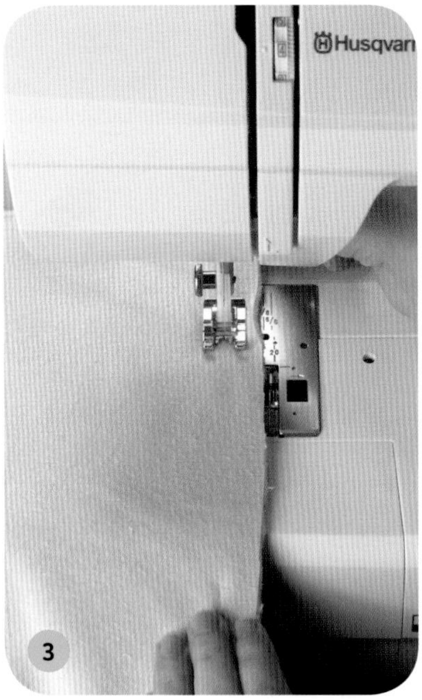

Sew the body. Sew the pillow body across the long seam, leaving an opening, as the pattern indicates, for turning the pillow right side out. Also, leave the two ends of the body open.

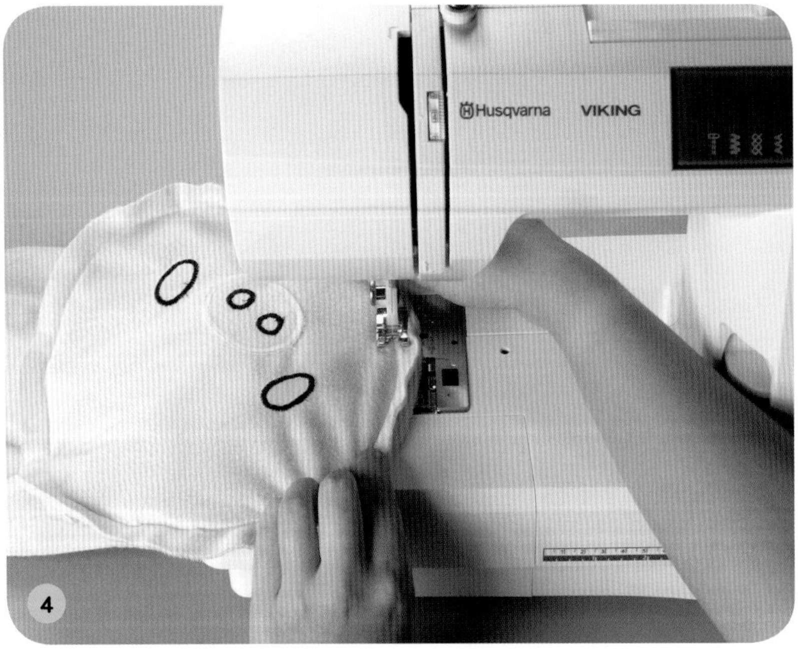

Sew the front and back. Sew the front and back circles to each end of the body, including ears where indicated by the pattern. Use the markings from the pattern to match up the center top and bottom of the face.

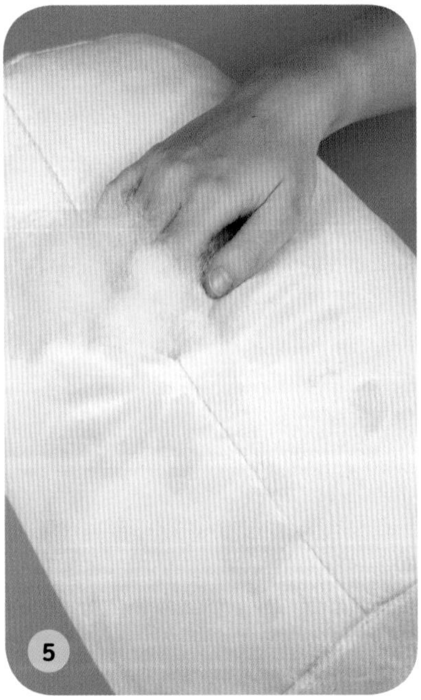

Finish. Turn the pillow right side out, stuff it firmly, and hand-sew the opening closed.

Square Pillow

Difficulty: Very Easy to Experienced Beginner

This project is another very simple shape that can be customized easily into all sorts of characters. The small and flat shape makes it a great travel or throw pillow. A knit plush fabric, such as fleece, minky, or faux fur, works best for this project. The challenge will come if you attempt the Squid, which calls for some tricky pivoting with corners (see sidebar on page 54). Take full advantage of the stretchy quality of fleece to make this work. Also, consider rounding your corners if necessary to make the process easier. The patterns provide guides to make a Squid, Raccoon, and Bear pillow. The patterns and measurements are made for fabric that is 60" (1525mm) wide, the common width for fleece and minky.

Patterns on pages 166–167.

Materials

- For Squid:
  ¾ yd. (¾m) plush fabric
- For Bear or Raccoon:
  ½ yd. (½m) plush fabric
- For Raccoon:
  ⅛ yd. (⅛m) black and white or contrasting fabric
- Fabric for appliqué
- Batting
- Fusible web
- Stabilizer
- Thread to match main plush fabric
- Thread to match contrasting fabric
- Thread to match appliqué fabric

Tools

- Fabric marker
- Fabric scissors
- Fabric pins
- Hand-sewing needle

Square Pillow

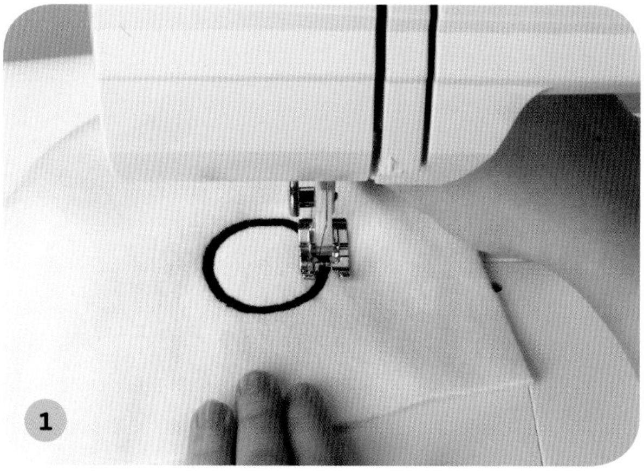

Appliqué. Cut the pattern pieces from your fabric and make all applicable markings. Apply fusible web to the appliqué pieces. Iron the appliqué pieces to the main fabric following the pattern guidelines. Sew along the edges of the fabric.

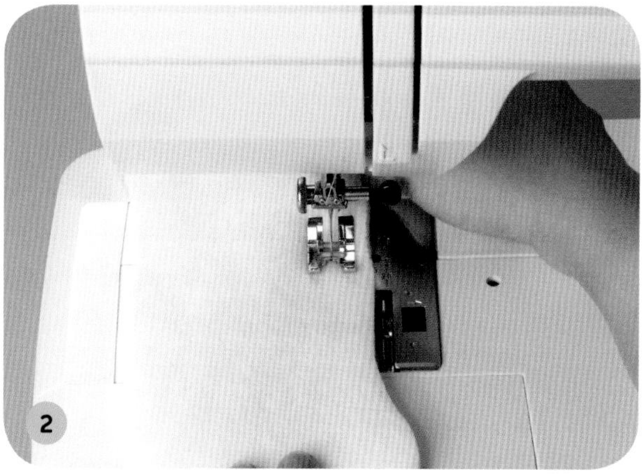

Sew the arms, ears, tentacles, and hood. Sew any arm and ear [For Squid: tentacle and hood] pieces together, leaving the straight edges open. Turn them right side out.

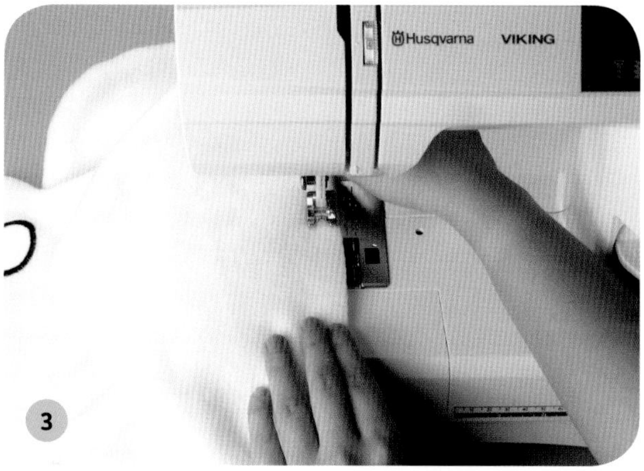

Baste the squid hood. For Squid: Pin the straight edges of the Squid hood around the top of the pillow front, matching the corners together. Clip the seam allowances in the hood to help it reach all the way around. Use a basting stitch to hold it in place for the next step. If the fabric puckers while doing this, try rounding the corners instead for an easier transition.

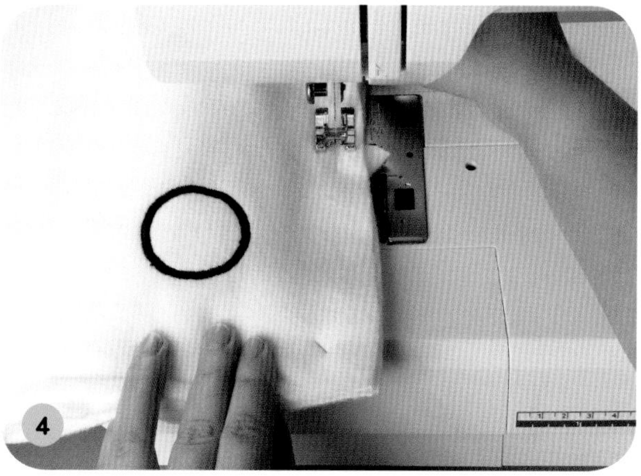

Sew the front to the back. Pin the front of the pillow to the back, inserting all arms, ears, and tentacles as indicated by the pattern. Sew them all in place, leaving an opening as indicated for turning it right side out.

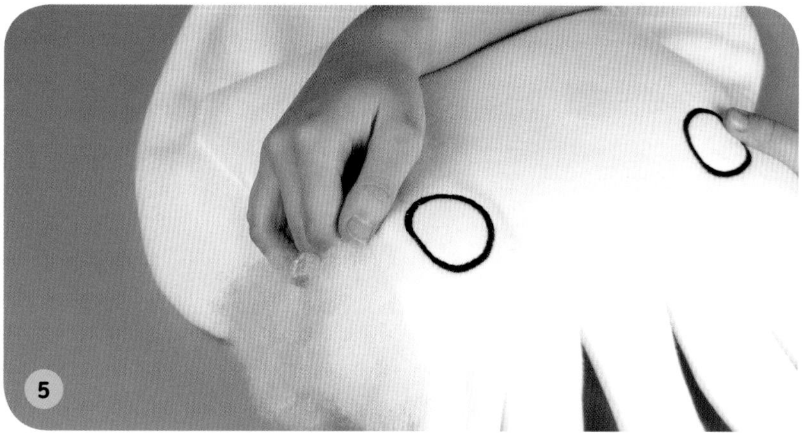

Finish. Turn the pillow right side out, stuff it firmly, and hand-sew the opening closed.

Towel Caddy

Difficulty: Experienced Beginner

Have you ever found yourself with a towel rack in your bathroom that you never use because its height or location is awkward? Here's a great way to finally utilize it. You can fill this caddy with all your commonly used toiletries and create space elsewhere. This project works best with terry cloth. Other medium-weight fabrics would work as well, but not be quite as perfect for the bathroom as terry cloth is. The challenge in this project can come from working with the terry cloth itself. The many shaggy fibers can get threads caught up and knotted. If you have this problem, use a zigzag instead of a straight stitch to tack some of the fibers down, and iron the fabric to flatten the fibers temporarily. You can always fluff the fabric again with your fingers or a quick wash.

Patterns on pages 168–170.

Materials

- ¾ yd. (¾m) terry cloth
- Fabric for appliqué
- Hook-and-loop tape
- Thread to match terry cloth
- Thread to match appliqué fabric
- Fusible web
- Stabilizer

Tools

- Fabric marker
- Fabric scissors
- Fabric pins
- Hand-sewing needle

Brushing Kitty

Bubble Bunny

Bathing Platypus

Bath: お風呂
Ofuro (oh-FOO-roh)

Learn to Speak Japanese

Towel Caddy

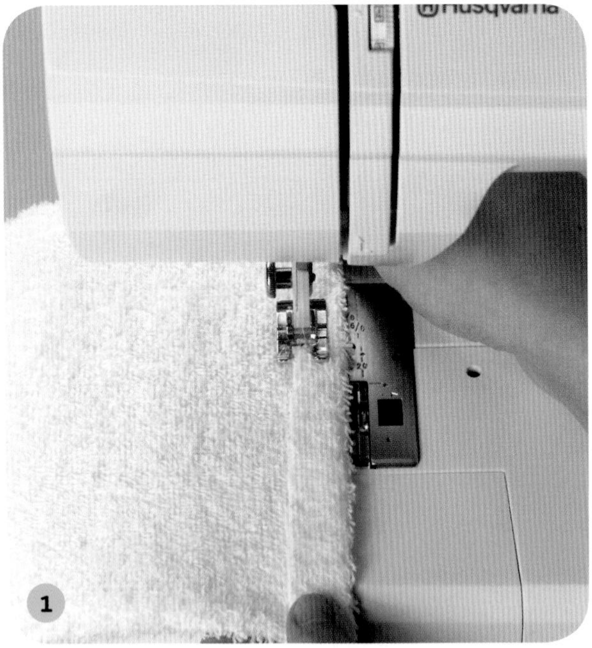

Hem the pockets. Cut the pattern pieces from your fabric and make all applicable markings. Apply fusible web to the appliqué pieces. Fold over ⅝" (15mm) around all edges of each pocket and iron them flat. Sew along only the top edge of each pocket to hem them.

Appliqué. Iron the appliqué pieces to the pockets as shown in the illustrations. Sew the pieces down along the fabric edges and along any lines as indicated by the pattern.

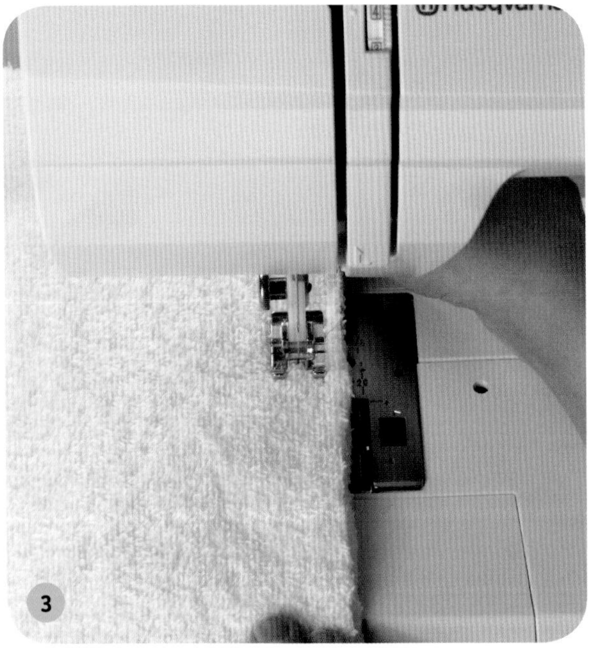

Sew the main body. Sew the two pieces of the caddy body together along all edges, leaving a small opening, as indicated by the pattern, to turn it right side out.

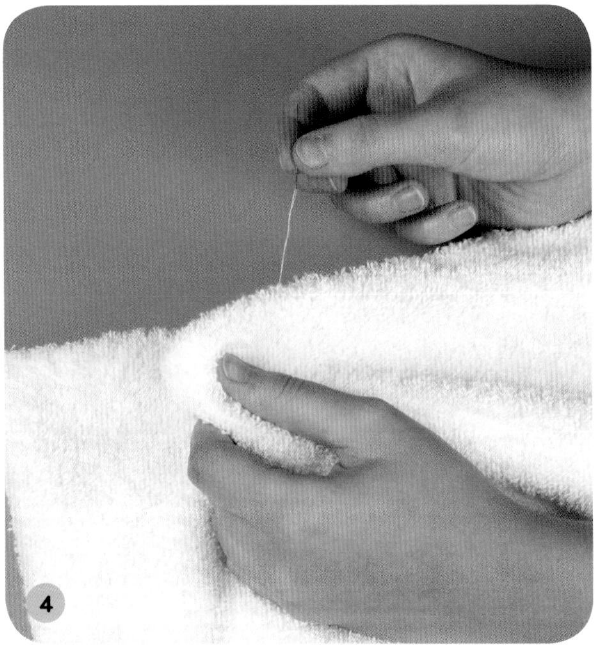

Turn and sew the body closed. Turn the body right side out and hand-sew the opening closed.

Apply the hook-and-loop tape. Sew the hook side of the hook-and-loop tape to the top back of the body, and the loop side to the middle back of the body, as indicated by the pattern.

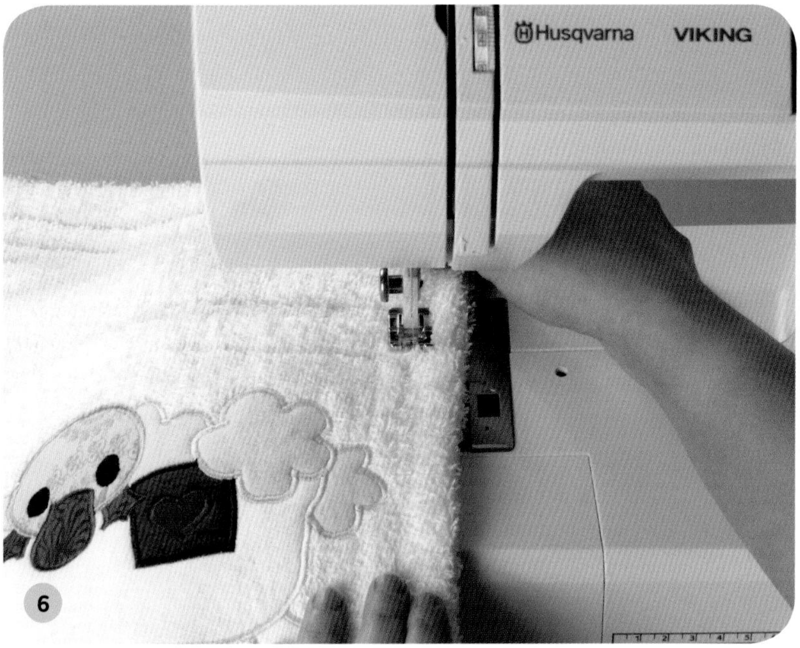

Apply the pockets. Pin the pockets to the locations indicated by the pattern to the front of the body. Sew them in place along the sides and the bottom, leaving the top sides open.

Technique: Cutting Numerous Appliqué Pieces

In this project, you'll be assembling a picture from numerous tiny appliqué pieces. It can be a chore to cut out each individual bit of fusible web.

An easier way to manage this task and prevent your fabrics from flying everywhere is to lay all your pieces out on a sheet of parchment paper, wrong side facing up. Then unroll the fusible web over the pieces and iron it down. Make sure the fusible web does not overreach the parchment paper or you will get adhesive on your ironing board! When the paper cools, you can pull it off, and all the fabric bits will be adhered to the fusible web in one sheet, ready to be cut out whenever you need them!

Sushi Quilt

Difficulty: Experienced Beginner

This last project is definitely the ultimate in kawaii sewing. It looks wonderful hanging on the wall or draped over your couch, ready to provide a bit of extra warmth. Most quilts use a consistent (and tiny) ¼" (5mm) seam allowance, but this project has a ⅜" (10mm) seam allowance to make it easier for beginners. You can use this quilt to study your sushi know-how and be the envy of your friends! Quilting cotton is the best fabric for this project, due to its stability and softness. Picking out the fabric for the quilt is lots of fun—it's enjoyable searching for just the right patterns and colors. The challenge in this project comes from the time and patience you'll need to make it, though it's quite worth it. Be sure that your seam allowance is very consistent, so all of your pieces line up. Also, if you have difficulty fitting the full quilt under your sewing machine, rolling up the sides will make maneuvering much easier.

Materials

- 1 yd. (1m) light brown (like pine wood) cotton
- ⅔ yd. (⅔m) white cotton
- 1¼ yds. (1¼m) pickled ginger–pink cotton
- 1½ yds. (1½m) wasabi-green cotton
- 1½ (1½m) yds. 60" (1525mm)-wide quilt backing fabric
- Quilt batting
- Thread to match all main and appliqué fabric colors
- Fusible web
- Stabilizer

Appliqué fabrics:

- Fat quarter (¼m) of nori (seaweed) dark green cotton
- Fat quarter (¼m) of salmon-pink cotton
- Fat quarter (¼m) of cucumber-green cotton
- Fat quarter (¼m) of avocado-green cotton
- Fat quarter (¼m) of roe (fish eggs) dark orange cotton
- Fat quarter (¼m) of eel–dark brown cotton
- Fat quarter (¼m) of egg-yellow cotton
- Fat quarter (¼m) of sea urchin–brownish-orange cotton
- Fat quarter (¼m) of solid black cotton

Tools

- Fabric marker
- Fabric scissors
- Fabric pins
- Safety pins

Patterns on pages 170–174.

- Tamago, page 170
- Uni, page 171
- Salmon Hand Roll, page 171
- Ikura, page 172
- Kappa Roll, page 172
- Ootoro, page 172
- California Roll, page 173
- Ebi, page 173
- Unagi, page 174

Fish: 魚
Sakana (SAH-KAH-nah)

Learn to Speak Japanese

^ The whole sushi quilt!

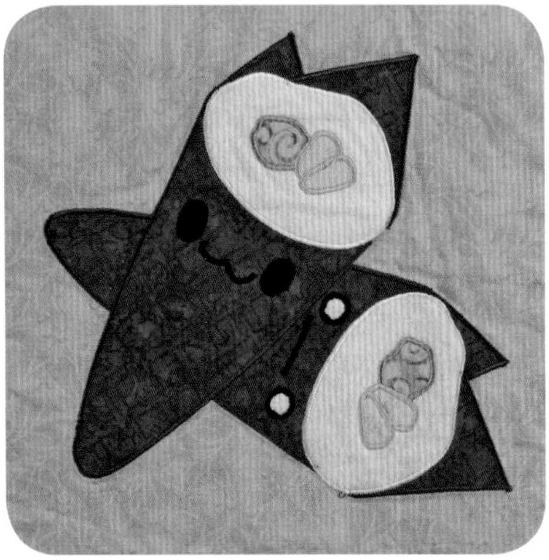

^ Salmon hand roll detail.

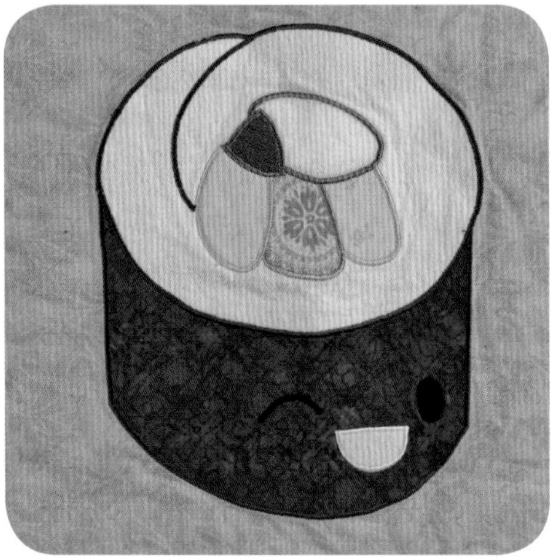

^ California roll detail.

^ Tamago (egg) roll detail.

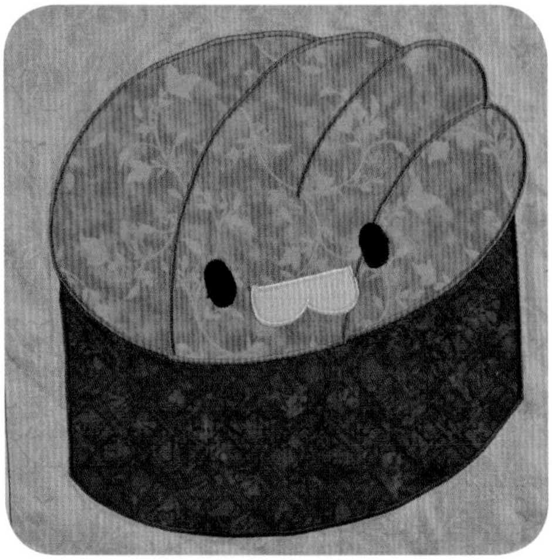

^ Uni (sea urchin) detail.

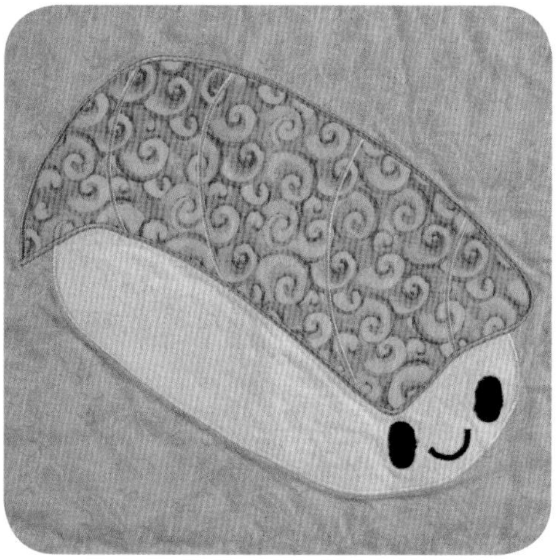

^ Ootoro (fatty tuna) roll detail.

^ Ikura (salmon roe) detail.

^ Ebi (shrimp on rice) detail.

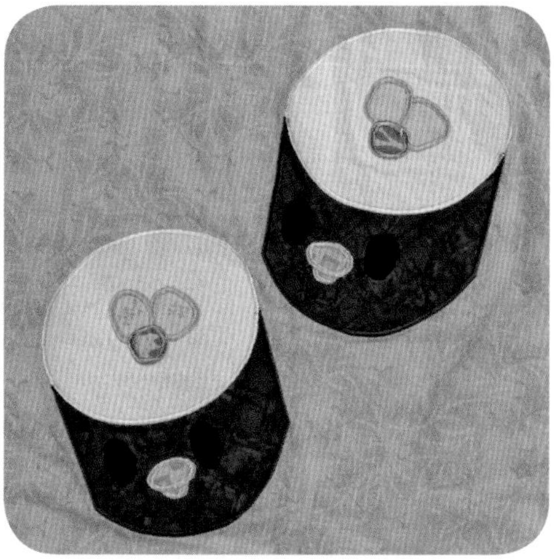

^ Kappa (cucumber) roll detail.

^ Unagi (eel) detail.

Quilt block and strip layout.

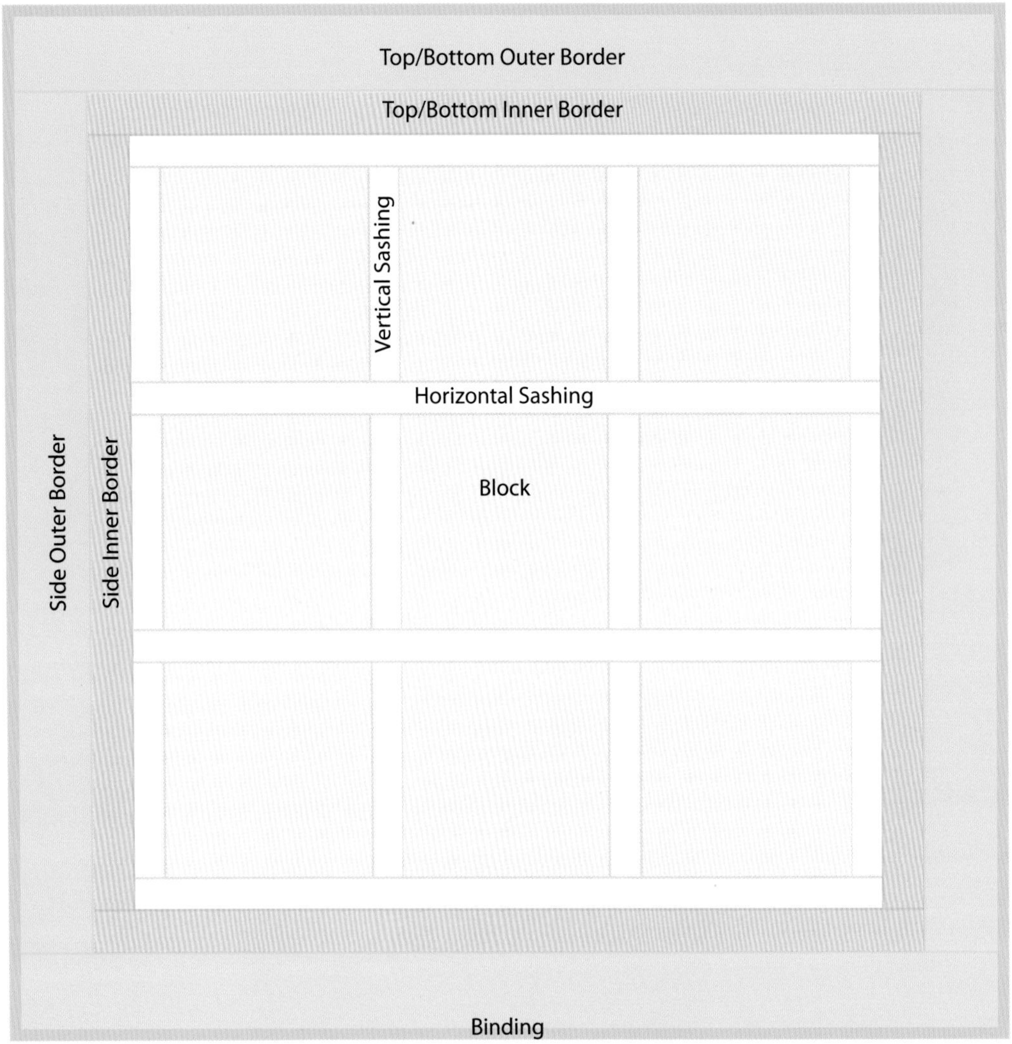

Pieces without a pattern

Cut with a ⅜" (10mm) seam allowance. See illustration (page 140) for more details.

Quilt Piece	Size	Quantity	Color
Block	10¾" x 10¾" (275 x 275mm)	9	Light brown (pine wood)
Backing	(At least) 48" x 48" (1220 x 1220mm)	1	Light brown (pine wood)
Vertical Sashing	2¼" x 10¾" (55 x 275mm)	12	White
Horizontal Sashing	36¾" x 2¼" (935 x 55mm)	4	White
Side Inner Border	2¾" x 36¾" (70 x 935mm)	2	Pink (pickled ginger)
Top/Bottom Inner Border	2¾" x 40¾" (70 x 1035mm)	2	Pink (pickled ginger)
Side Outer Border	4⅜" x 40¾" (111 x 1035mm)	2	Green (wasabi)
Top/Bottom Outer Border	48" x 4⅜" (1220 x 111mm)	2	Green (wasabi)
Binding	3¼" x 49¼" (85 x 1250mm)	4	Green (wasabi)

Sushi Quilt

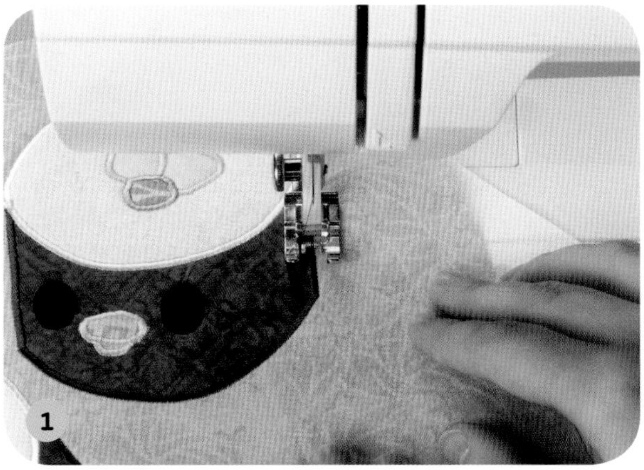

Appliqué. Cut the pattern pieces from your fabric and make all applicable markings. Apply fusible web to the appliqué pieces. See the sidebar on page 135 to make this simpler. Iron the appliqué pieces to the nine main squares as shown by the pattern illustrations. Sew the pieces down along the fabric edges and along any lines as the pattern indicates.

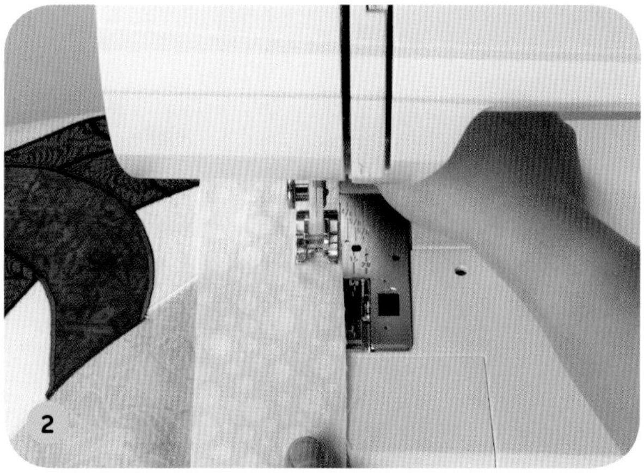

Sew the side white sashing strips. Attach the main squares to each other in rows of three, with small white vertical sashing strips in between and on the outside. When you finish, you should have three rows of three squares. Iron the seam allowances to one side.

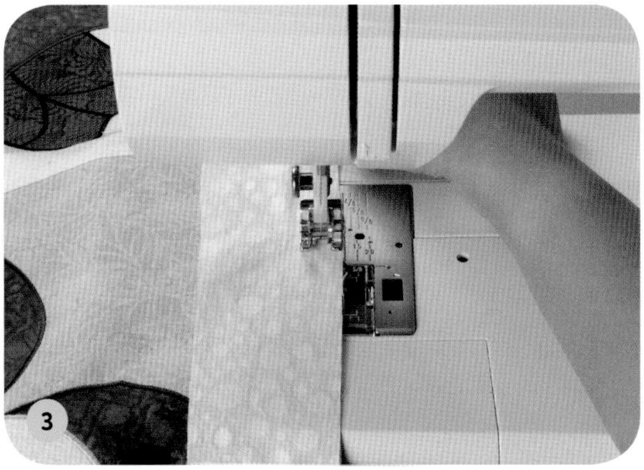

Sew the top white sashing strips. Attach the rows to each other from the top and bottom with the longer white horizontal sashing strips in between and on the outside. When you finish, you should have one large square with a white border. Iron the seam allowances to one side.

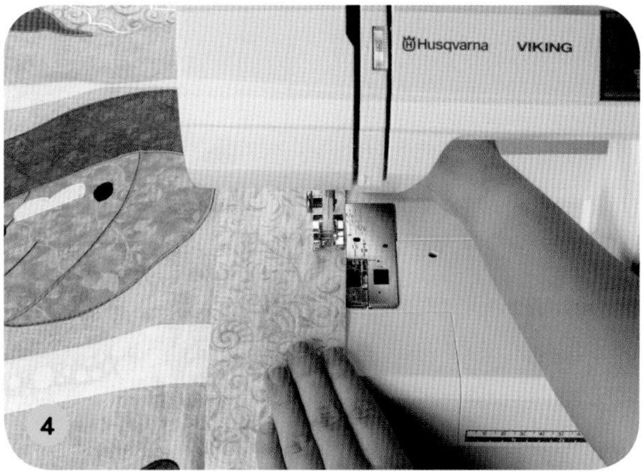

Sew the side pink borders. Sew the pink borders to the sides of the main square. Iron the seam allowances to one side.

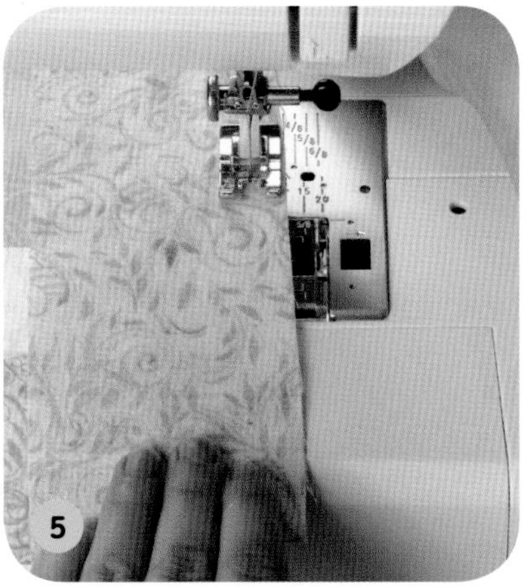

Sew the top and bottom pink borders. Sew the pink borders to the top and bottom of the main square. Iron the seam allowances to one side.

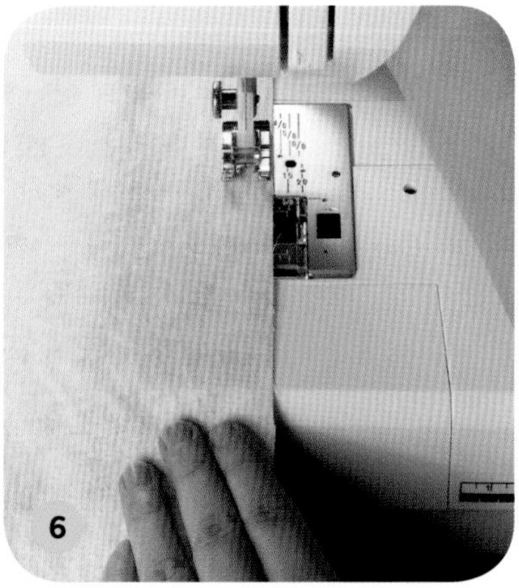

Sew the green side borders. Sew the green borders to the sides of the main square. Iron the seam allowances to one side.

Sushi Quilt

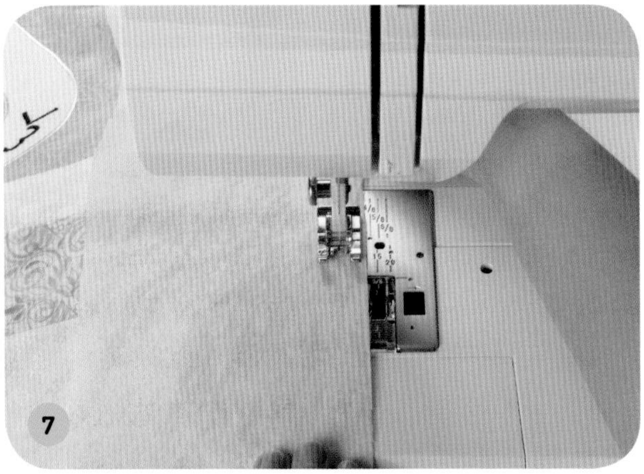

Sew the green top and bottom borders. Sew the green borders to the top and bottom of the main square. Iron the seam allowances to one side.

Baste the layers. Lay out the backing fabric, the quilt batting on top of it, and lastly your quilt top on top, making sure to smooth out any wrinkles. Using safety pins and starting from the middle, smooth out and pin the layers every 5" (125mm) until you reach the outer edges.

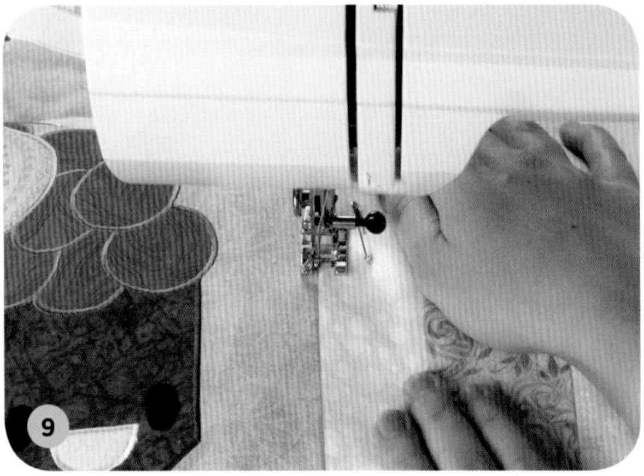

Quilt the layers. With a slightly longer stitch, sew through all the layers of your quilt along the edges of your squares and the borders. Work from the center outward and smooth the fabric constantly as you go, making sure all the layers are perfectly even. When it's complete, trim the excess quilt batting and backing sticking out from the edges of the quilt top.

Attach the binding. Fold the binding strips in half along the fold line and iron them flat. Sew a strip along the left and right sides of the quilt. Fold it across and over to the other side and stitch it in place along the edge encasing the seam allowance. Trim any excess.

Finish the binding. Fold the remaining two binding strips in half and iron them flat. Sew the strips along the top and bottom as before. This time, fold the binding toward itself and sew the ends together about ⅛" (3mm) away from the edge of the quilt. Trim close to the seam and fold the binding over the quilt edge, encasing the corner. Stitch the binding in place as you did in Step 10.

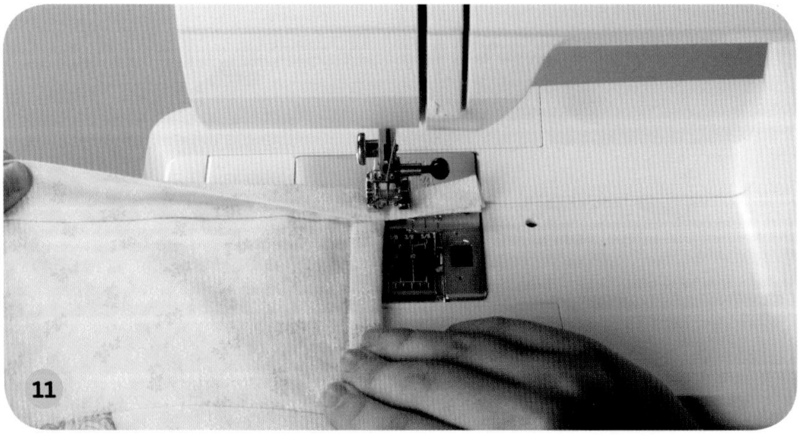

Patterns

This section contains all of the pattern pieces you'll need to create the projects in the front part of the book. Photocopy all the necessary pieces at 250% and get sewing!

Key Chains

Pages 30–37

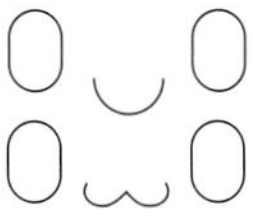

Eye
Cut 2

Strawberry and Layer Cake Key Chain Plush
Face templates
Cut 2 eyes; embroider mouth along line shown.

Strawberry Key Chain Plush
Leaves
Cut 1

Eye
Cut 2

Dumpling Key Chain Plush
Face template
Cut 2 eyes; embroider mouth along line shown.

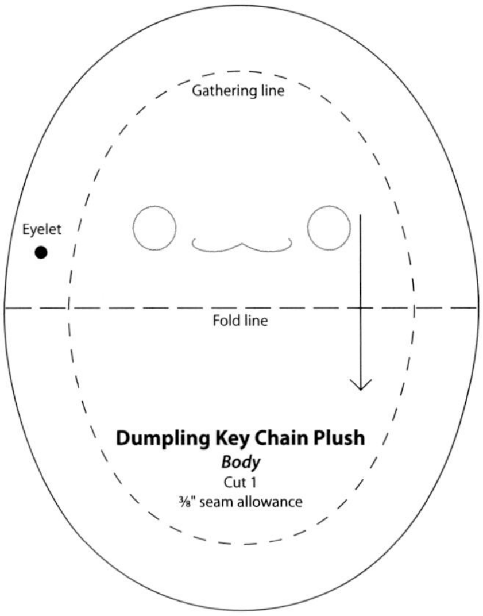

Dumpling Key Chain Plush
Body
Cut 1
⅜" seam allowance

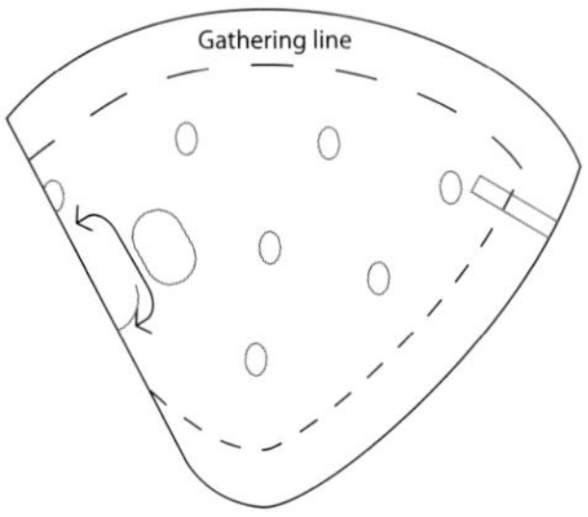

Strawberry Key Chain Plush
Body
Cut 1 on fold
⅜" seam allowance

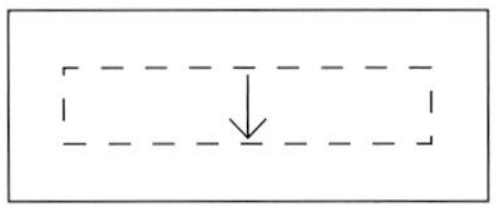

Layer Cake Key Chain Plush
Frosting layer
Cut 2 of contrast color
⅜" seam allowance

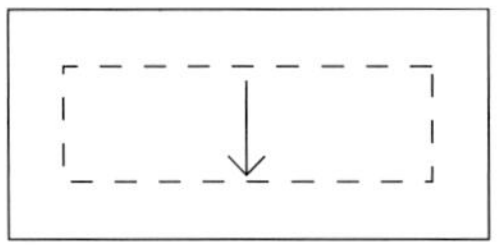

Layer Cake Key Chain Plush
Cake layer
Cut 4 of main color
⅜" seam allowance

Layer Cake Key Chain Plush
Top and bottom
Cut 1 of main color
Cut 1 of contrast color
⅜" seam allowance

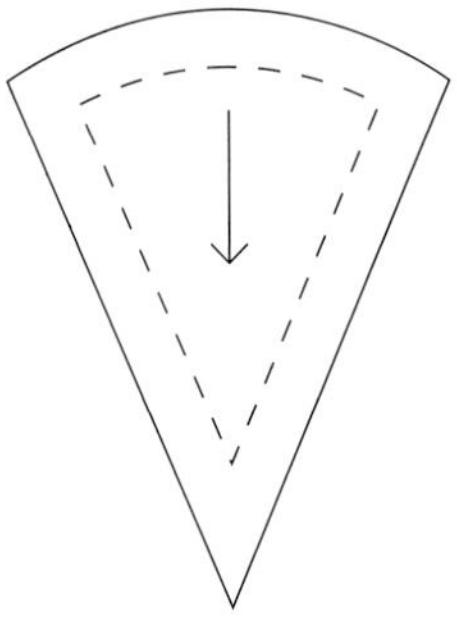

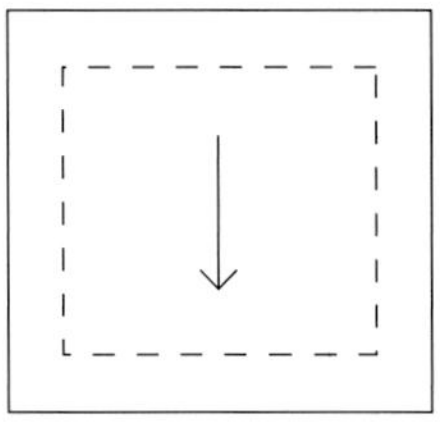

Layer Cake Key Chain Plush
Back
Cut 1 of contrast color
⅜" seam allowance

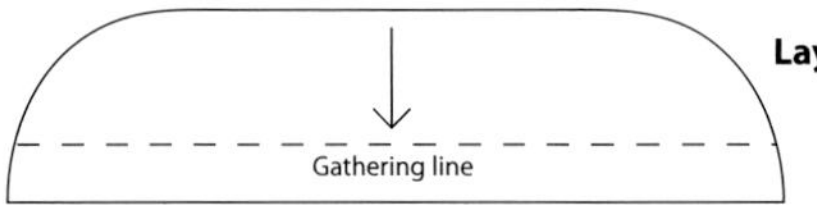

Layer Cake Key Chain Plush
Frosting ruffle
Cut 1 of contrast color
⅜" seam allowance

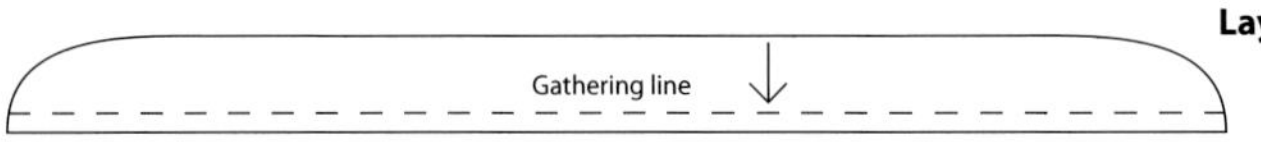

Layer Cake Key Chain Plush
Rosette
Cut 1 of contrast color
¼" seam allowance

Enlarge patterns 250% for actual size.

Electronics Cases

Pages 40–42

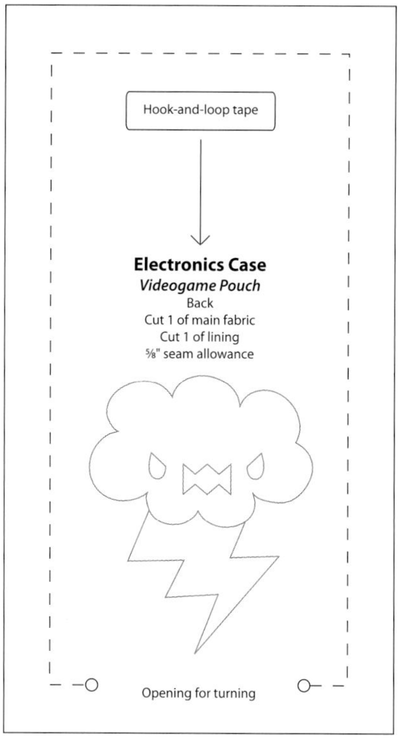

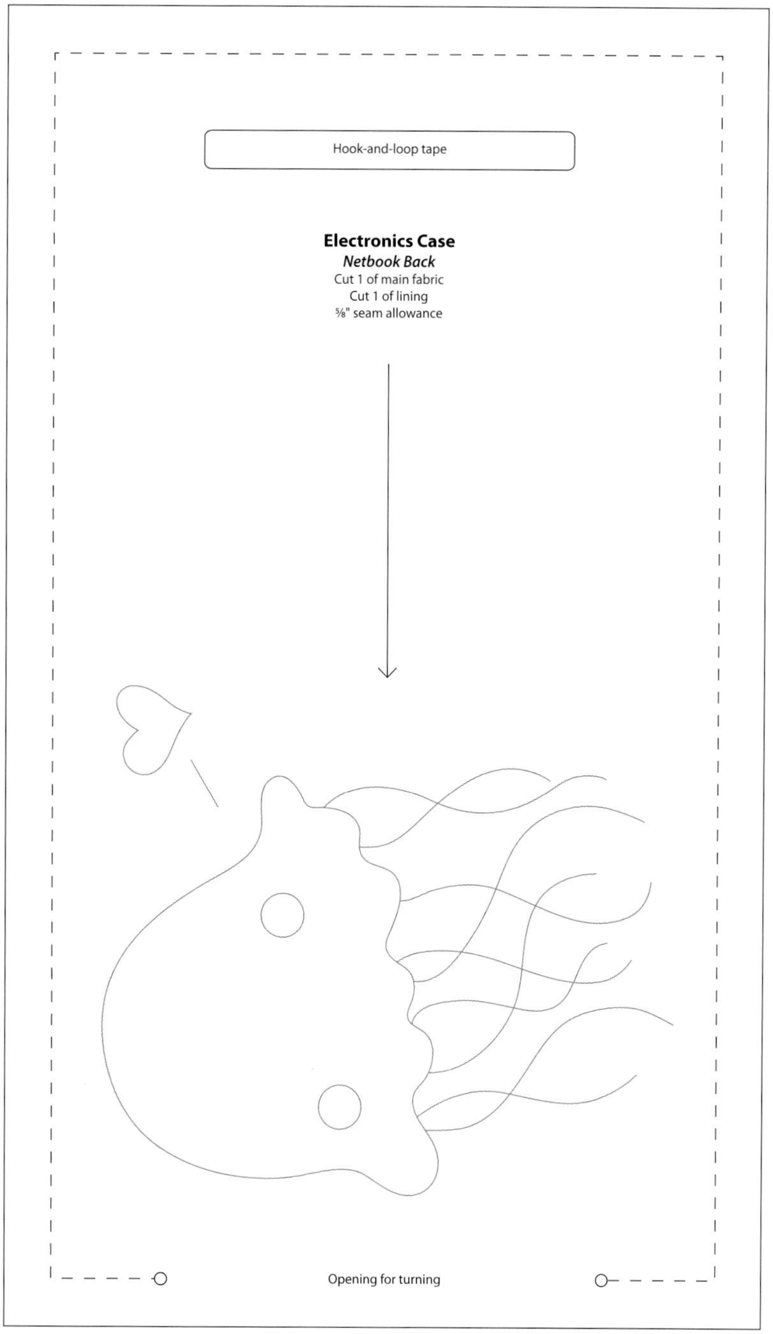

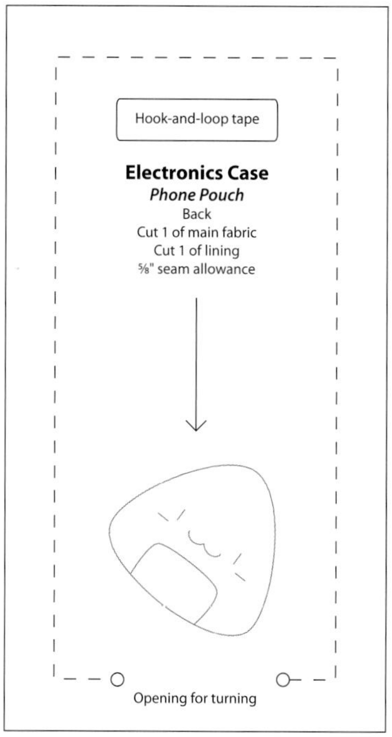

Onigiri motif

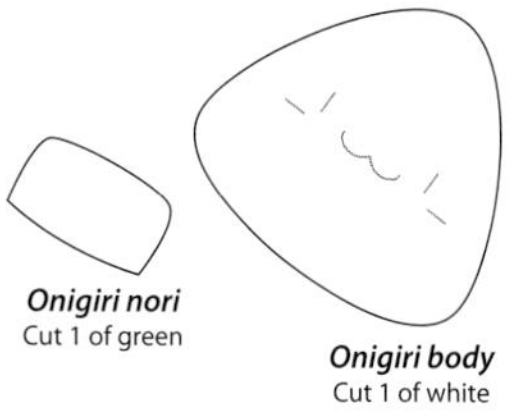

Thundercloud motif

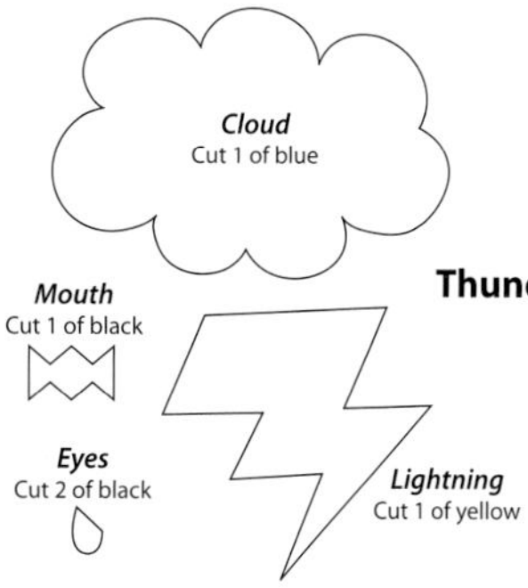

Enlarge patterns 250% for actual size.

Electronics Cases *(continued)*

Pages 40–42

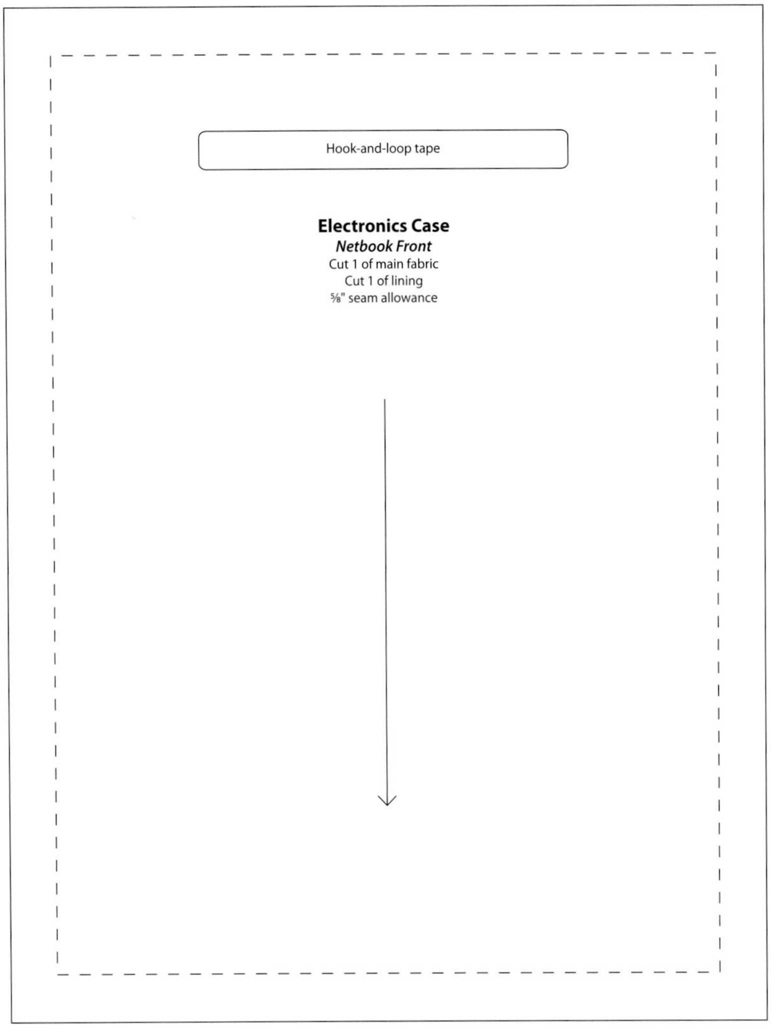

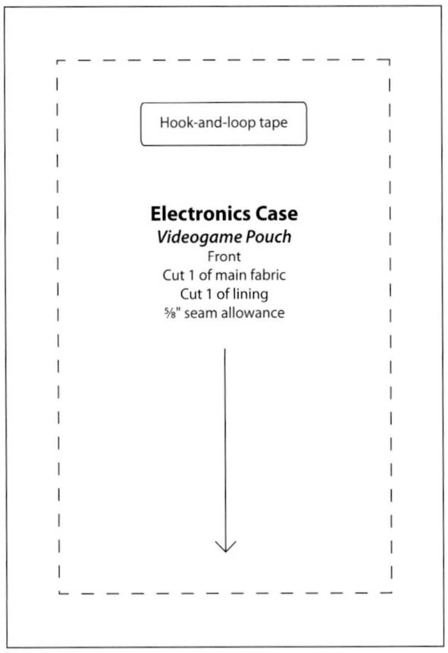

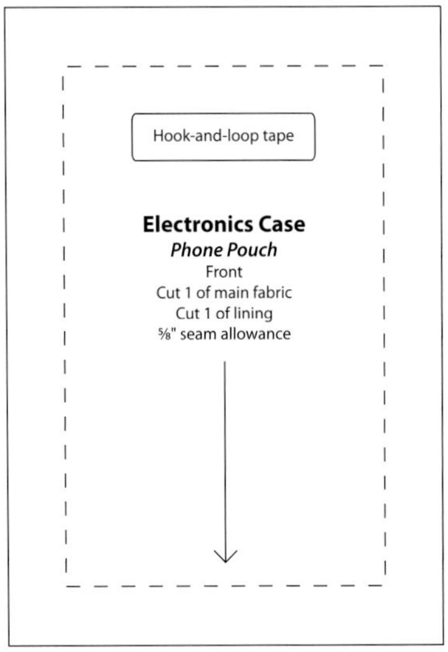

Jellyfish motif

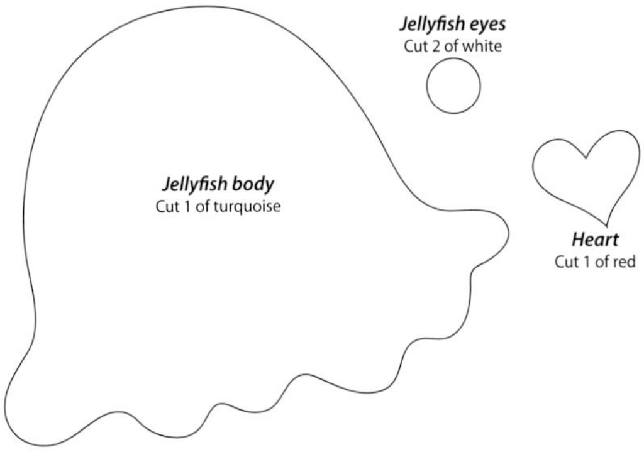

Enlarge patterns 250% for actual size.

Square Purse with Flap

Pages 43–45

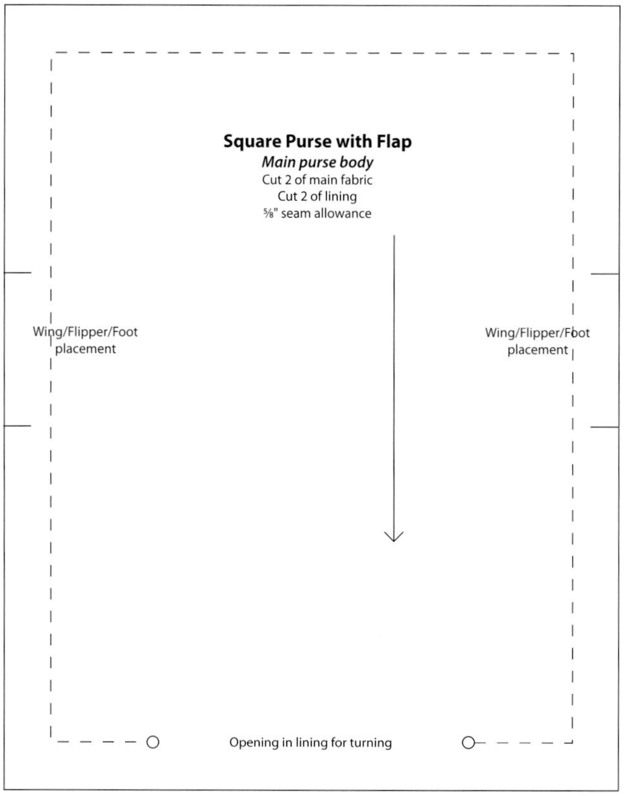

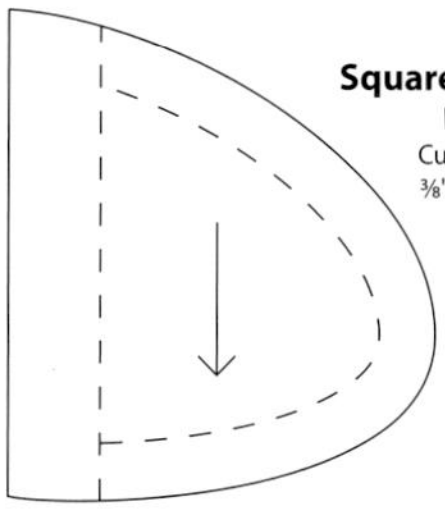

Square Purse with Flap
Wing/Flipper
Cut 4 of main fabric
⅜" seam allowance

Square Purse with Flap
Eye
Cut 2

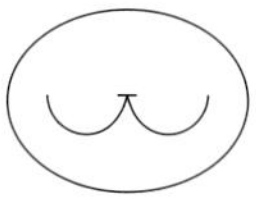

Square Purse with Flap
Muzzle
Cut 1

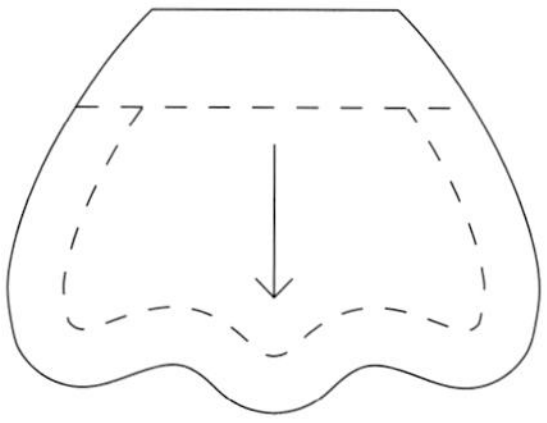

Square Purse with Flap
Platypus foot
Cut 4 of contrast color
⅜" seam allowance

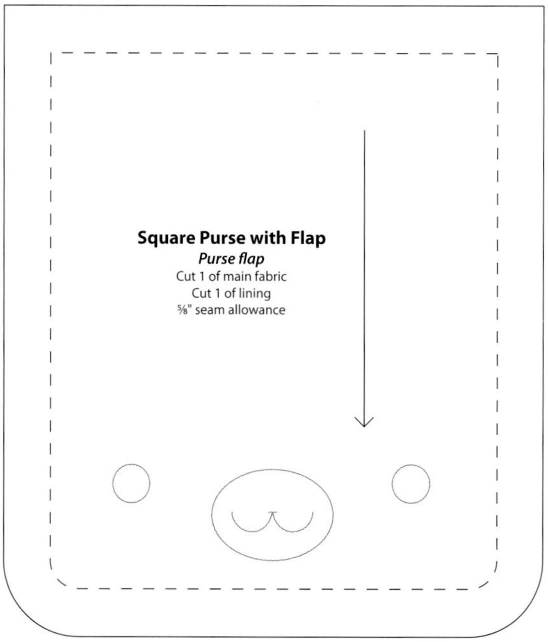

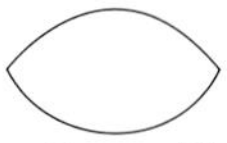

Square Purse with Flap
Beak top
Cut 1

Square Purse with Flap
Beak bottom
Cut 1

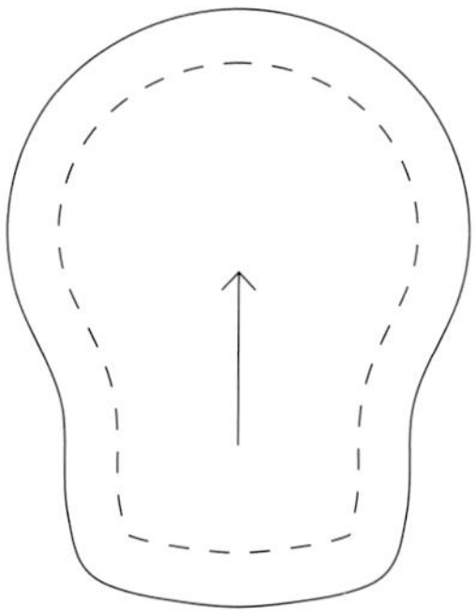

Square Purse with Flap
Platypus bill
Cut 2 of contrast color
⅜" seam allowance

Enlarge patterns 250% for actual size.

Jellyfish Purse

Pages 46–50

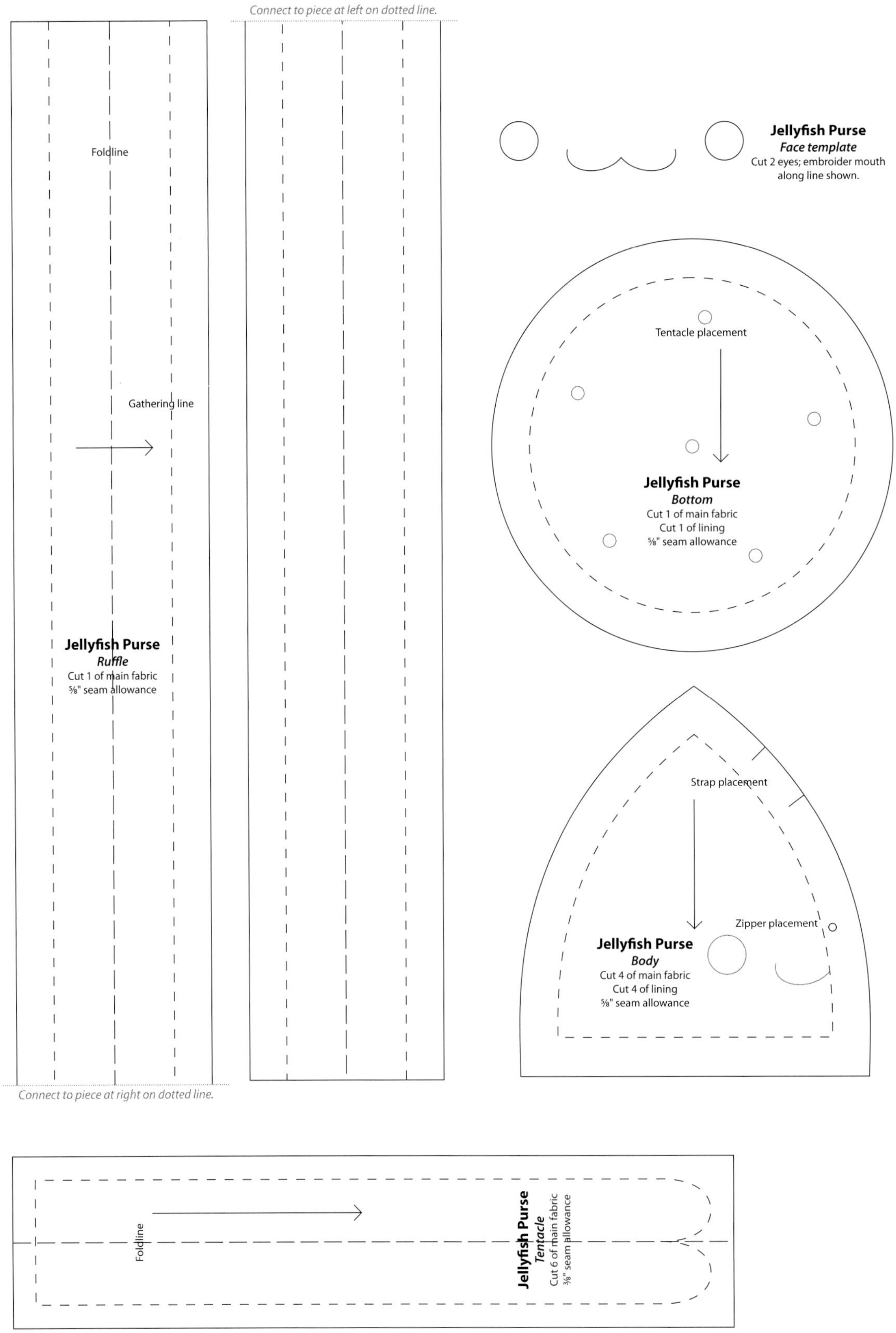

Enlarge patterns 250% for actual size.

Cube Purse

Pages 51–55

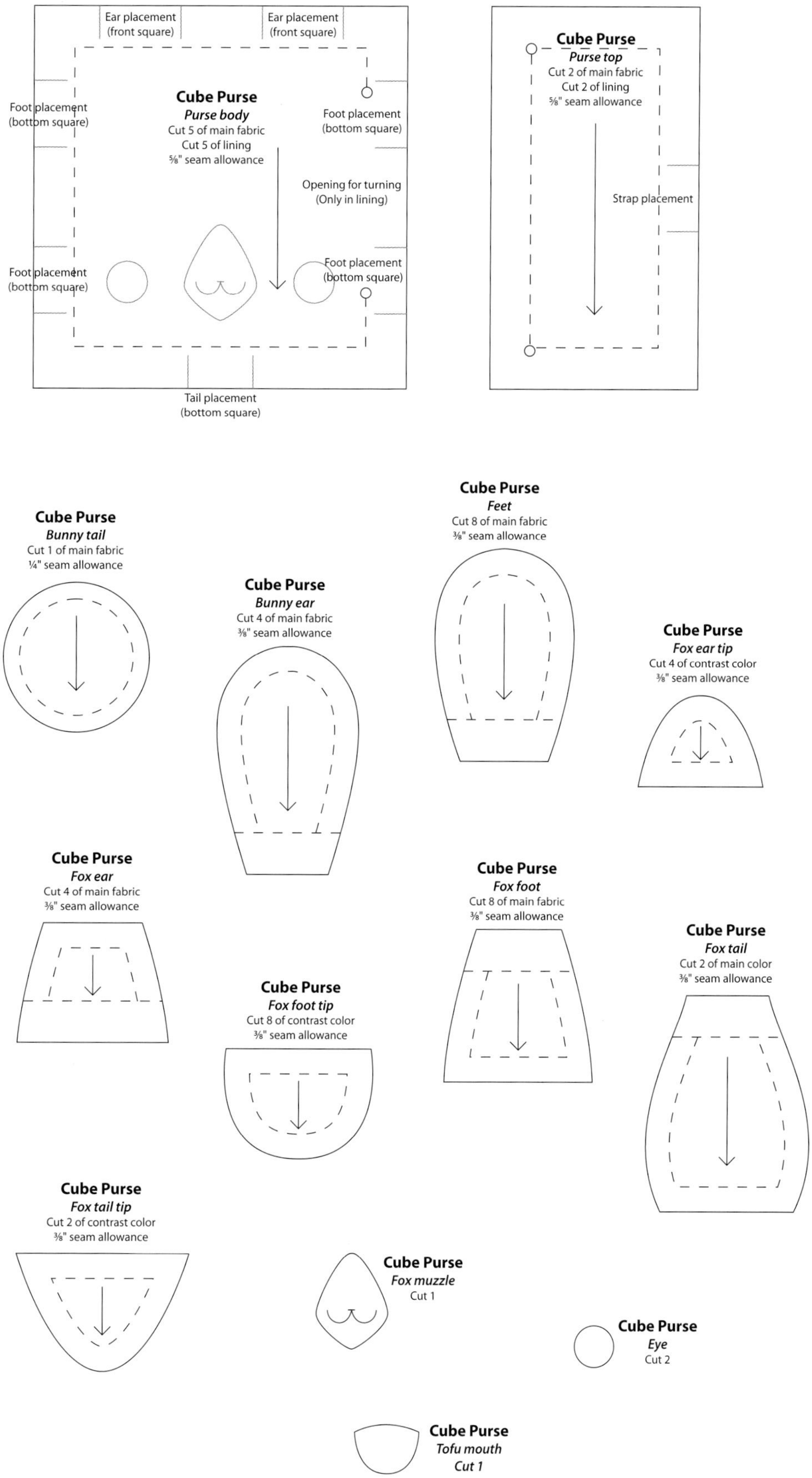

Enlarge patterns 250% for actual size.

Character Hats

Pages 58–63

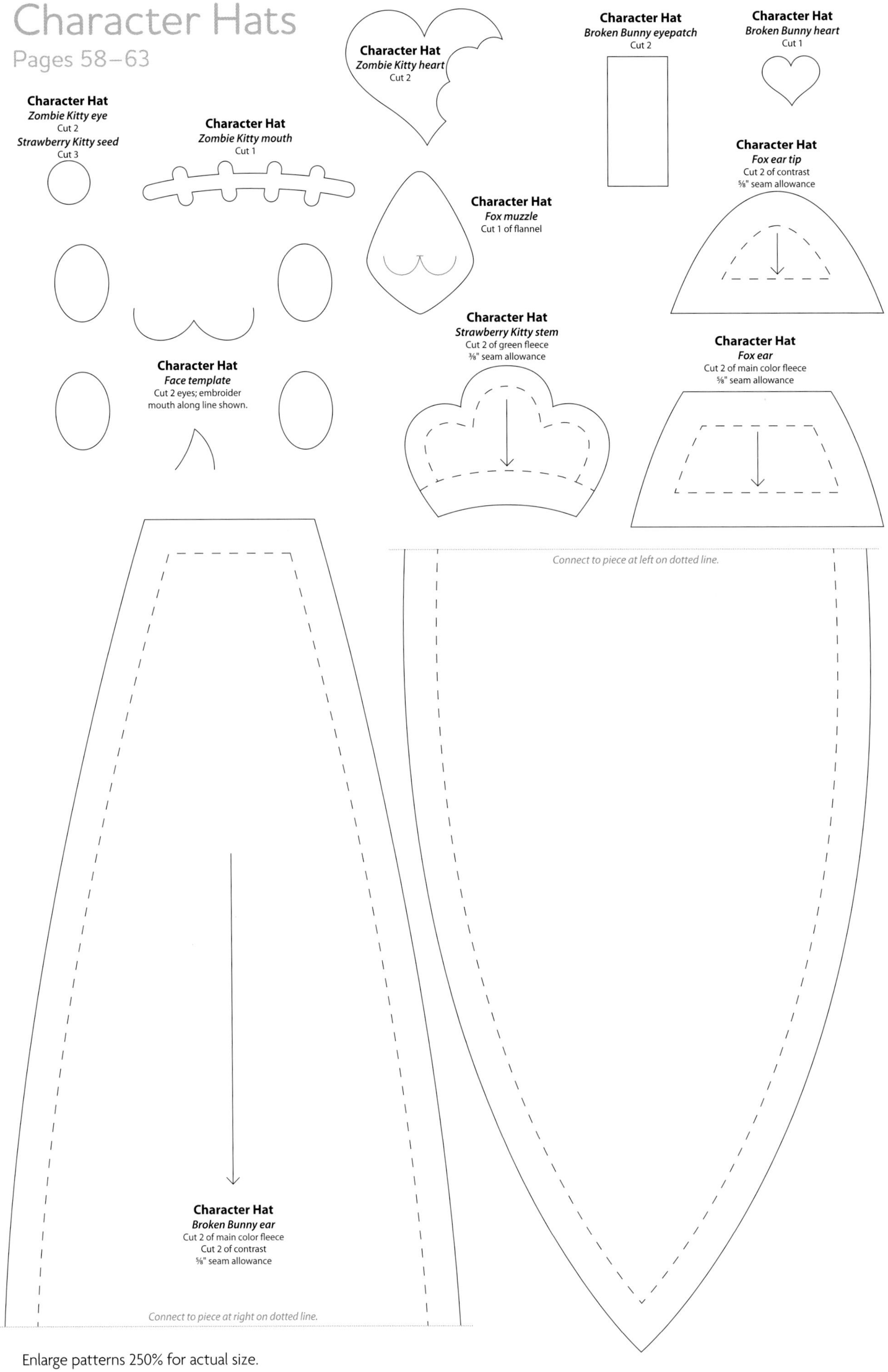

Enlarge patterns 250% for actual size.

Character Hats *(continued)*

Pages 58–63

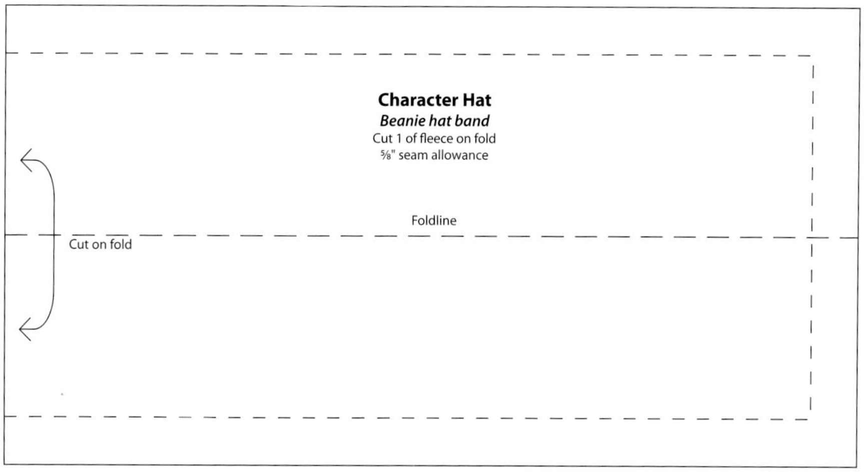

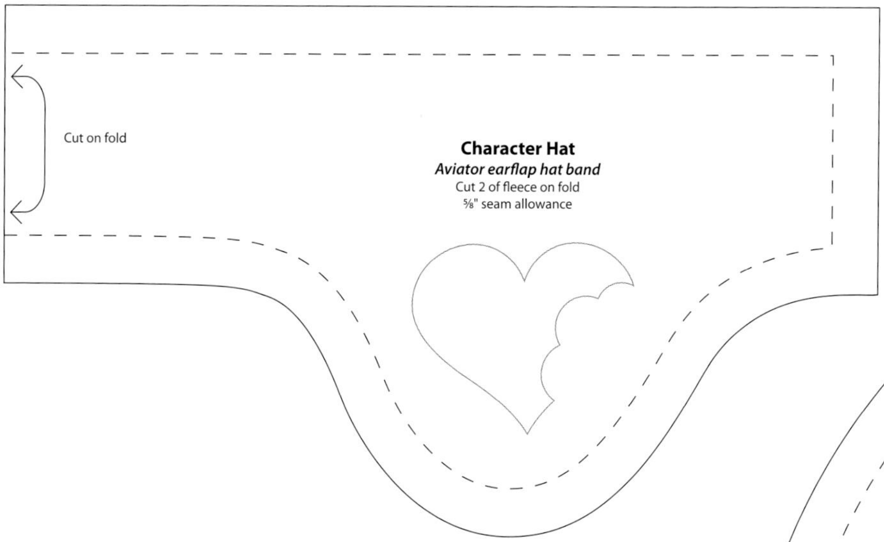

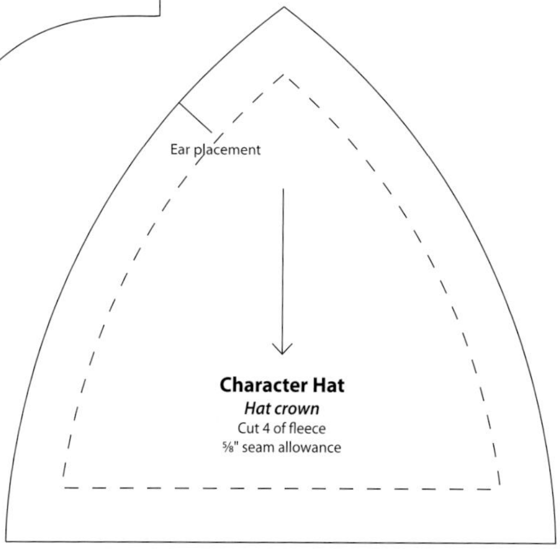

Character Hat
Zombie Kitty/Strawberry Kitty ear
Cut 2 of main color fleece
Cut 2 of contrast
⅝" seam allowance

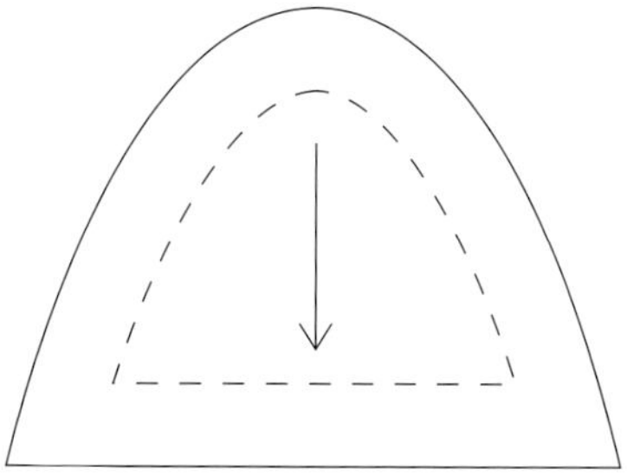

Enlarge patterns 250% for actual size.

Arm & Leg Warmers

Pages 64–69

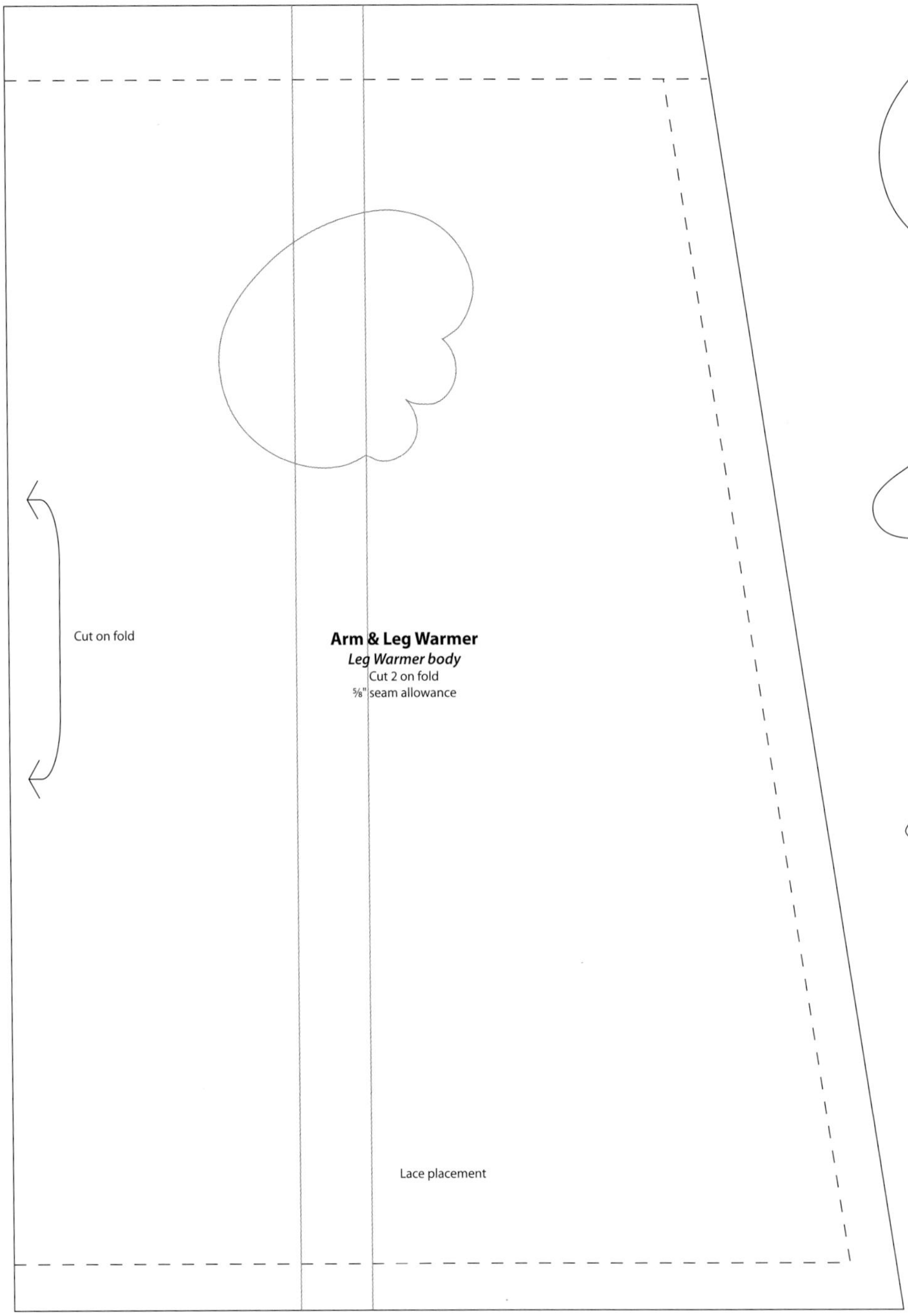

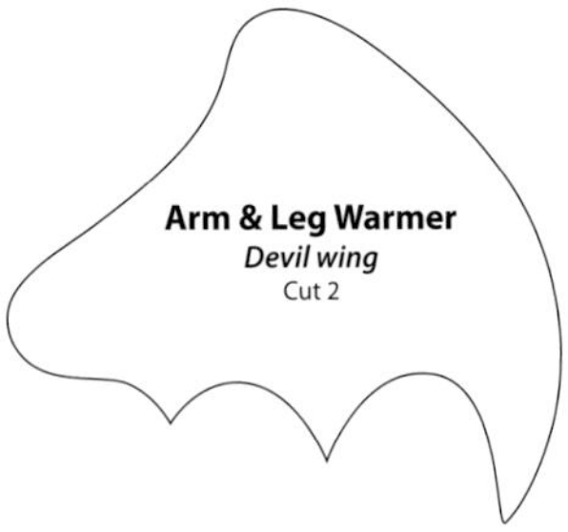

Arm & Leg Warmer
Strawberry stem
Cut 2

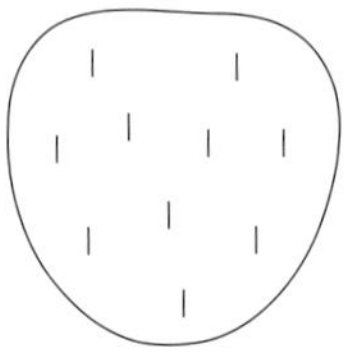

Arm & Leg Warmer
Strawberry
Cut 2

Enlarge patterns 250% for actual size.

Arm & Leg Warmers *(continued)*

Pages 64–69

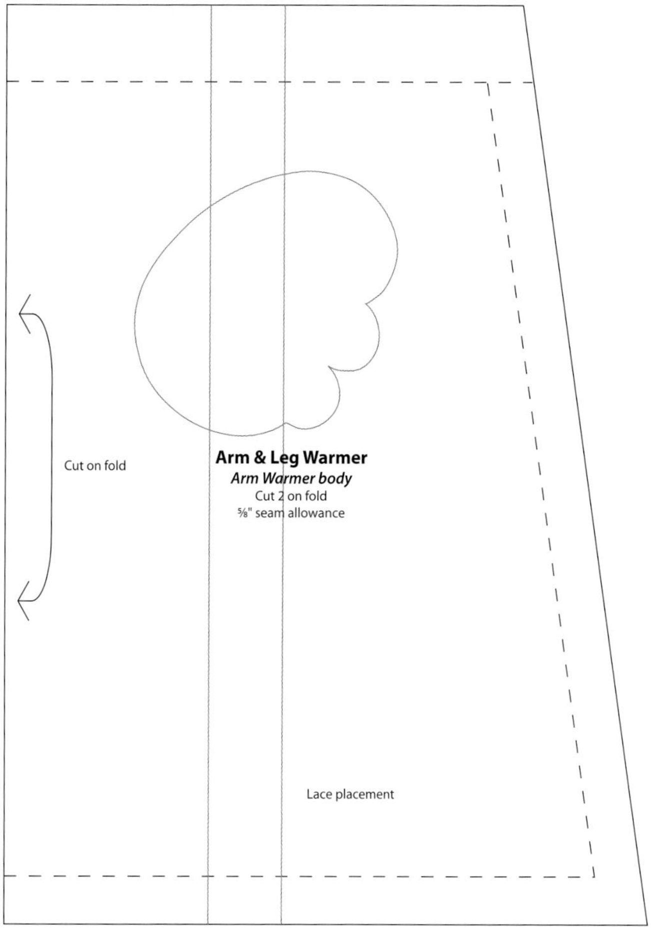

Enlarge patterns 250% for actual size.

Animal Scarf

Pages 70–75

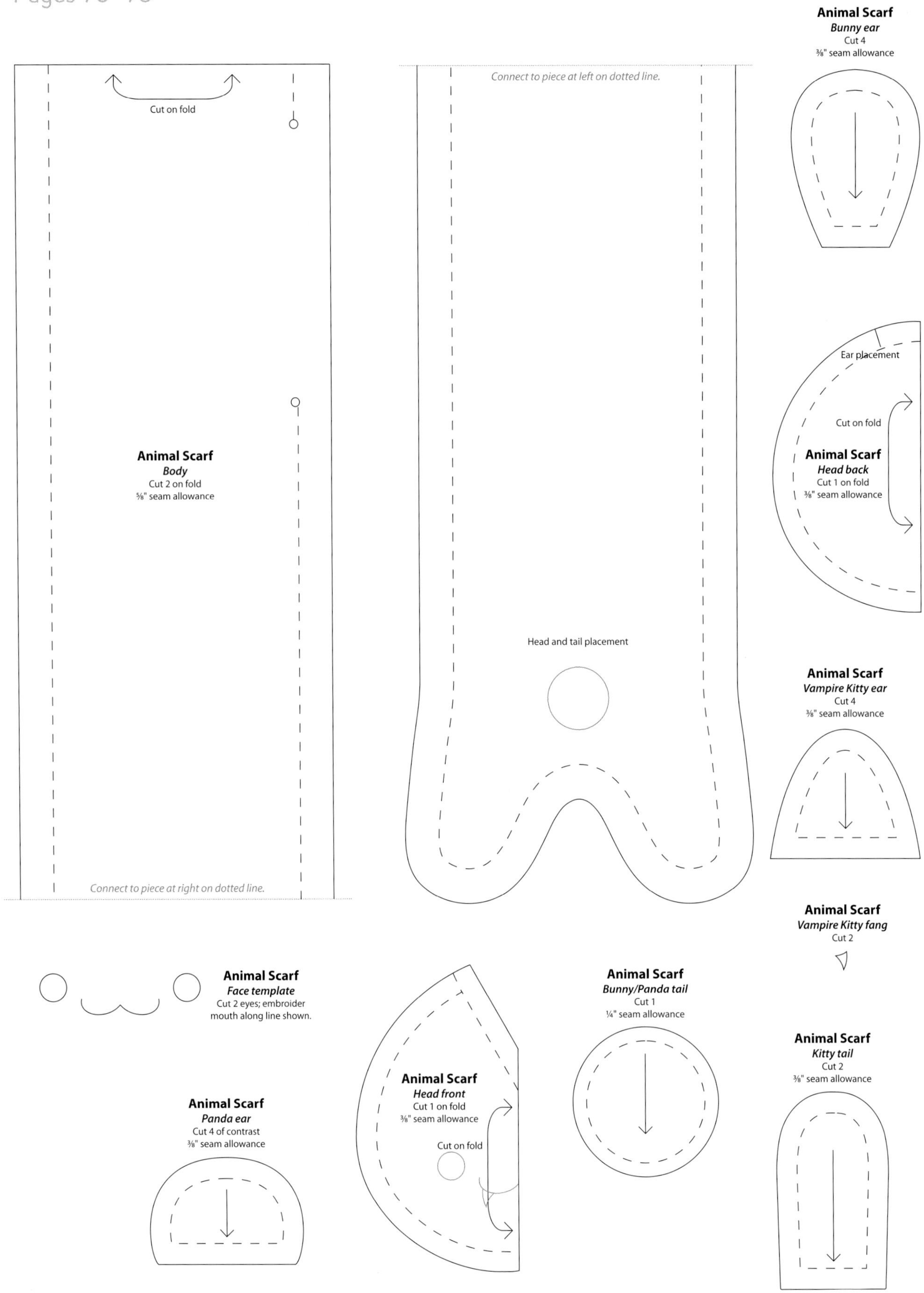

Enlarge patterns 250% for actual size.

Blob Plush

Pages 78–81

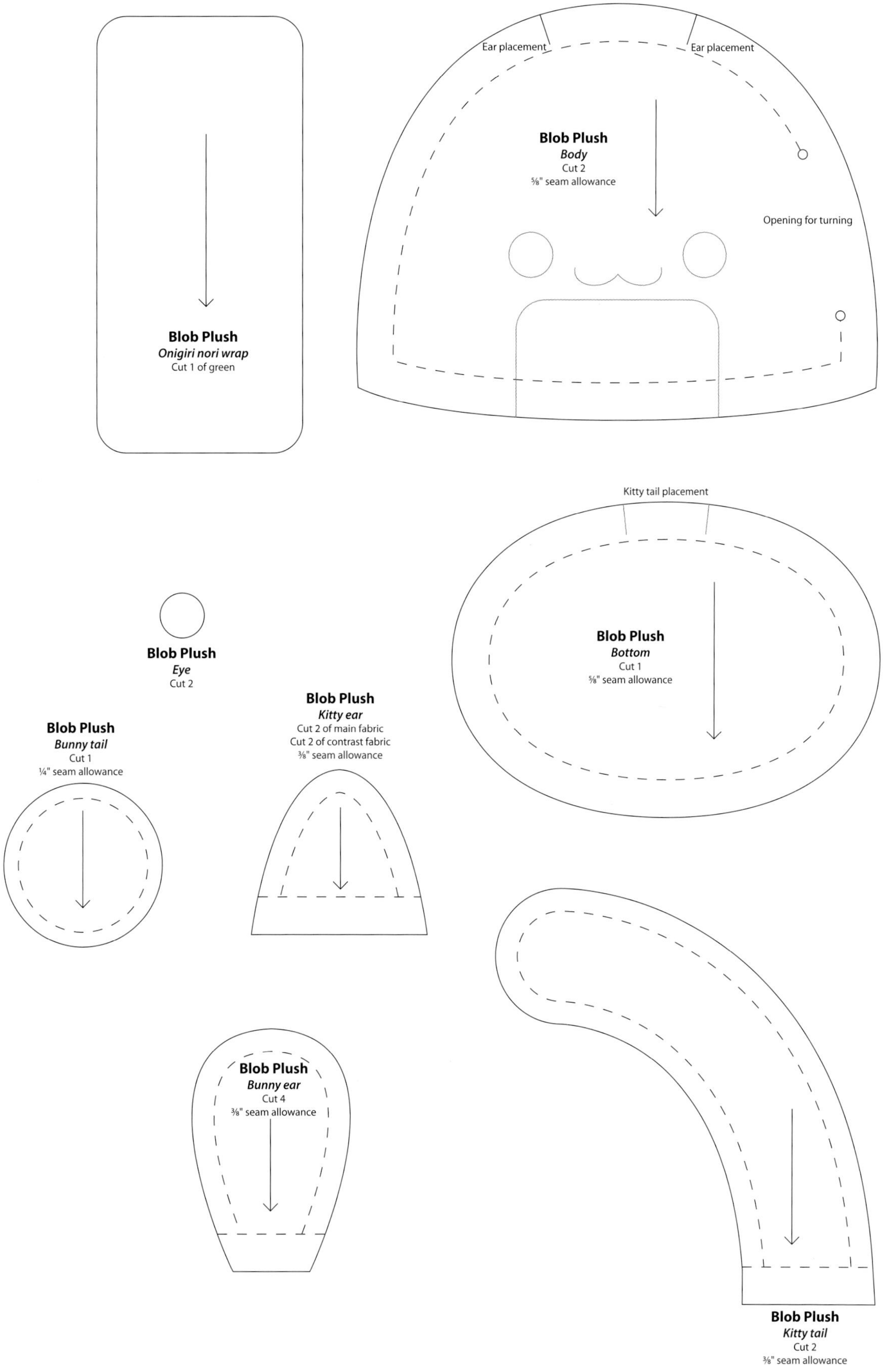

Enlarge patterns 250% for actual size.

Octopus Plush

Pages 82–86

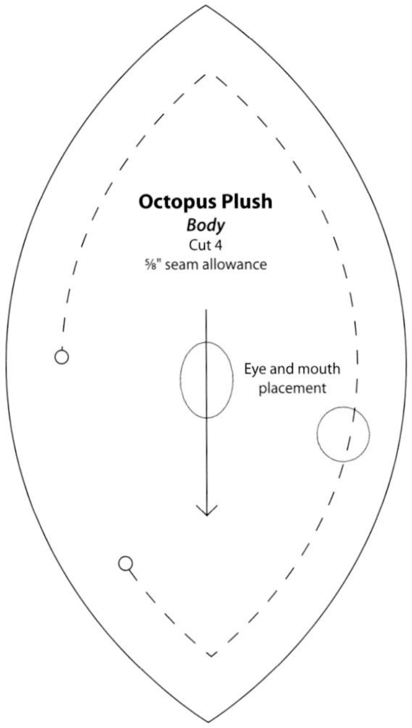

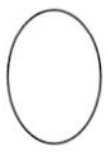

Octopus Plush
Eye
Cut 2

Octopus Plush
Mouth
Cut 1
3/8" seam allowance

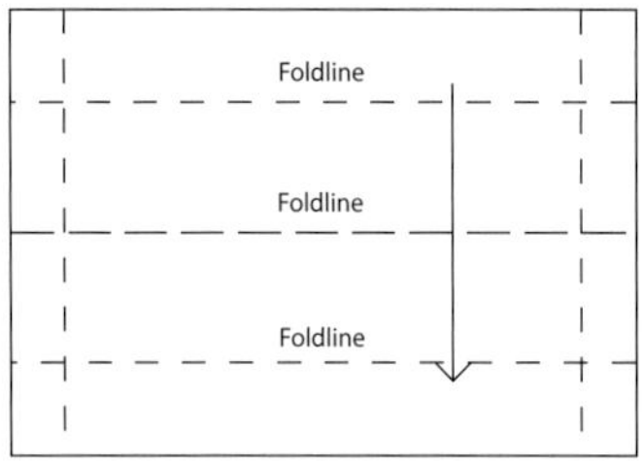

Octopus Plush
Legs
Cut 16 (or 2 for each leg needed)
3/8" seam allowance

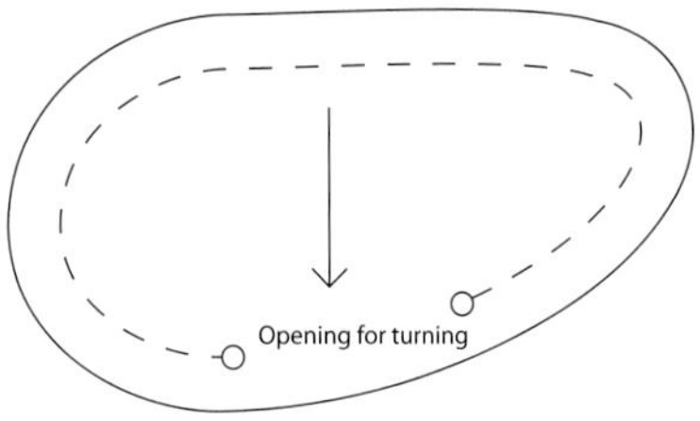

Enlarge patterns 250% for actual size.

Platypus Plush

Pages 87–90

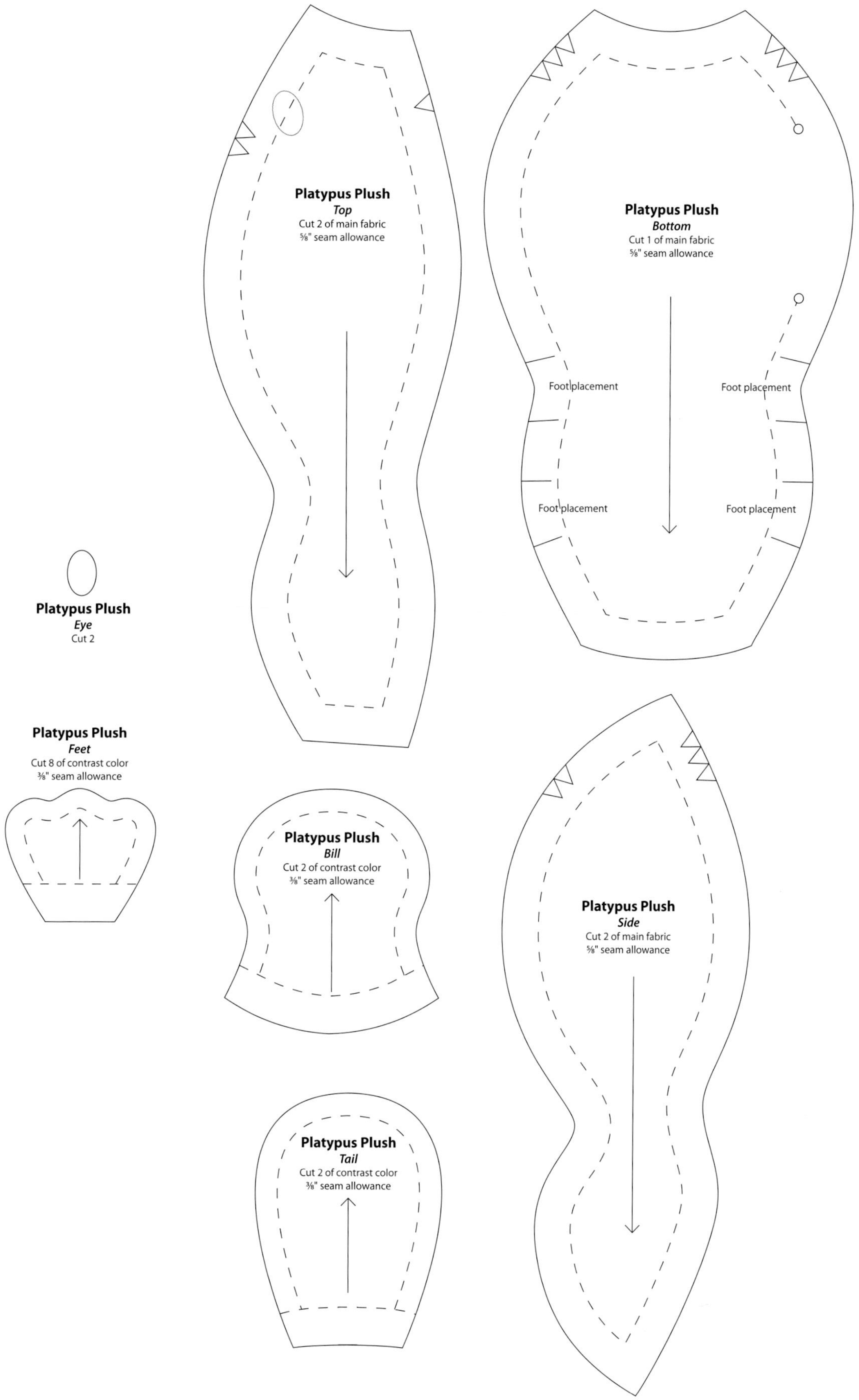

Enlarge patterns 250% for actual size.

Sitting Plush

Pages 91–95

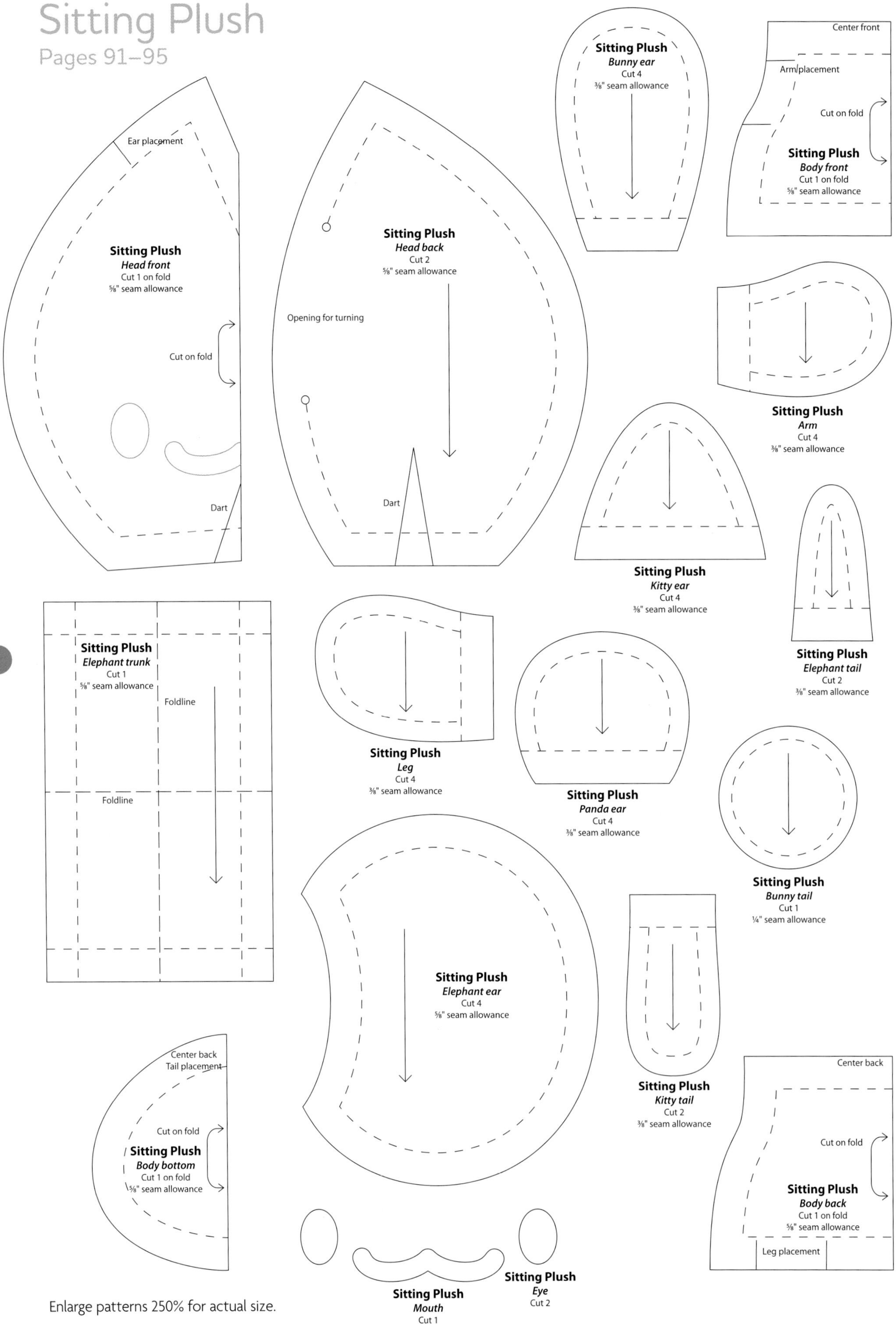

Enlarge patterns 250% for actual size.

Llama Plush

Pages 96–99

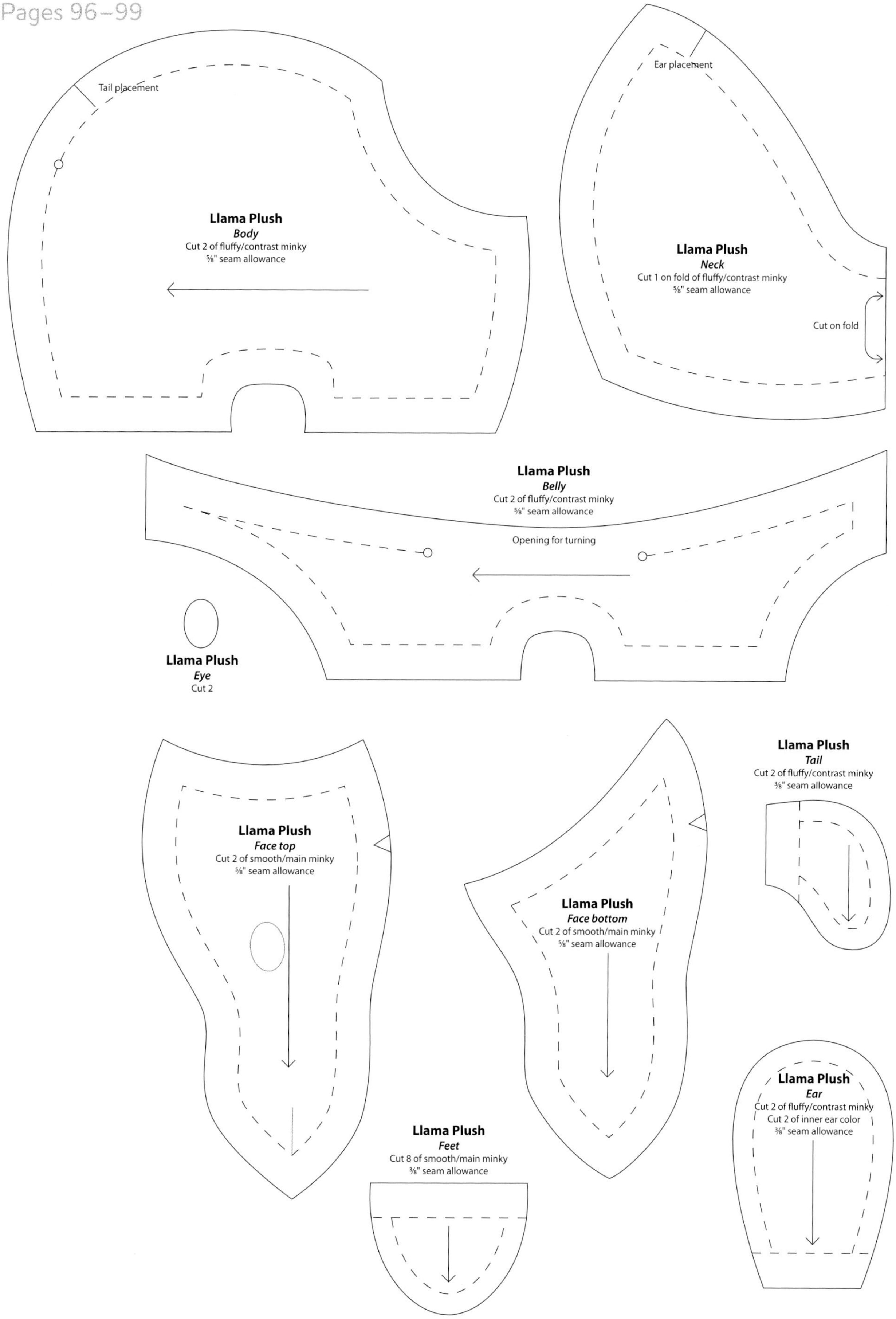

Enlarge patterns 250% for actual size.

Character Hoodie

Pages 102–109

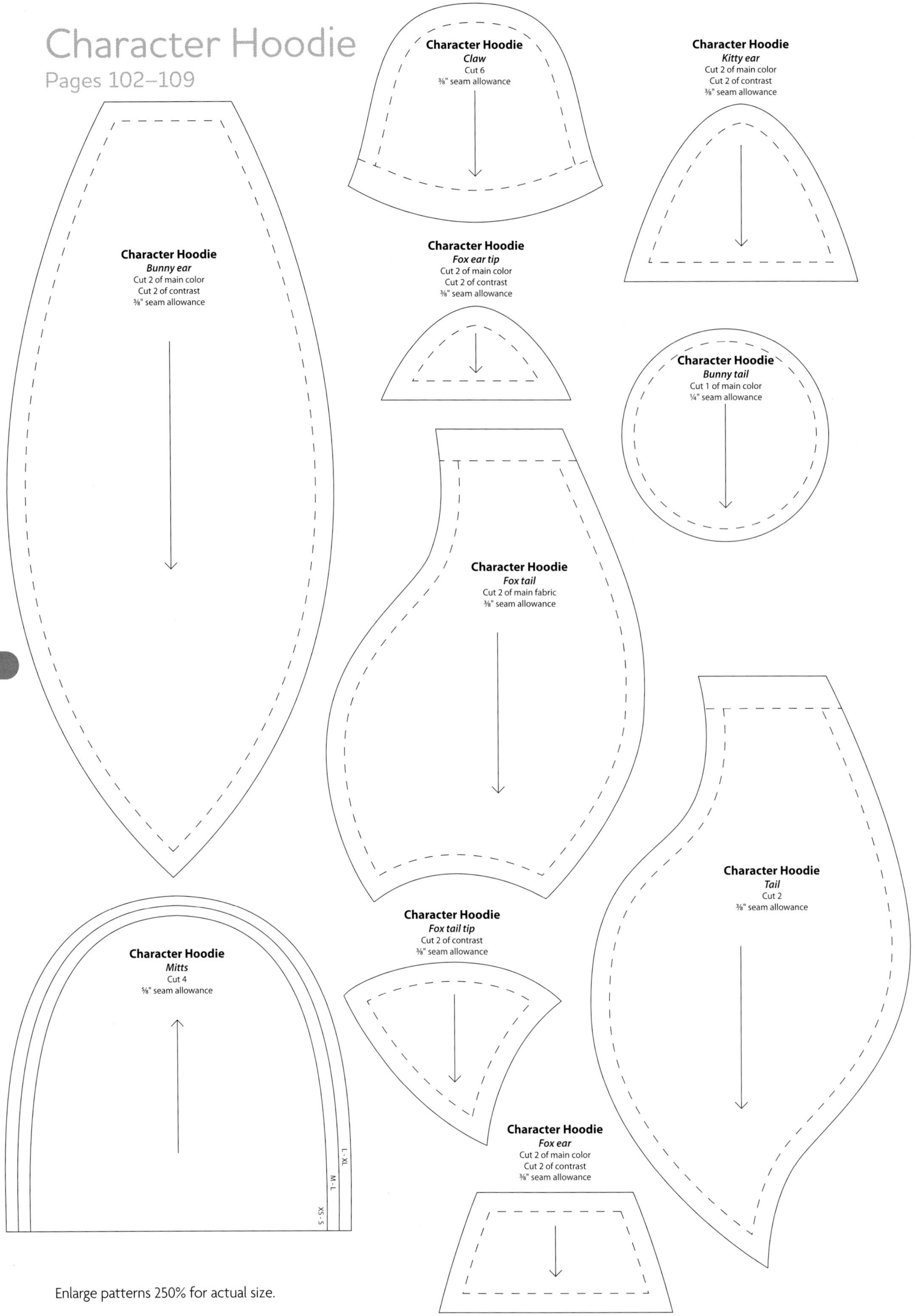

Enlarge patterns 250% for actual size.

Poncho

Pages 110–115

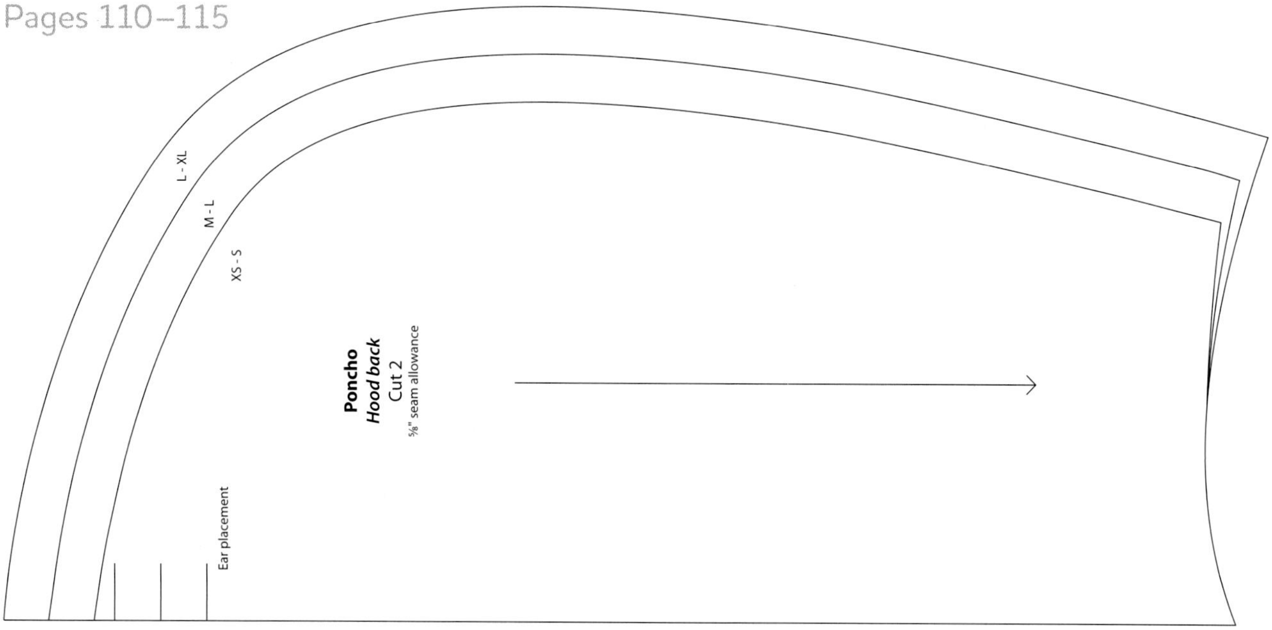

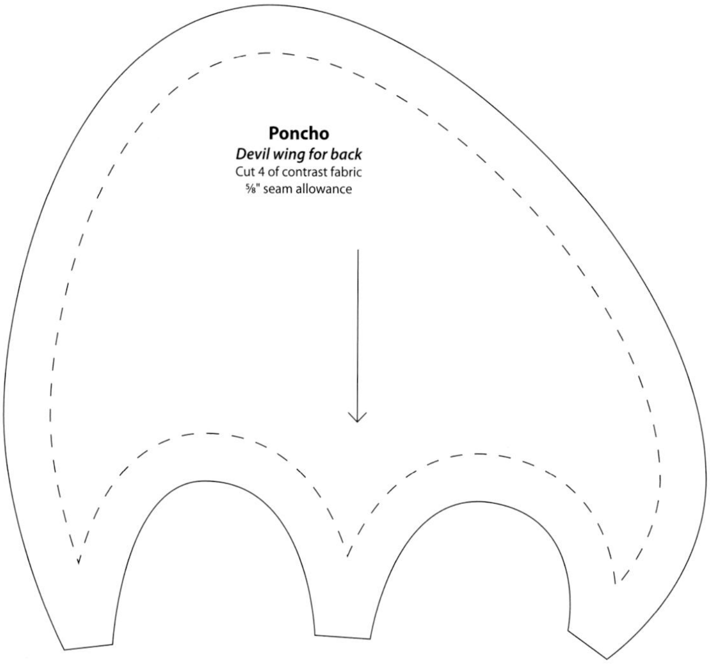

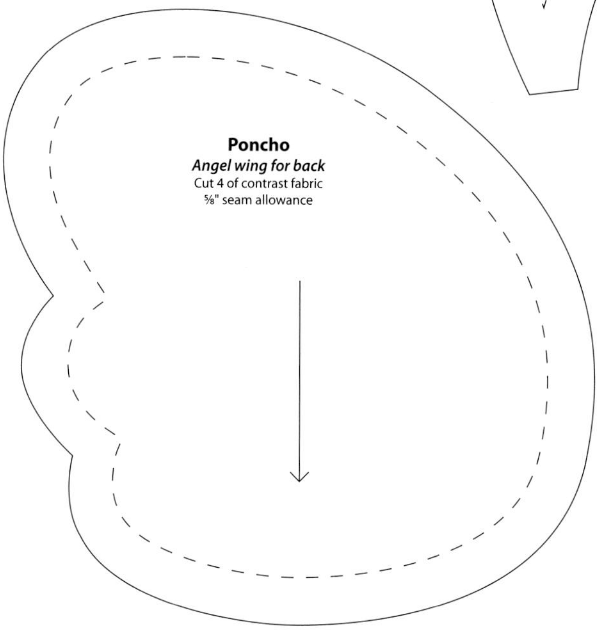

Enlarge patterns 250% for actual size.

Poncho *(continued)*

Pages 110–115

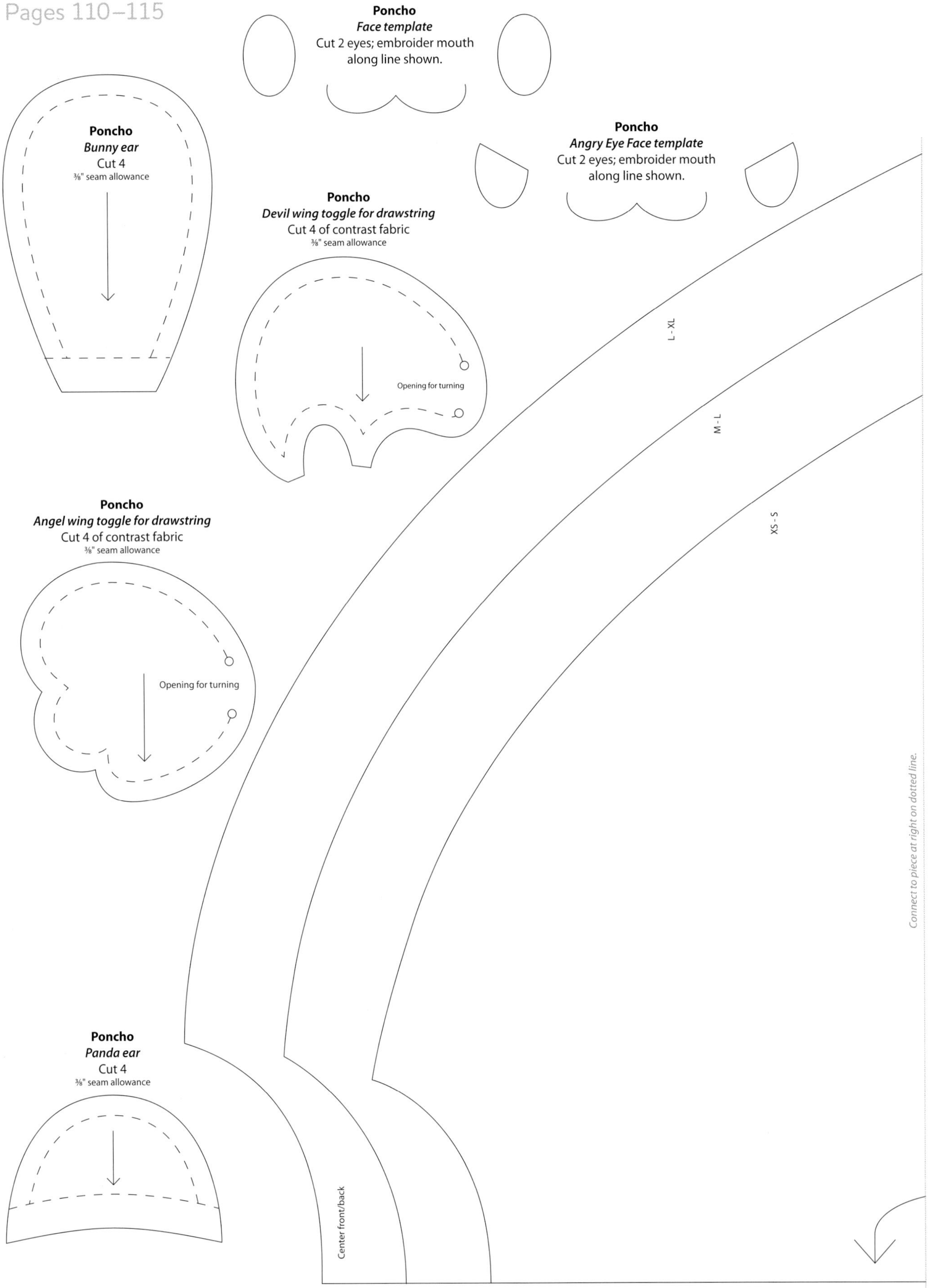

Enlarge patterns 250% for actual size.

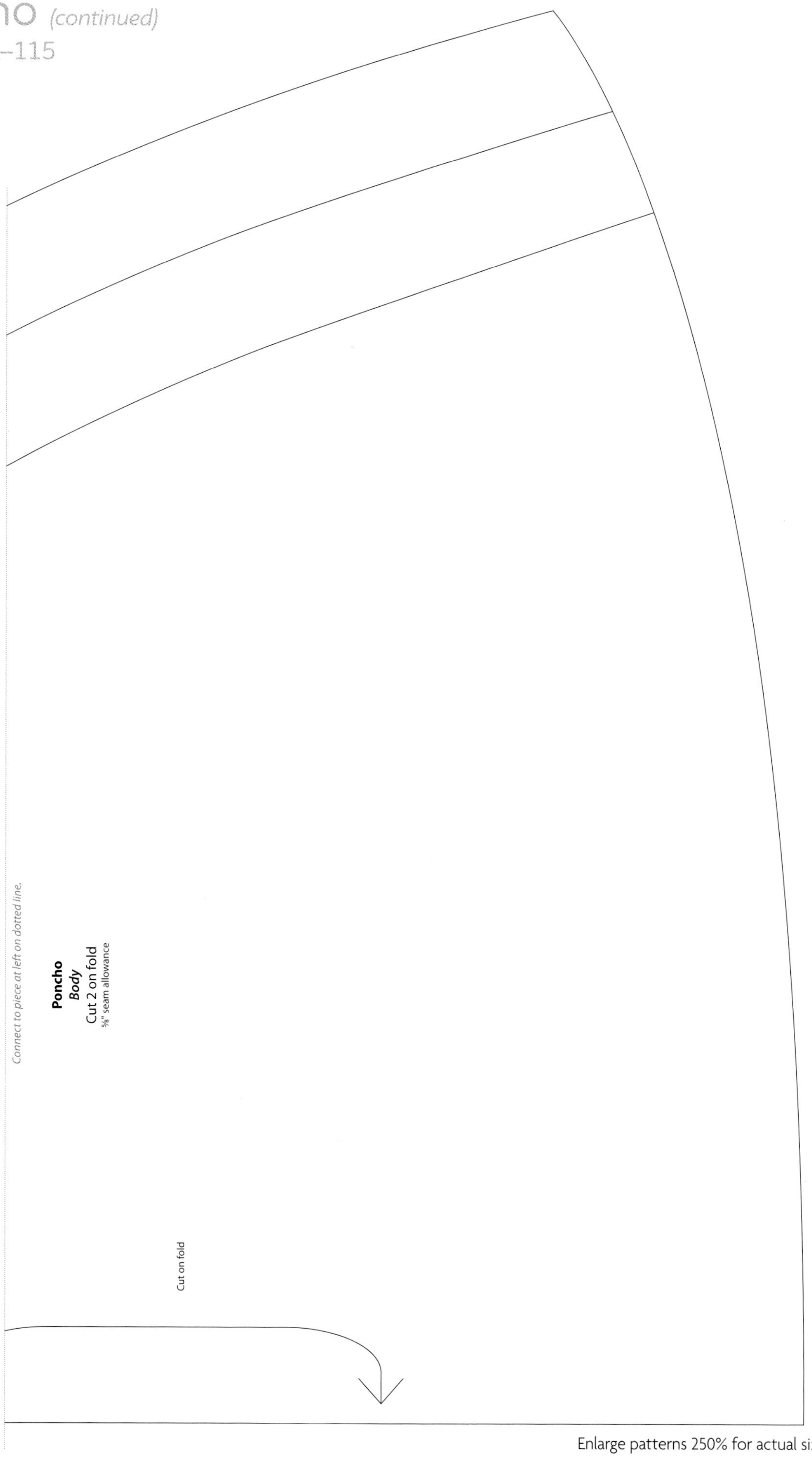

Enlarge patterns 250% for actual size.

Poncho *(continued)*

Pages 110–115

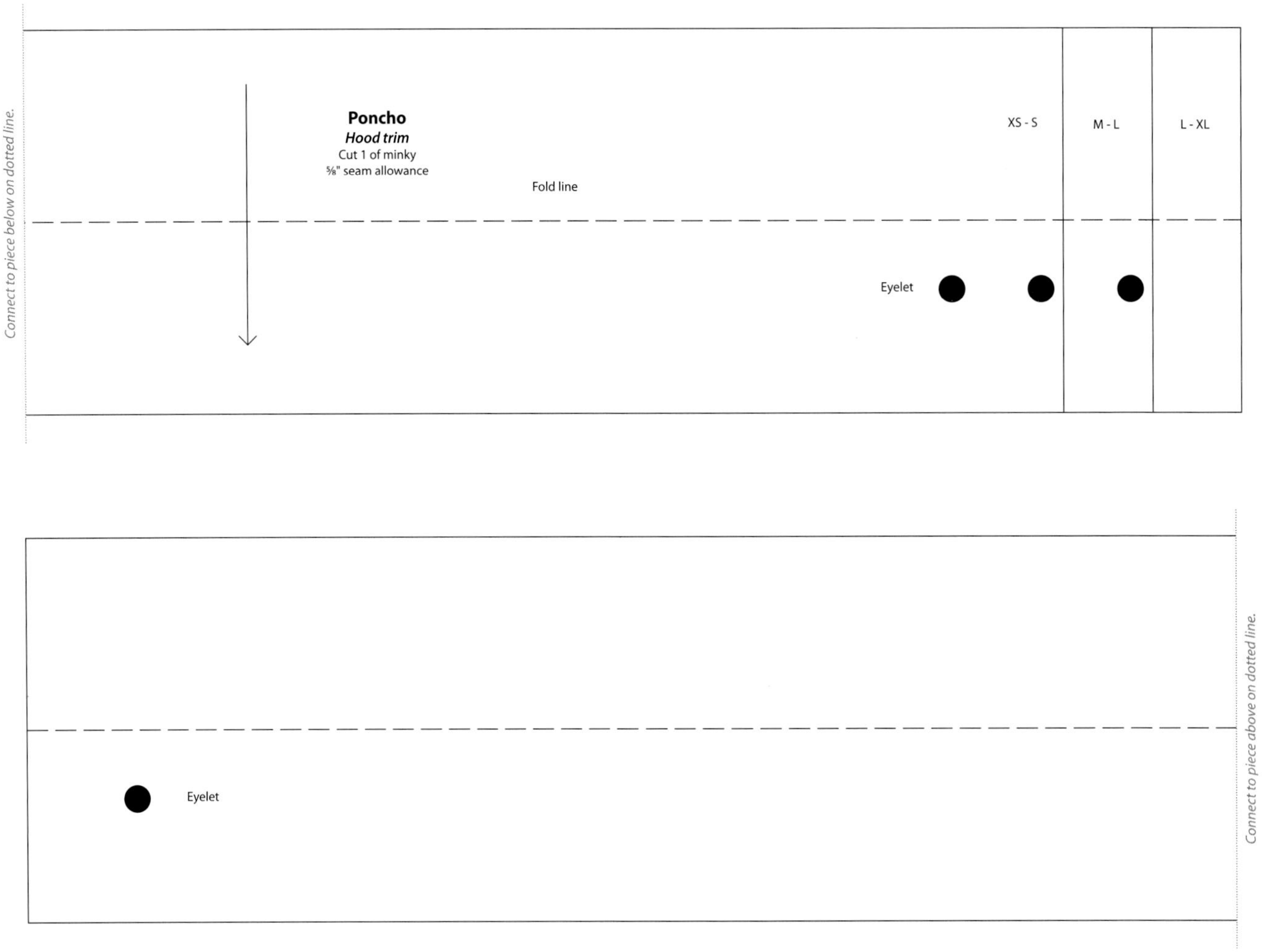

Enlarge patterns 250% for actual size.

Log Pillow

Pages 126–128

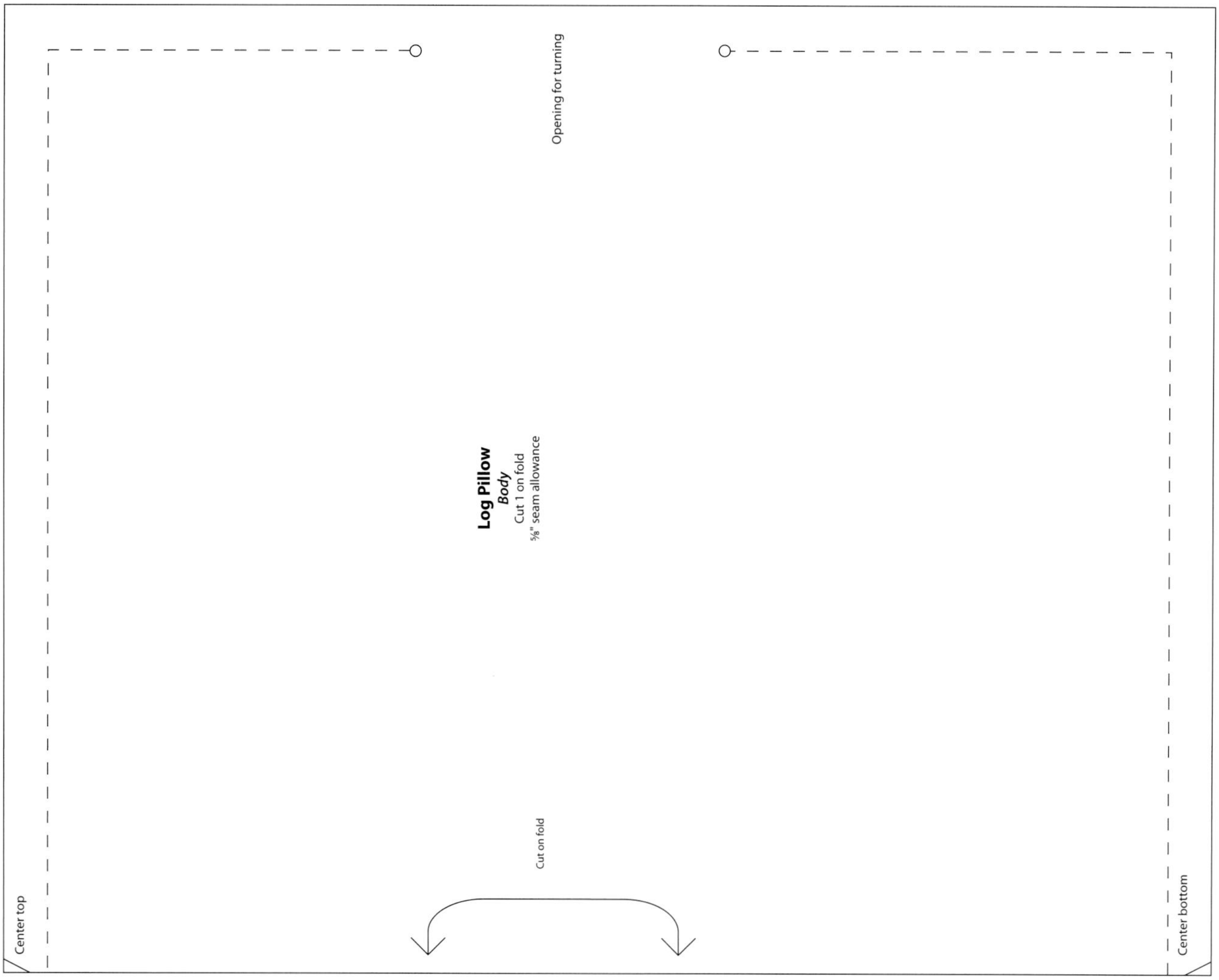

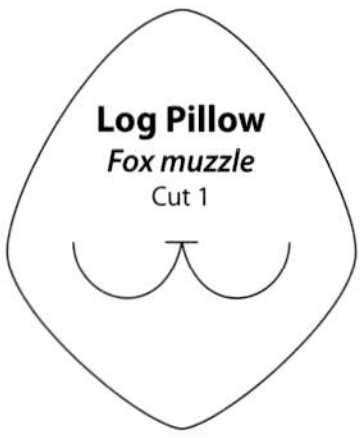

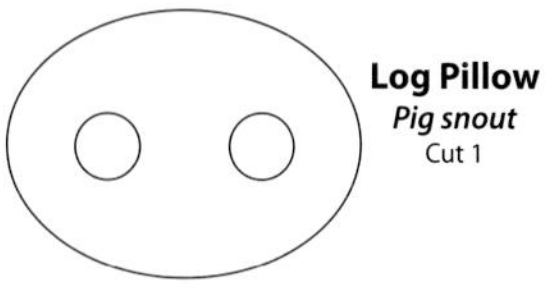

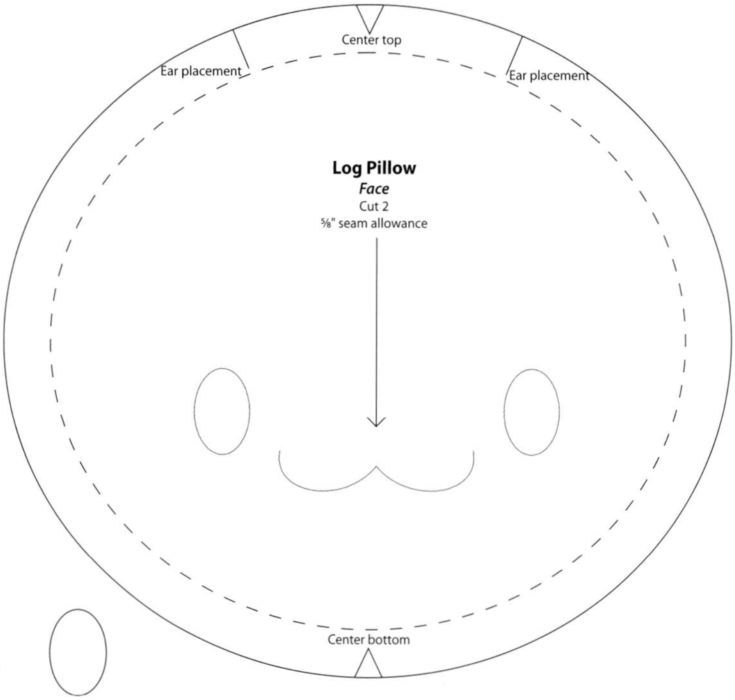

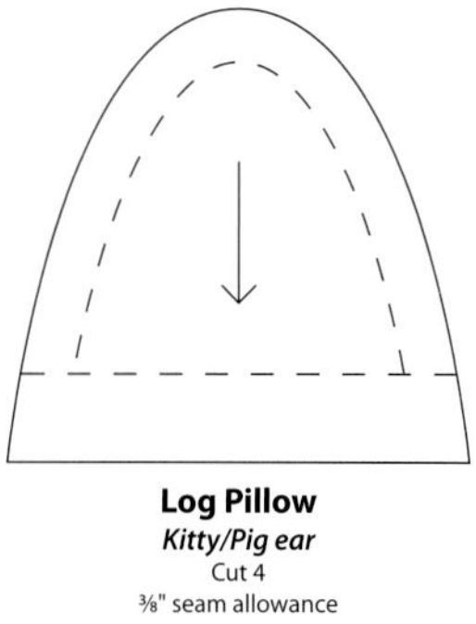

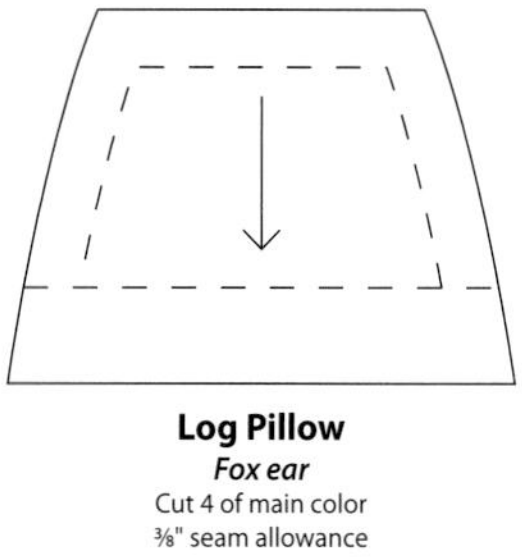

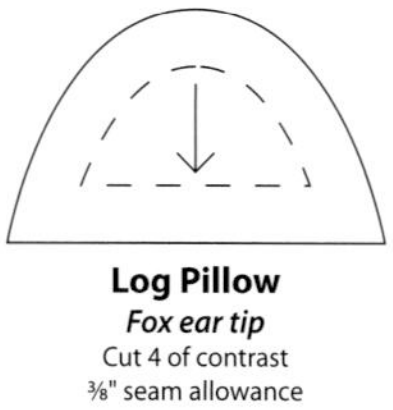

Enlarge patterns 250% for actual size.

Square Pillow

Pages 129–131

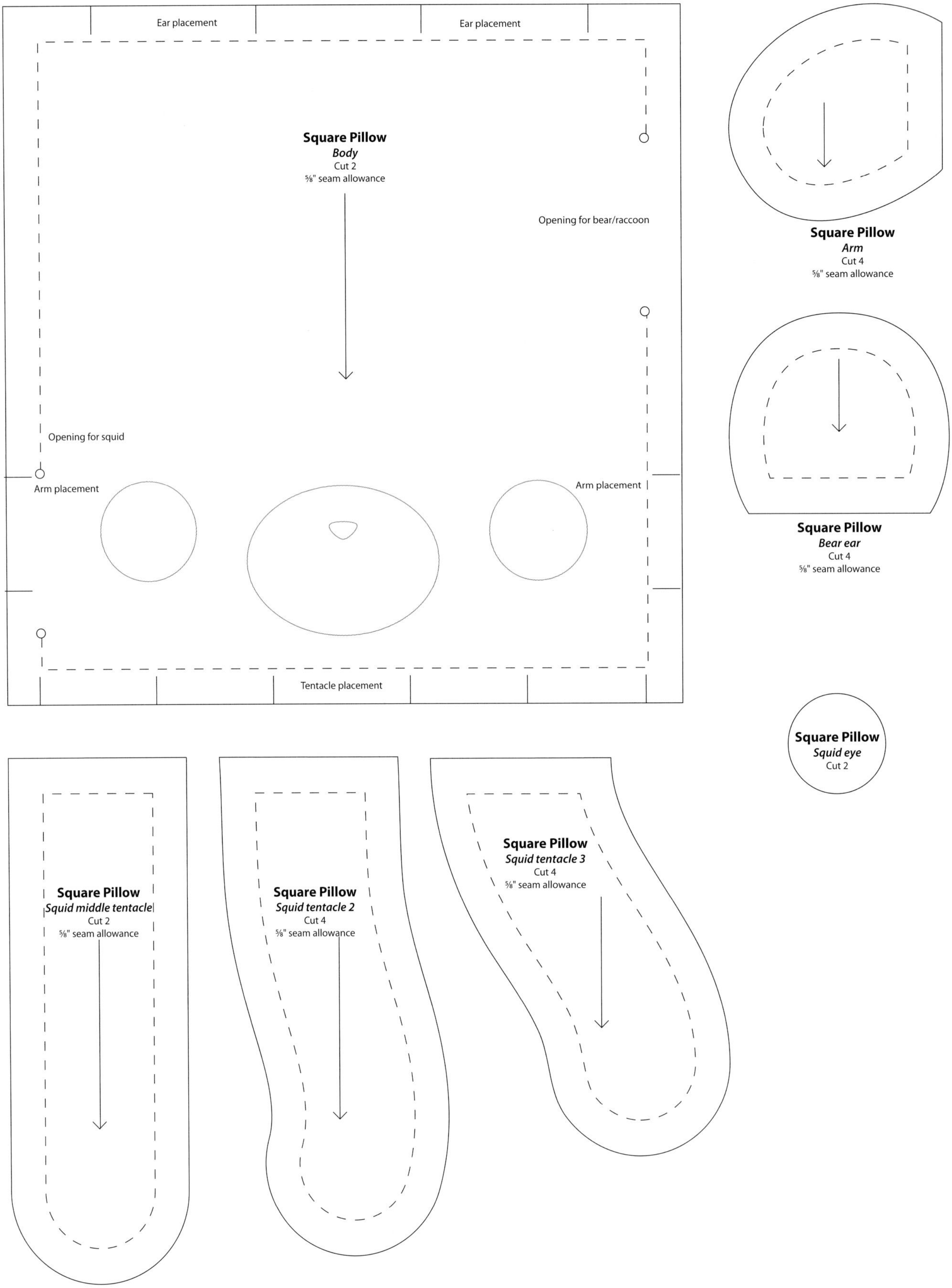

Enlarge patterns 250% for actual size.

Square Pillow *(continued)*

Pages 129–131

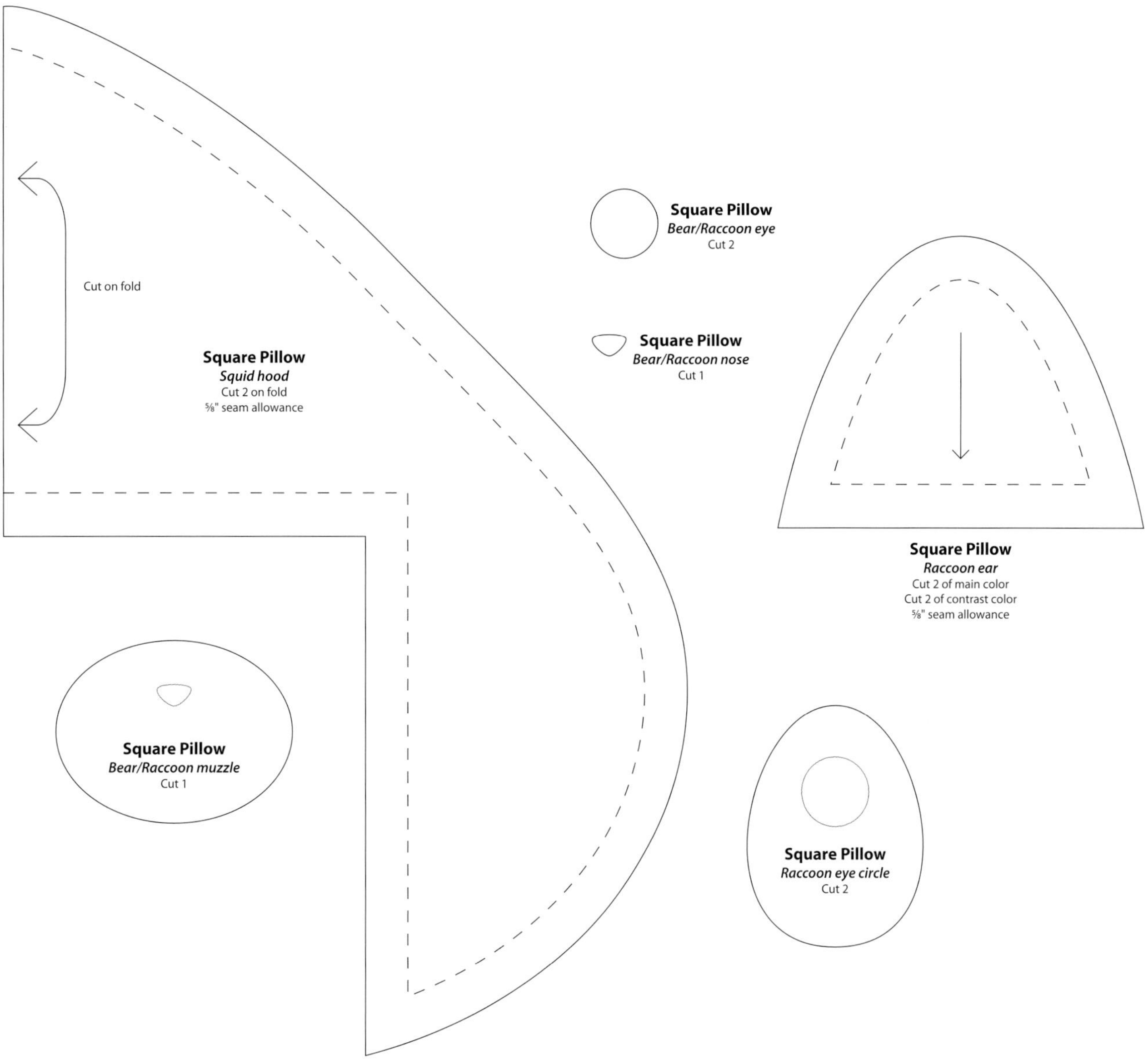

Enlarge patterns 250% for actual size.

Towel Caddy

Pages 132–135

Enlarge patterns 250% for actual size.

Towel Caddy *(continued)*

Pages 132–135

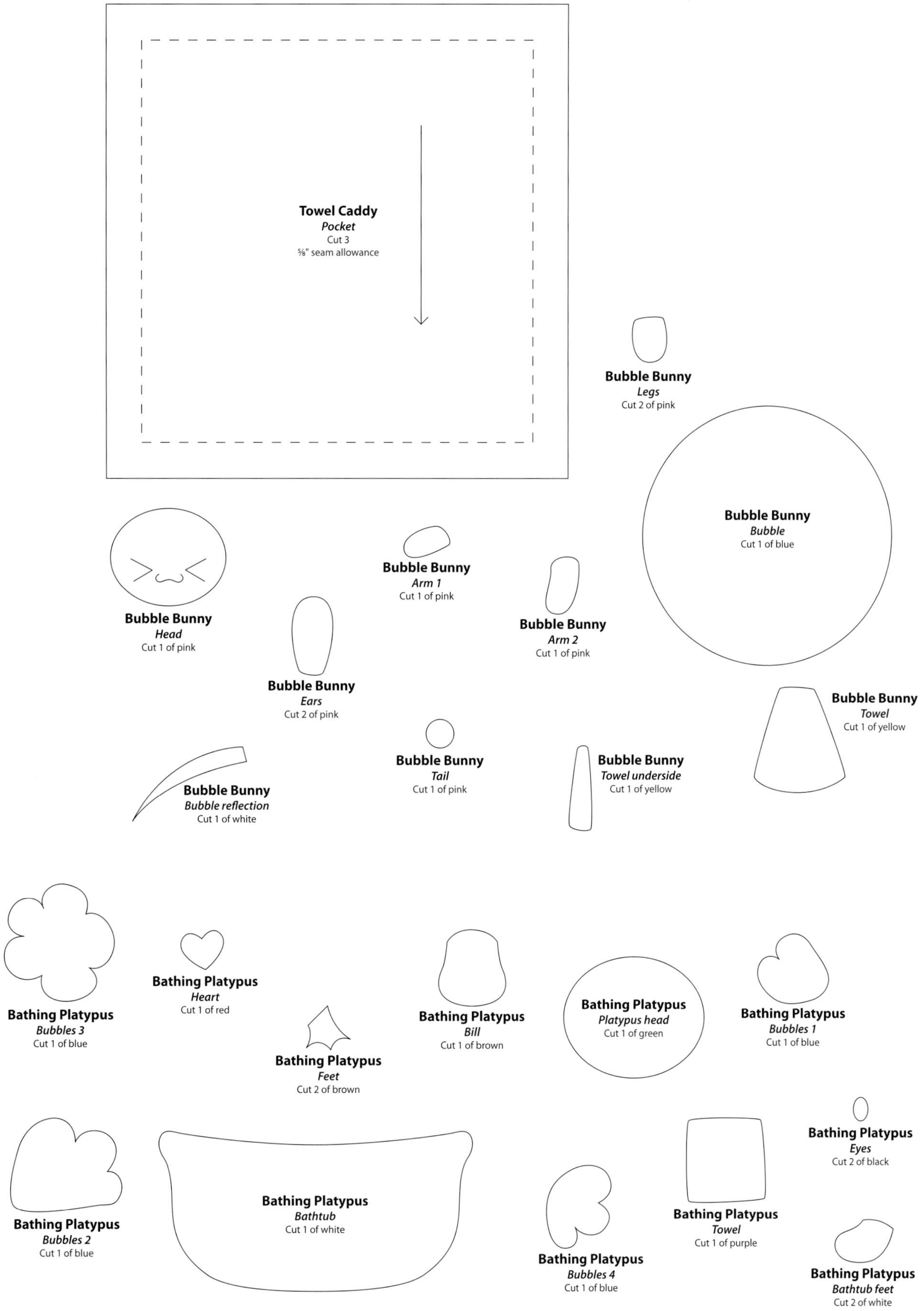

Enlarge patterns 250% for actual size.

Towel Caddy *(continued)*

Pages 132–135

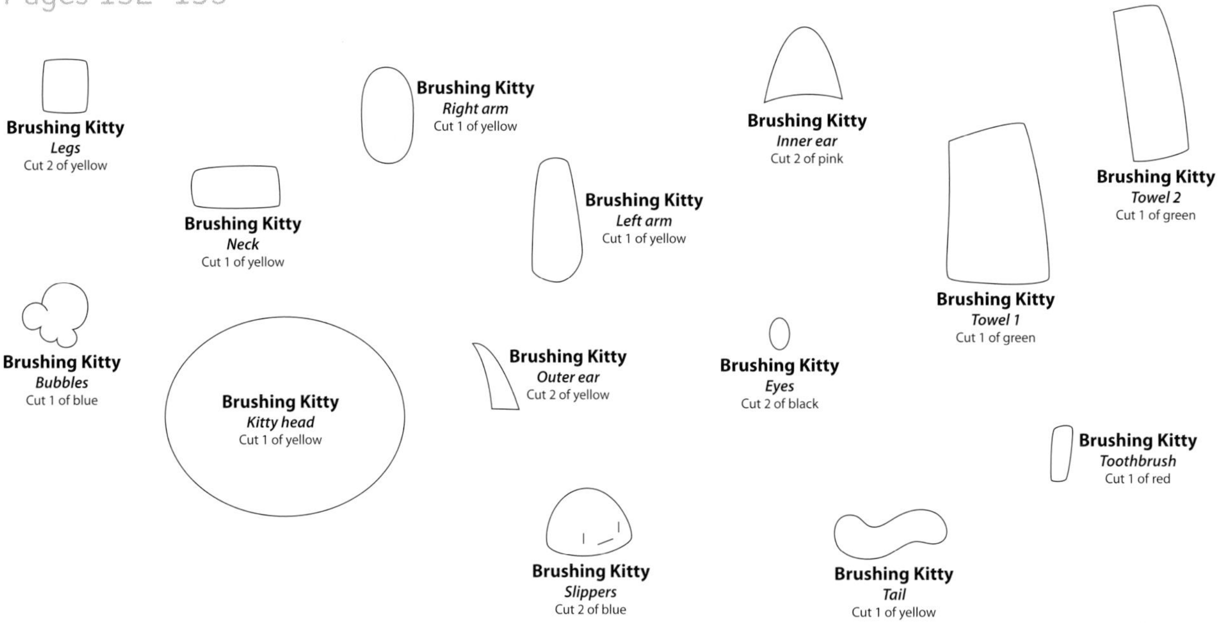

Sushi Quilt

Pages 136–142

Tamago (Egg)

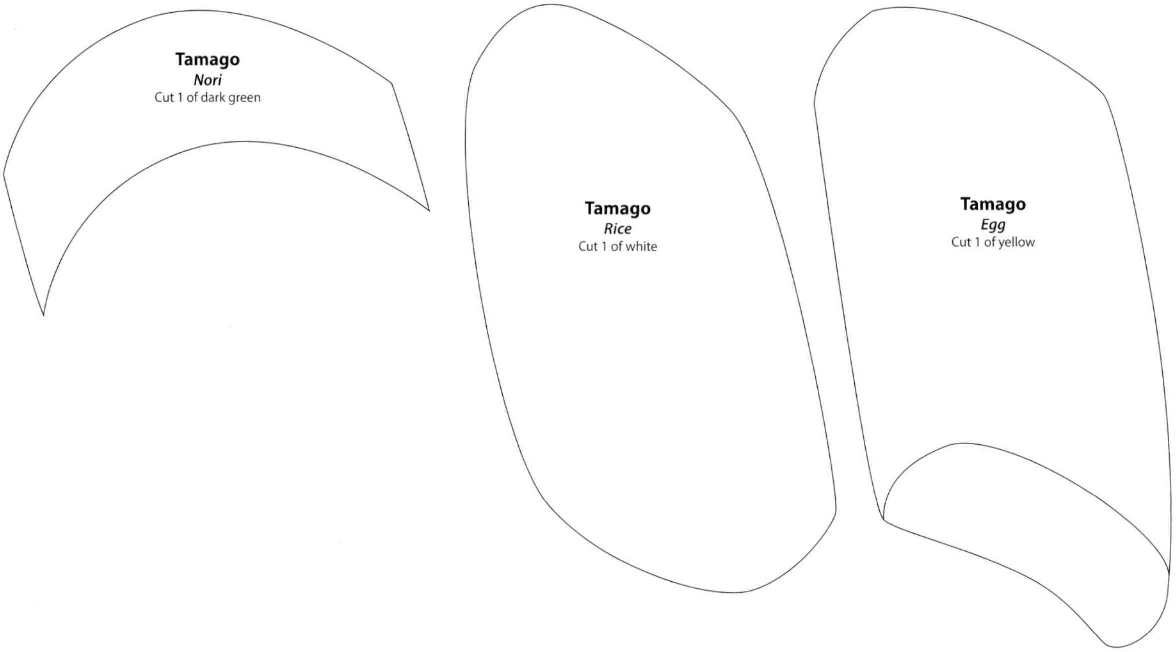

Enlarge patterns 250% for actual size.

Sushi Quilt *(continued)*

Pages 136–142

Uni (Sea Urchin)

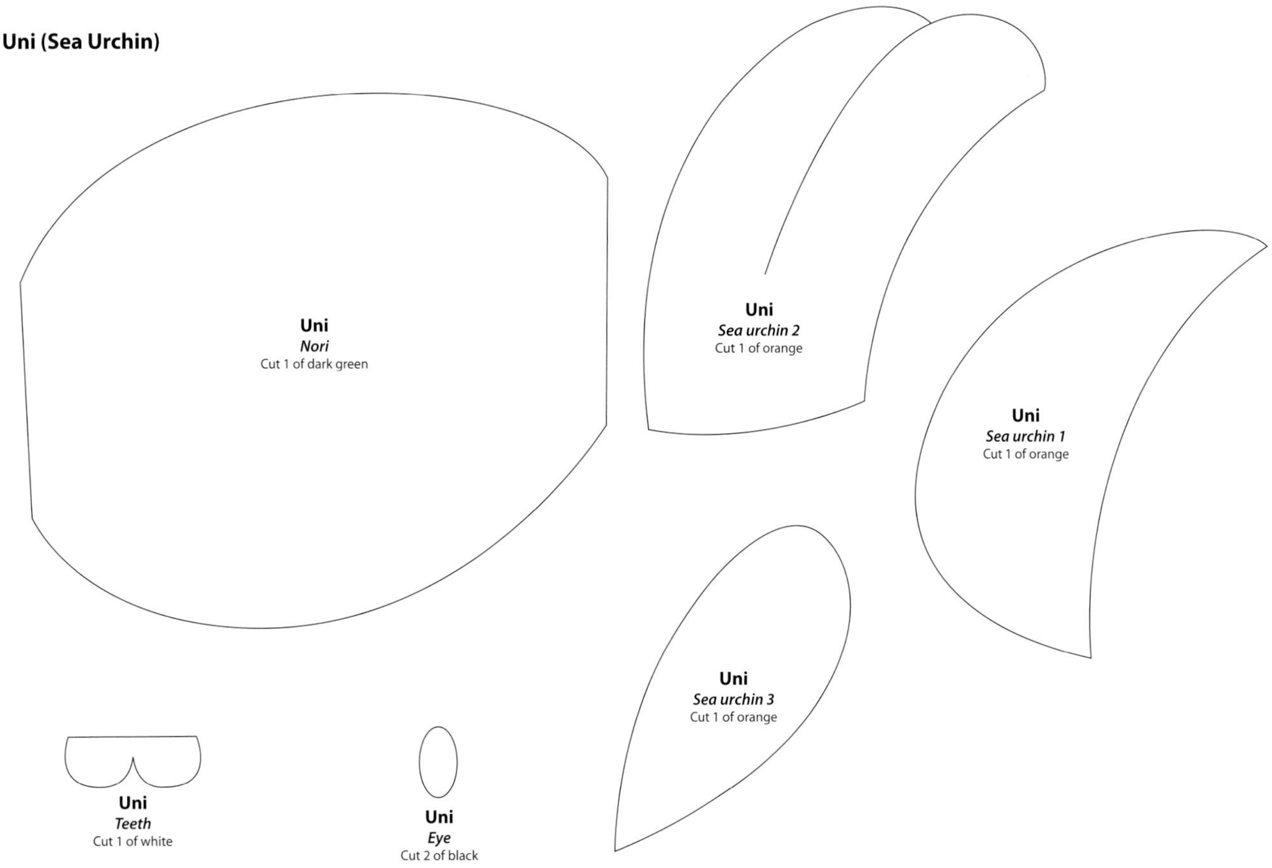

Salmon Hand Roll

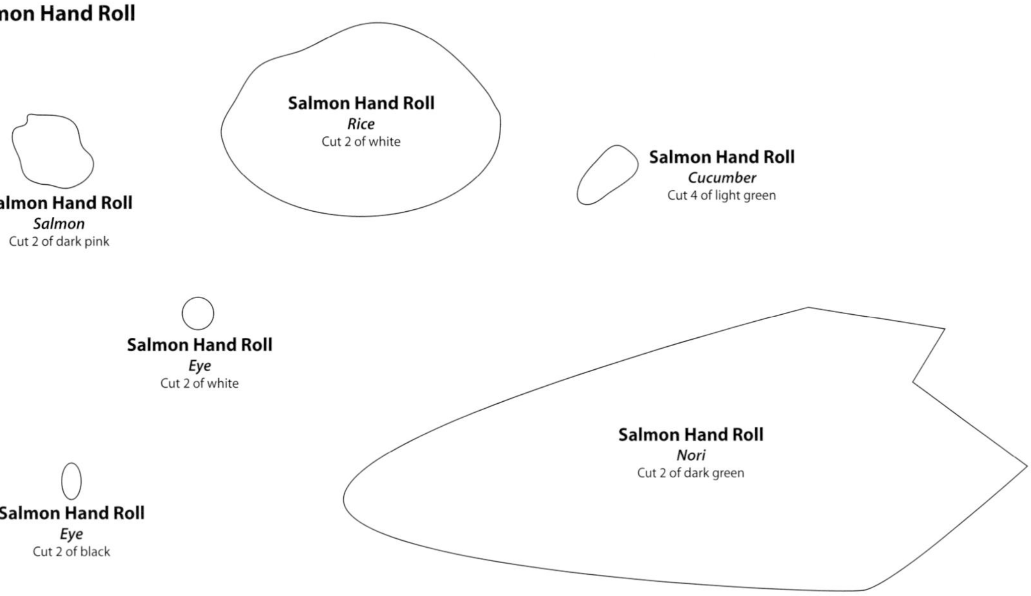

Enlarge patterns 250% for actual size.

Sushi Quilt *(continued)*

Pages 136–142

Ikura (Salmon Roe)

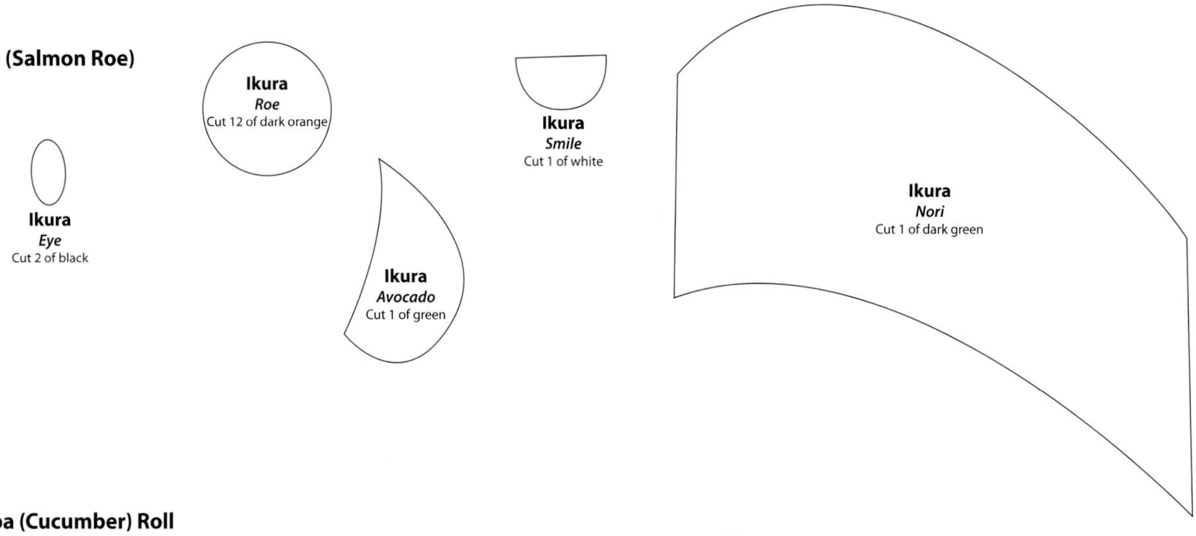

Kappa (Cucumber) Roll

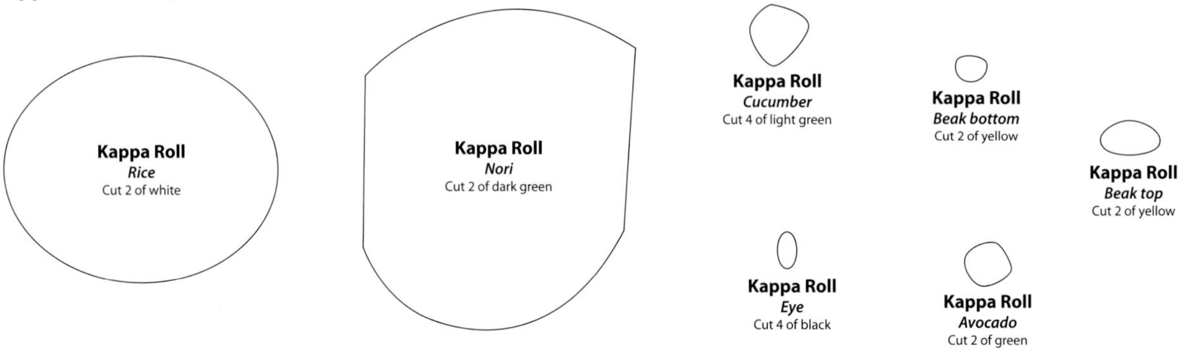

Ootoro (Fatty Tuna)

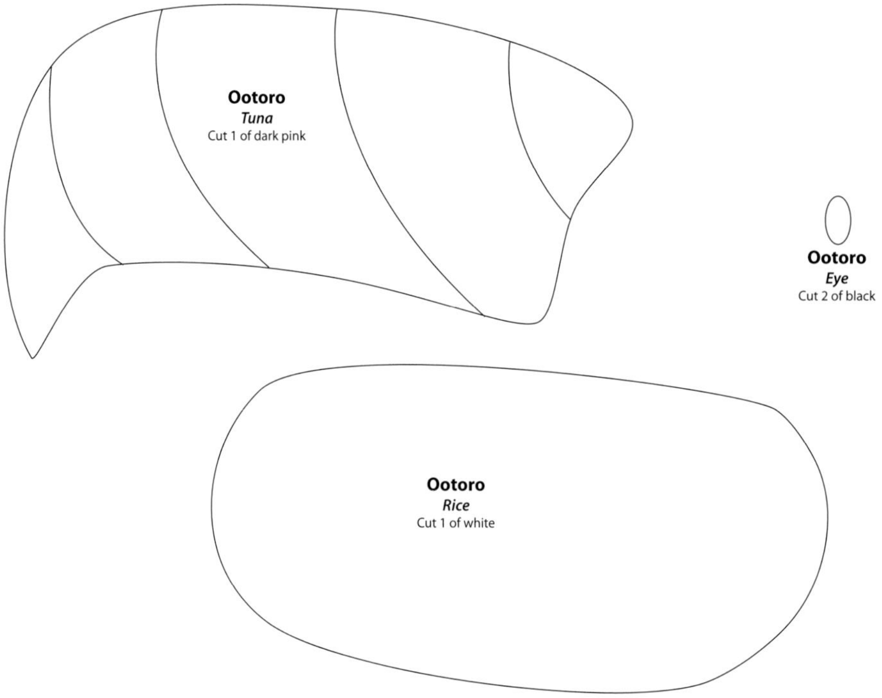

Enlarge patterns 250% for actual size.

Sushi Quilt *(continued)*

Pages 136–142

California Roll

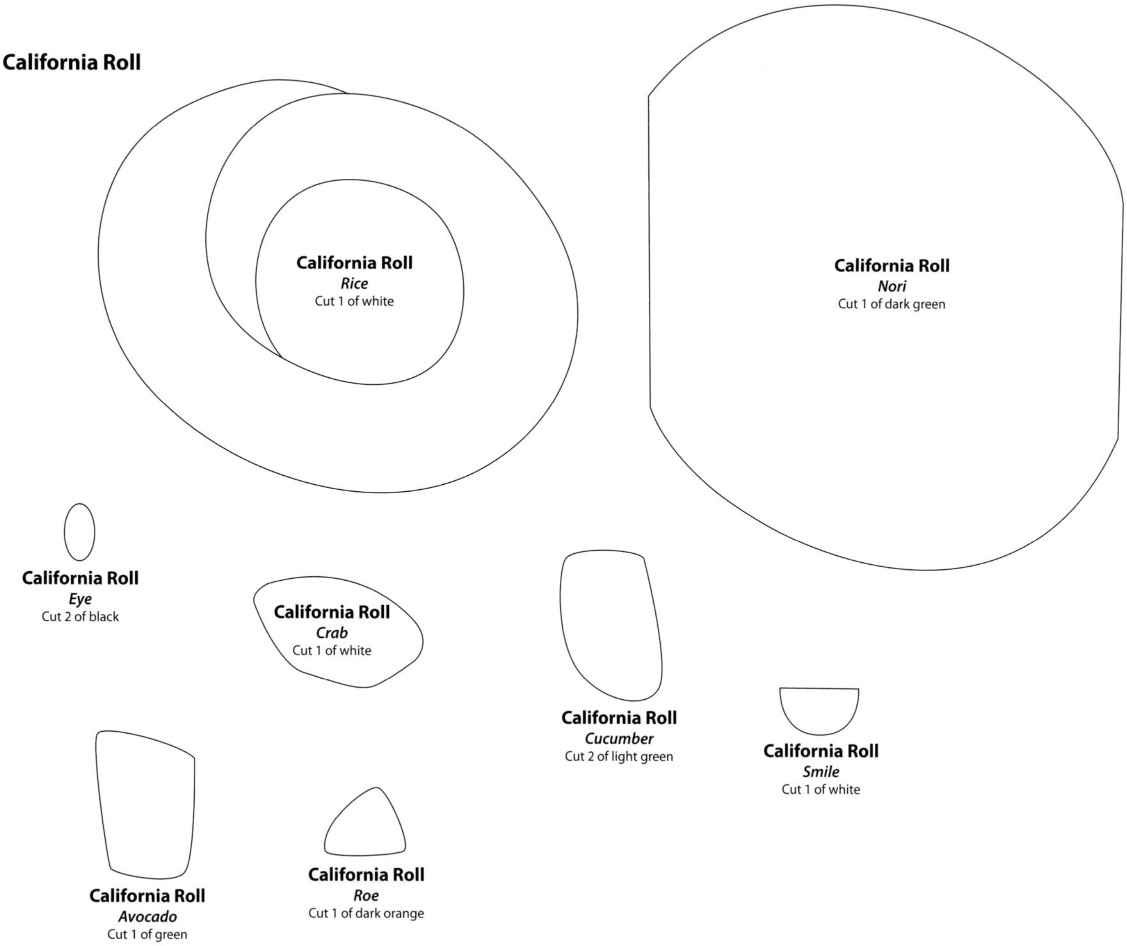

Ebi (Shrimp)

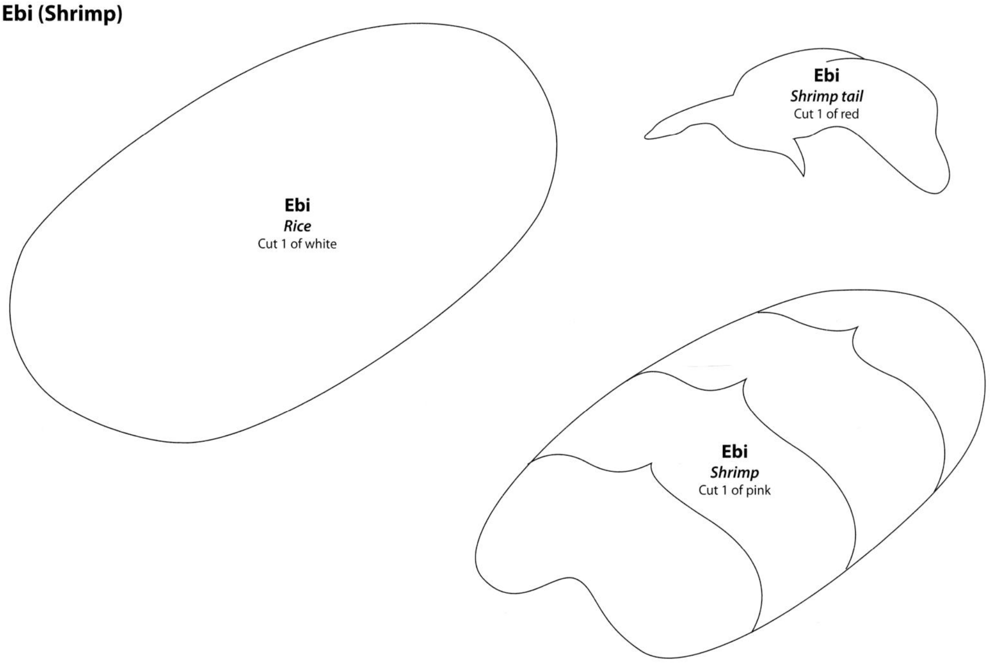

Enlarge patterns 250% for actual size.

Sushi Quilt *(continued)*

Pages 136–142

Unagi (Eel)

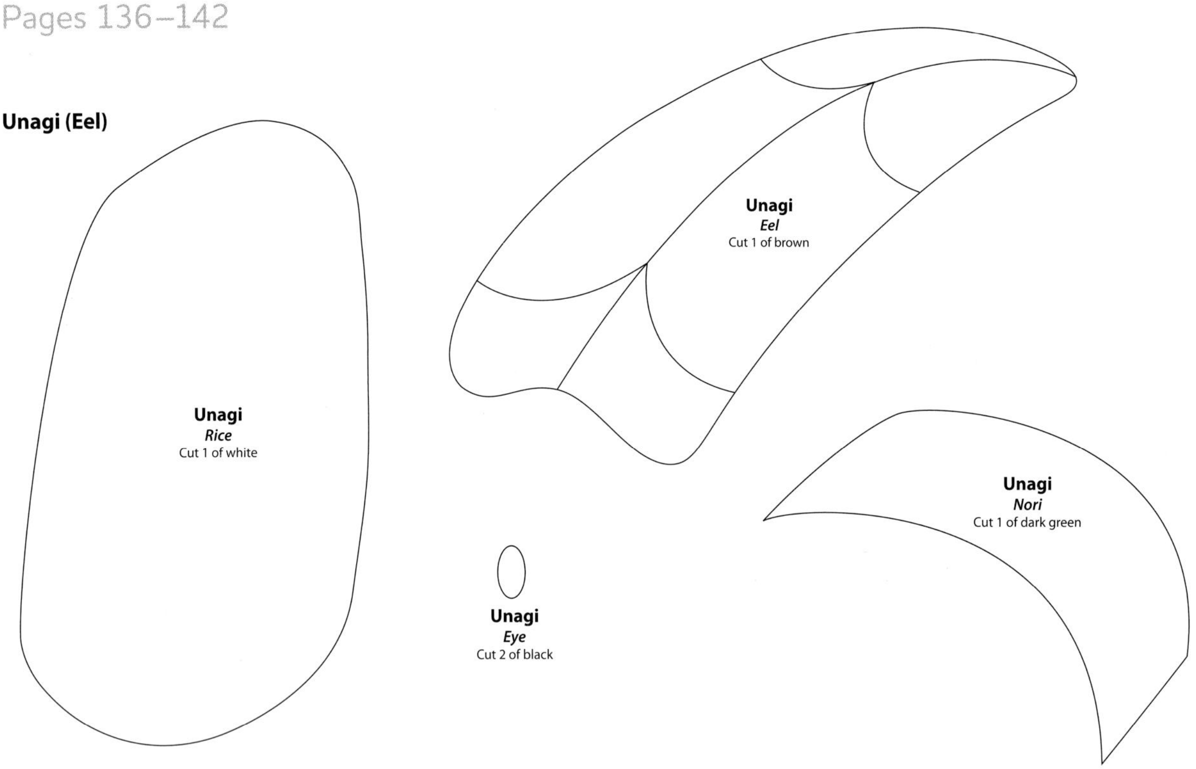

Enlarge patterns 250% for actual size.

Index

Acquisition and book editor
Kerri Landis

Copy editor
Paul Hambke

Cover and book designer
Lindsay Hess

Cover and gallery photographer
Scott Kriner

Layout
Wil Younger

Proofreader
Debbie Henry

Step-by-step photographer
Matthew McClure

More Great Books from Fox Chapel Publishing

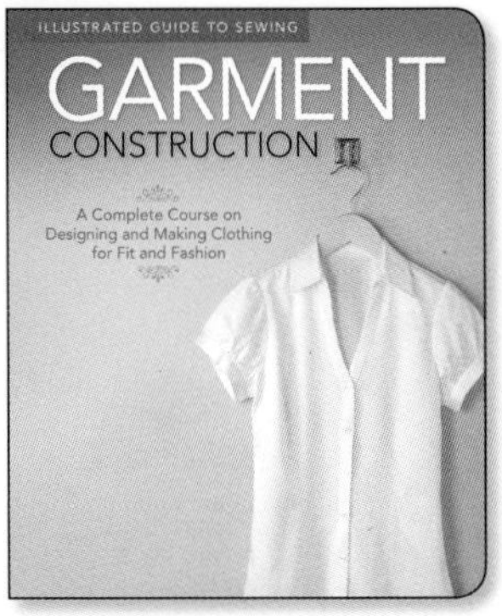

Illustrated Guide to Sewing: Garment Construction
A Complete Course on Designing and Making Clothing for Fit and Fashion
Edited by Mindy Kinsey

Learn to make the building blocks of a great wardrobe, from the basic order of constructing a garment to troubleshooting common fit problems.

ISBN: 978-1-56523-509-0
$19.95 • 176 Pages

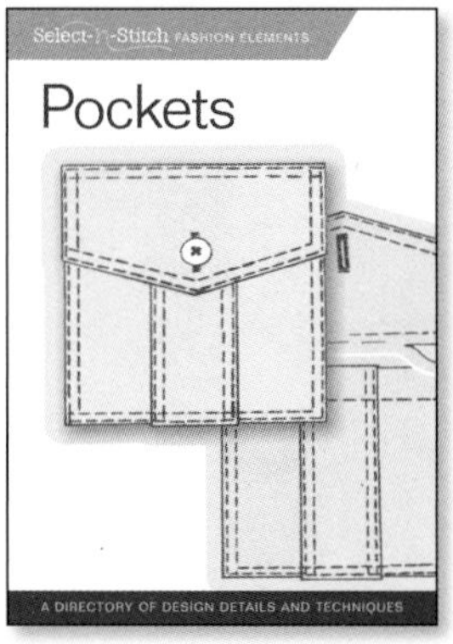

Select-n-Stitch: Pockets
A Directory of Design Details and Techniques
Edited by Mindy Kinsey

Learn the best methods and techniques to ensure your pockets are properly positioned, flat, and neatly sewn.

ISBN: 978-1-56523-553-3
$12.95 • 152 Pages

Simple Beginnings: Beading
A Step-by-Step Guide for Creating Your Own Custom Jewelry
By Suzann Sladcik Wilson

Starting at the beginning of the beading process, this book teaches you everything you need to know to become an accomplished beading artist.

ISBN: 978-1-56523-677-6
$19.95 • 144 Pages

Teach Yourself Henna Tattoo
Making Mehndi Art with Easy-to-Follow Instructions, Patterns, and Projects
By Brenda Abdoyan

Bring the tradition of henna tattooing into your own world and create designs for your own celebrations.

ISBN: 978-1-56523-672-1
$19.95 • 128 Pages

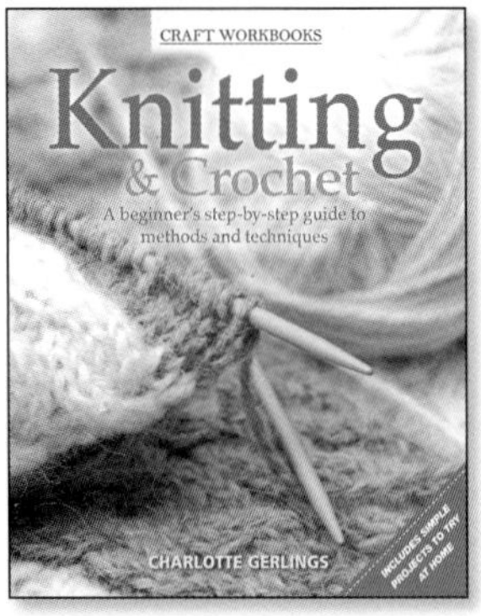

Knitting & Crochet
A Beginner's Step-by-Step Guide to Methods and Techniques
By Charlotte Gerlings

Two of the most popular needlecrafts are both easy to learn with the methods and techniques in this book.

ISBN: 978-1-56523-683-7
$9.95 • 48 Pages

Handmade Music Factory
The Ultimate Guide to Making Foot-Stompin'-Good Instruments
By Mike Orr

Author Mike Orr takes you inside the growing trend of handmade music and shows you how with a little creativity and some salvaged parts, you can create your own arsenal of instruments that look good, sound great, and deliver some foot stompin' fun!

ISBN: 978-1-56523-559-5
$22.95 • 160 Pages

Natural Wooden Toys
75 Easy-to-Make and Kid-Safe Designs to Inspire Imaginations & Creative Play
By Erin Freuchtel-Dearing

Make safe, colorful, and irresistible imagination-building wooden toys with a stay-at-home mom turned woodworker! Step-by-step instructions show you how to make 75 charming designs, and how to create natural, non-toxic finishes.

ISBN: 978-1-56523-524-3
$19.95 • 184 Pages

Easy & Elegant Beaded Copper Jewelry
How to Create Beautiful Fashion Accessories from a Few Basic Steps
By Lora S. Irish

Make your own affordable and stylish copper wire jewelry with a few simple tools, some wire, and beads.

ISBN: 978-1-56523-514-4
$24.95 • 256 Pages